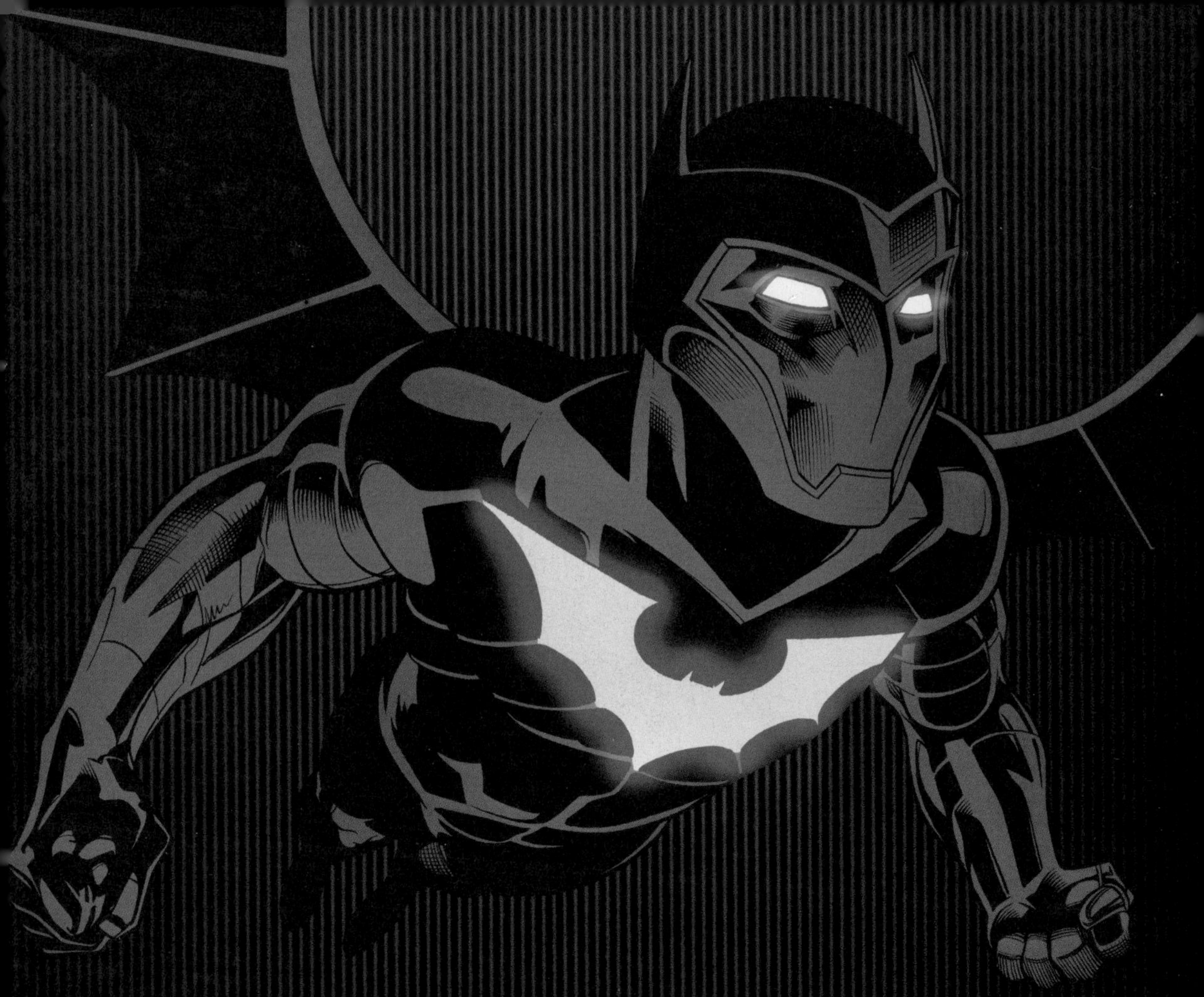

THE NEXT BATMAN
SECOND SON

JOHN RIDLEY
writer

TRAVEL FOREMAN with TONY AKINS
pencillers

NORM RAPMUND | MARK MORALES
LE BEAU UNDERWOOD | JOHN LIVESAY
inkers

REX LOKUS
colorist

ANDWORLD DESIGN
letterer

Collection cover art by **JORGE MOLINA**

BATMAN created by **BOB KANE** with **BILL FINGER**

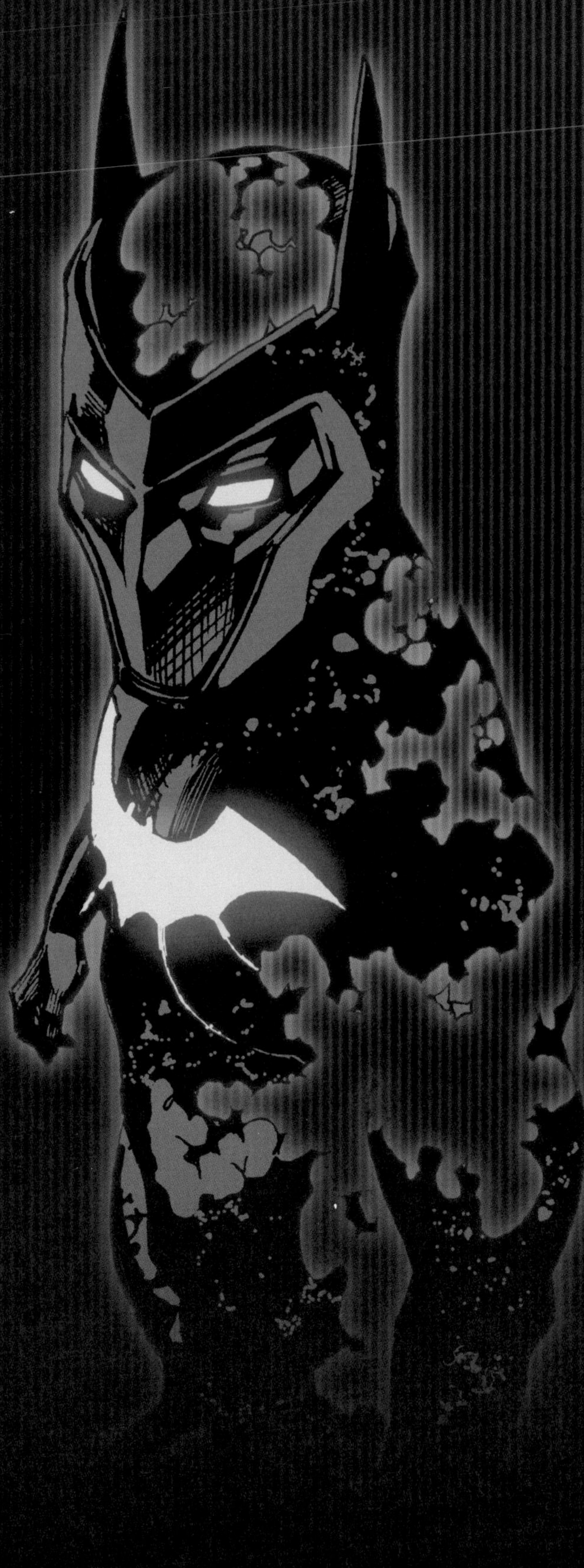

BEN ABERNATHY
Editor – Original Series & Collected Edition
STEVE COOK
Design Director – Books
CURTIS KING JR.
Publication Design
SUZANNAH ROWNTREE
Publication Production

MARIE JAVINS
Editor-in-Chief, DC Comics

DANIEL CHERRY III
Senior VP – General Manager
JIM LEE
Publisher & Chief Creative Officer
JOEN CHOE
VP – Global Brand & Creative Services
DON FALLETTI
VP – Manufacturing Operations & Workflow Management
LAWRENCE GANEM
VP – Talent Services
ALISON GILL
Senior VP – Manufacturing & Operations
NICK J. NAPOLITANO
VP – Manufacturing Administration & Design
NANCY SPEARS
VP – Revenue

THE NEXT BATMAN: SECOND SON

DC Comics, 2900 West Alameda Ave., Burbank, CA 91505
Printed by Transcontinental Interglobe, Beauceville, QC, Canada. 7/30/21. First Printing.
ISBN: 978-1-77951-360-1

Library of Congress Cataloging-in-Publication Data is available.

PEFC Certified
This product is from sustainably managed forests and controlled sources
PEFC
PEFC/01-31-106
www.pefc.org

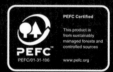

The Next Batman: Second Son #1
Cover Art by **DOUG BRAITHWAITE**

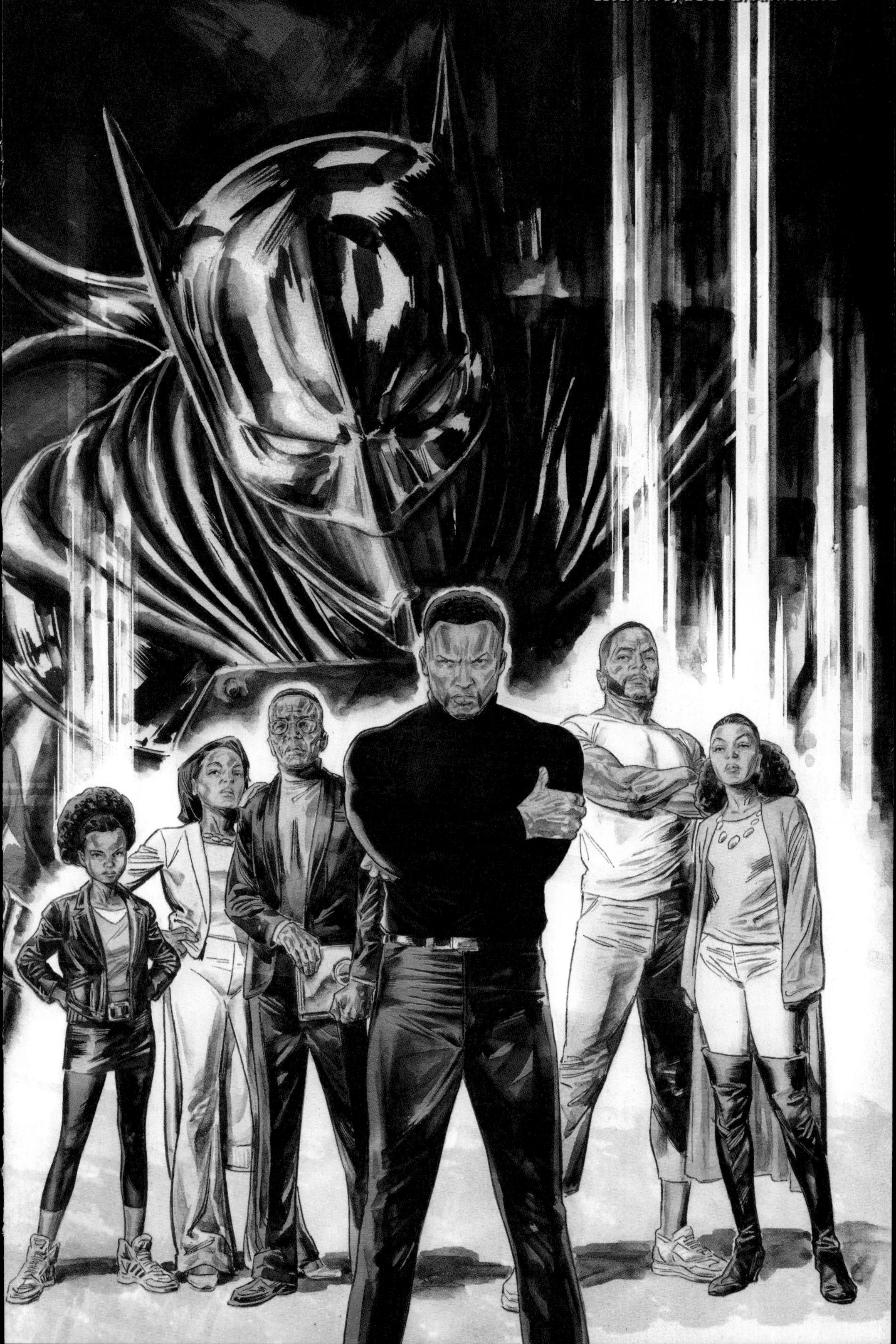

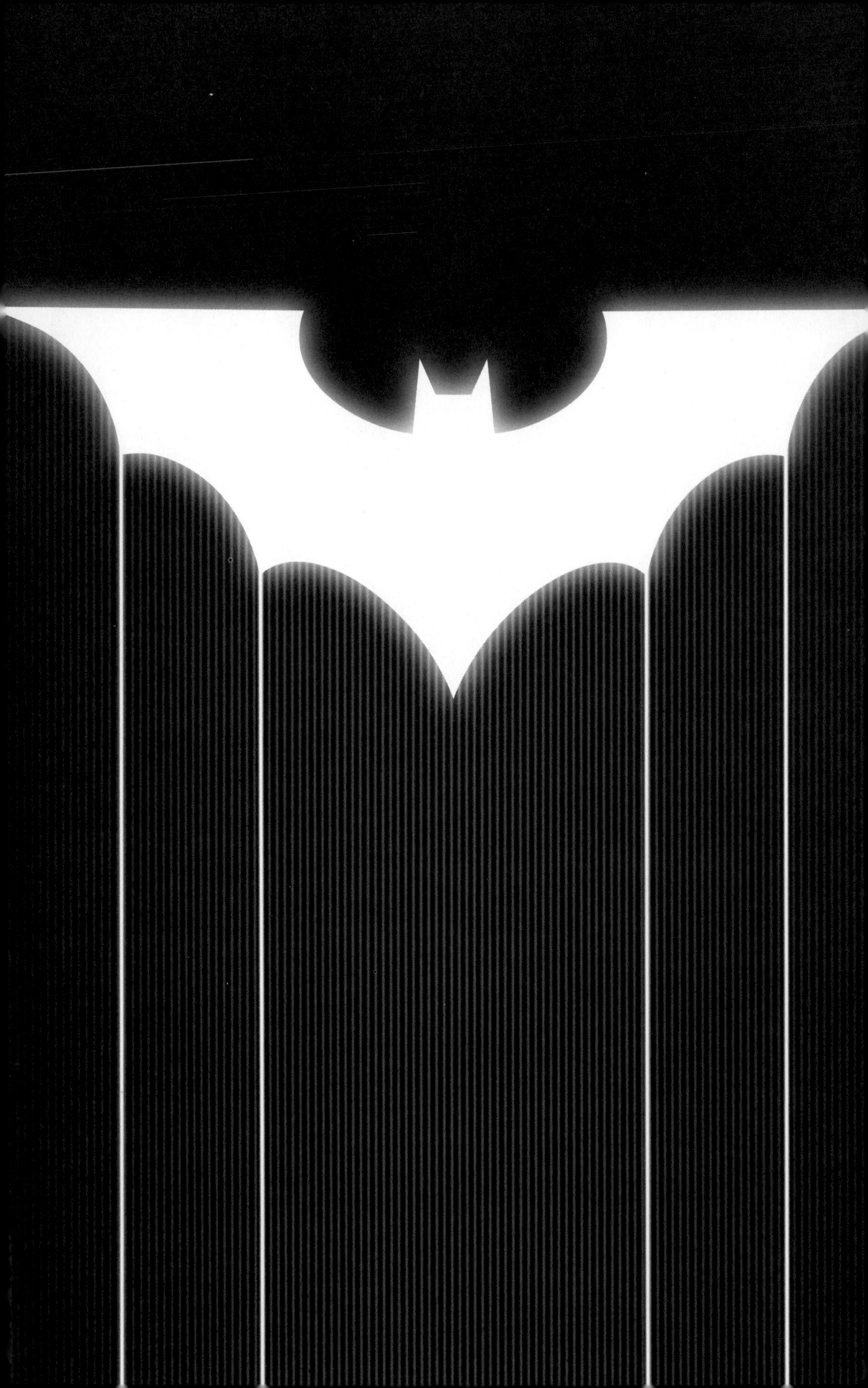

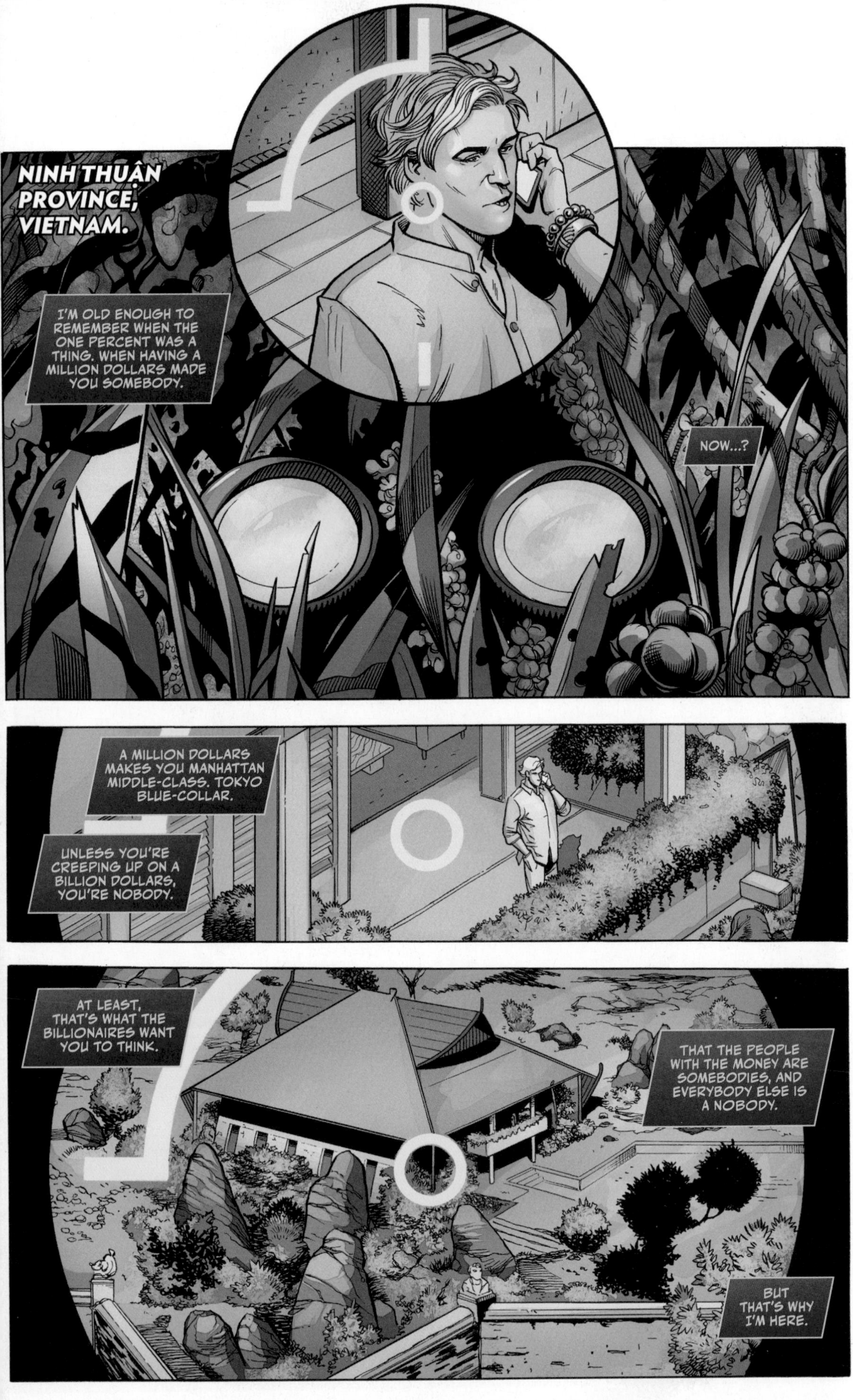
NINH THUẬN PROVINCE, VIETNAM.
I'M OLD ENOUGH TO REMEMBER WHEN THE ONE PERCENT WAS A THING. WHEN HAVING A MILLION DOLLARS MADE YOU SOMEBODY.
NOW...?
A MILLION DOLLARS MAKES YOU MANHATTAN MIDDLE-CLASS. TOKYO BLUE-COLLAR.
UNLESS YOU'RE CREEPING UP ON A BILLION DOLLARS, YOU'RE NOBODY.
AT LEAST, THAT'S WHAT THE BILLIONAIRES WANT YOU TO THINK.
THAT THE PEOPLE WITH THE MONEY ARE SOMEBODIES, AND EVERYBODY ELSE IS A NOBODY.
BUT THAT'S WHY I'M HERE.

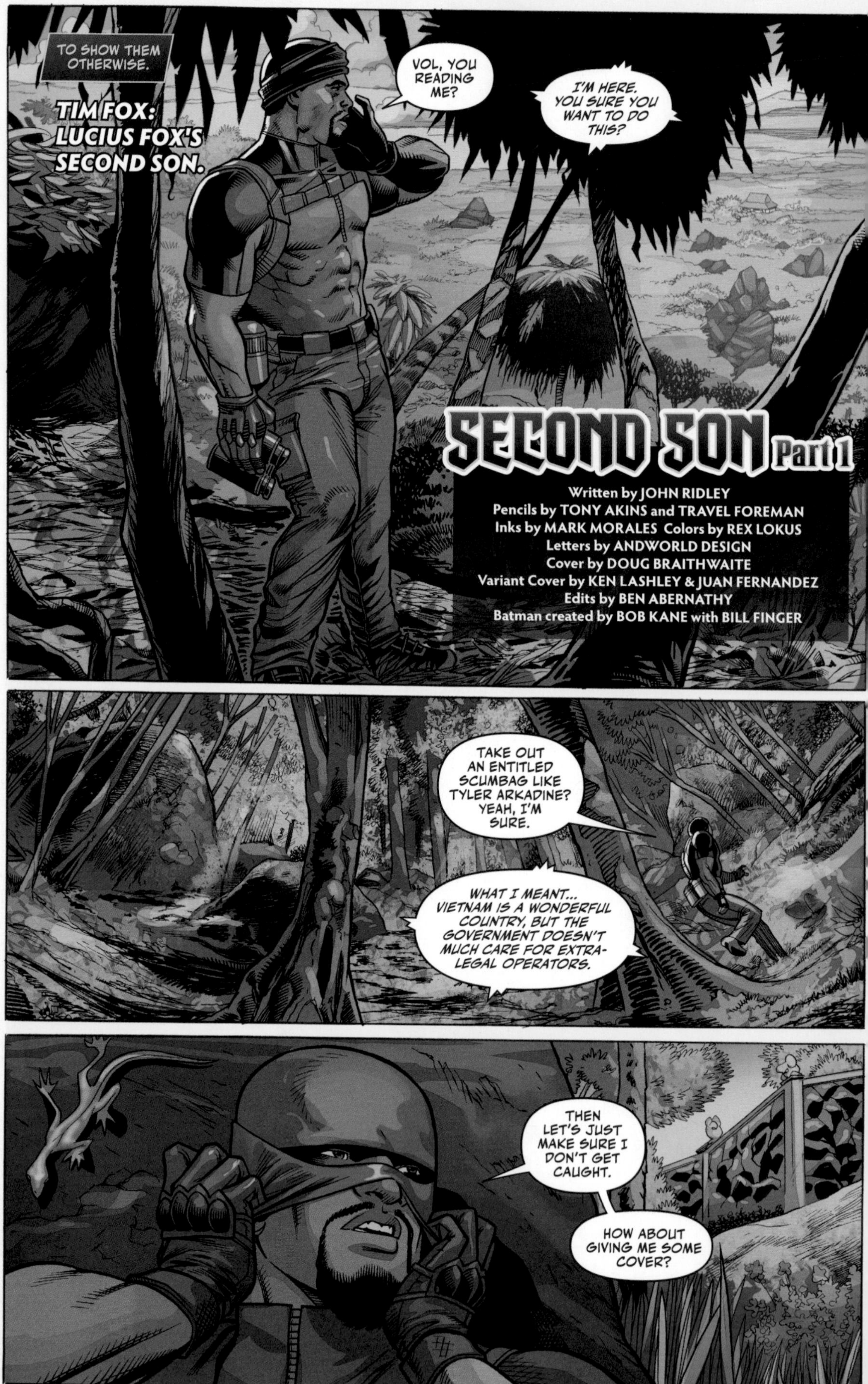

TO SHOW THEM OTHERWISE.
TIM FOX: LUCIUS FOX'S SECOND SON.
VOL, YOU READING ME?
I'M HERE. YOU SURE YOU WANT TO DO THIS?
SECOND SON Part 1
Written by JOHN RIDLEY
Pencils by TONY AKINS and TRAVEL FOREMAN
Inks by MARK MORALES Colors by REX LOKUS
Letters by ANDWORLD DESIGN
Cover by DOUG BRAITHWAITE
Variant Cover by KEN LASHLEY & JUAN FERNANDEZ
Edits by BEN ABERNATHY
Batman created by BOB KANE with BILL FINGER
TAKE OUT AN ENTITLED SCUMBAG LIKE TYLER ARKADINE? YEAH, I'M SURE.
WHAT I MEANT... VIETNAM IS A WONDERFUL COUNTRY, BUT THE GOVERNMENT DOESN'T MUCH CARE FOR EXTRA-LEGAL OPERATORS.
THEN LET'S JUST MAKE SURE I DON'T GET CAUGHT.
HOW ABOUT GIVING ME SOME COVER?

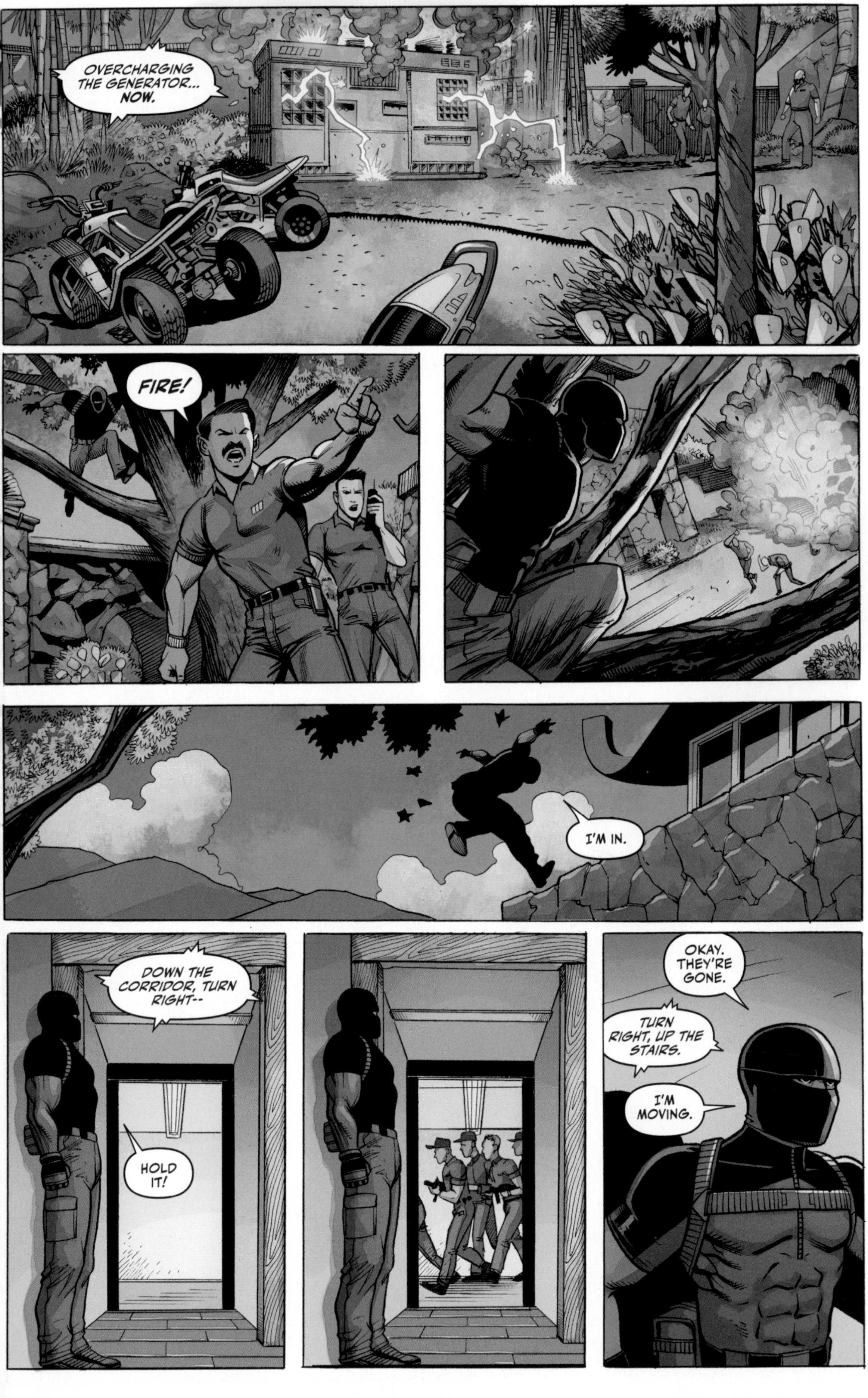
OVERCHARGING THE GENERATOR... NOW.
FIRE!
I'M IN.
DOWN THE CORRIDOR, TURN RIGHT--
HOLD IT!
OKAY. THEY'RE GONE.
TURN RIGHT, UP THE STAIRS.
I'M MOVING.

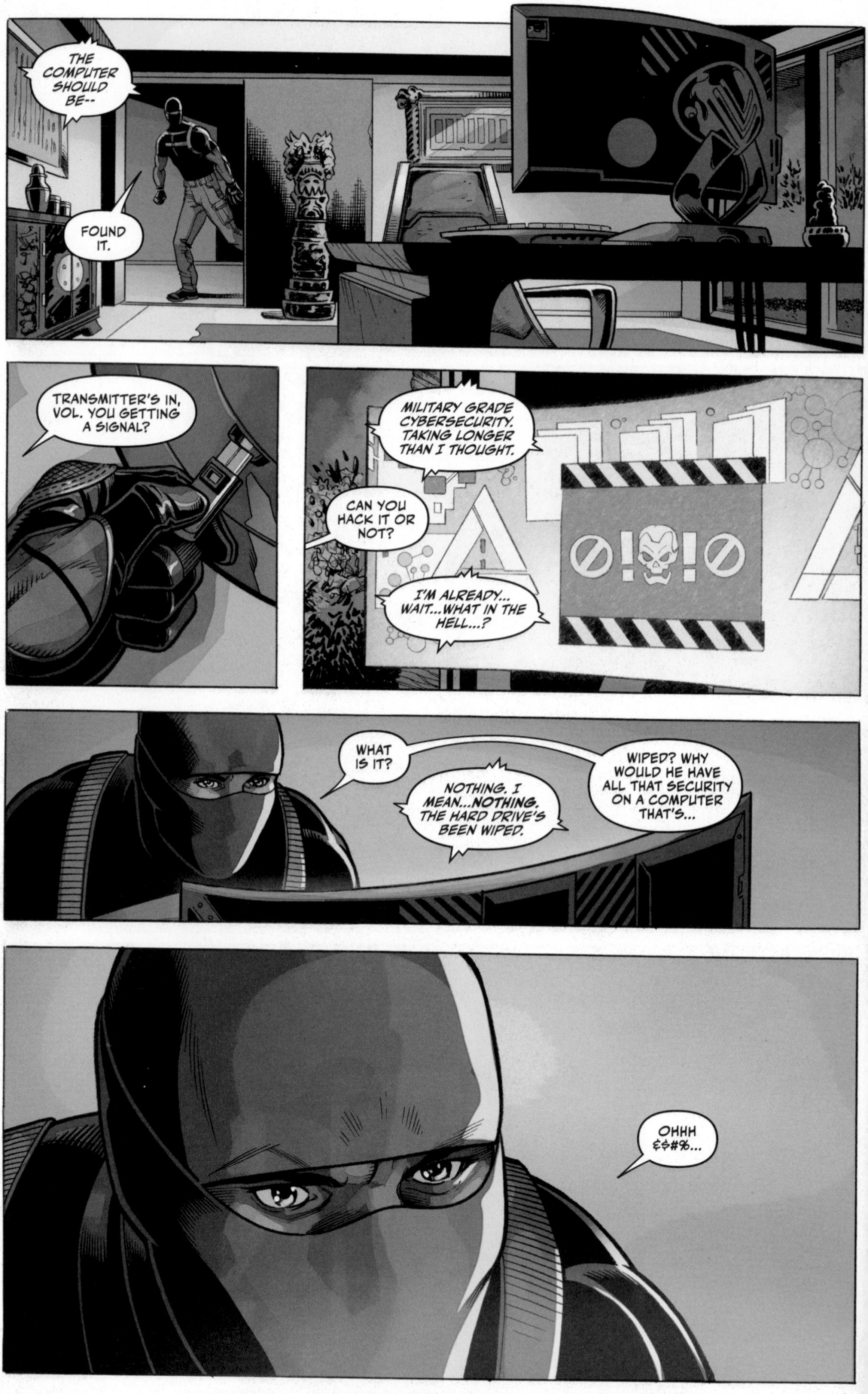
THE COMPUTER SHOULD BE--
FOUND IT.
TRANSMITTER'S IN, VOL. YOU GETTING A SIGNAL?
MILITARY GRADE CYBERSECURITY. TAKING LONGER THAN I THOUGHT.
CAN YOU HACK IT OR NOT?
I'M ALREADY... WAIT...WHAT IN THE HELL...?
WHAT IS IT?
NOTHING. I MEAN...NOTHING. THE HARD DRIVE'S BEEN WIPED.
WIPED? WHY WOULD HE HAVE ALL THAT SECURITY ON A COMPUTER THAT'S...
OHHH &$#%...

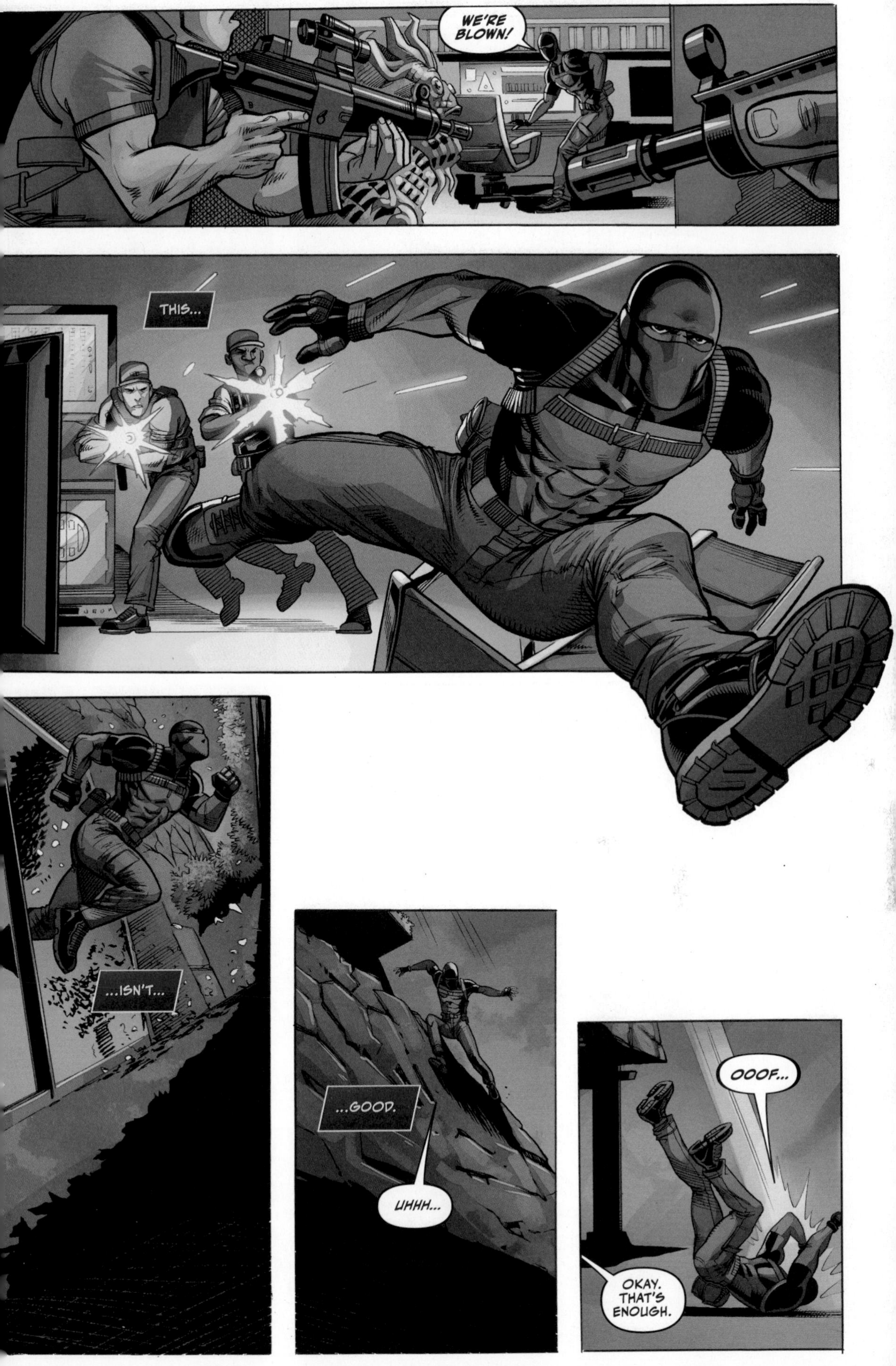
WE'RE BLOWN!
THIS...
...ISN'T...
...GOOD.
UHHH...
OOOF...
OKAY. THAT'S ENOUGH.

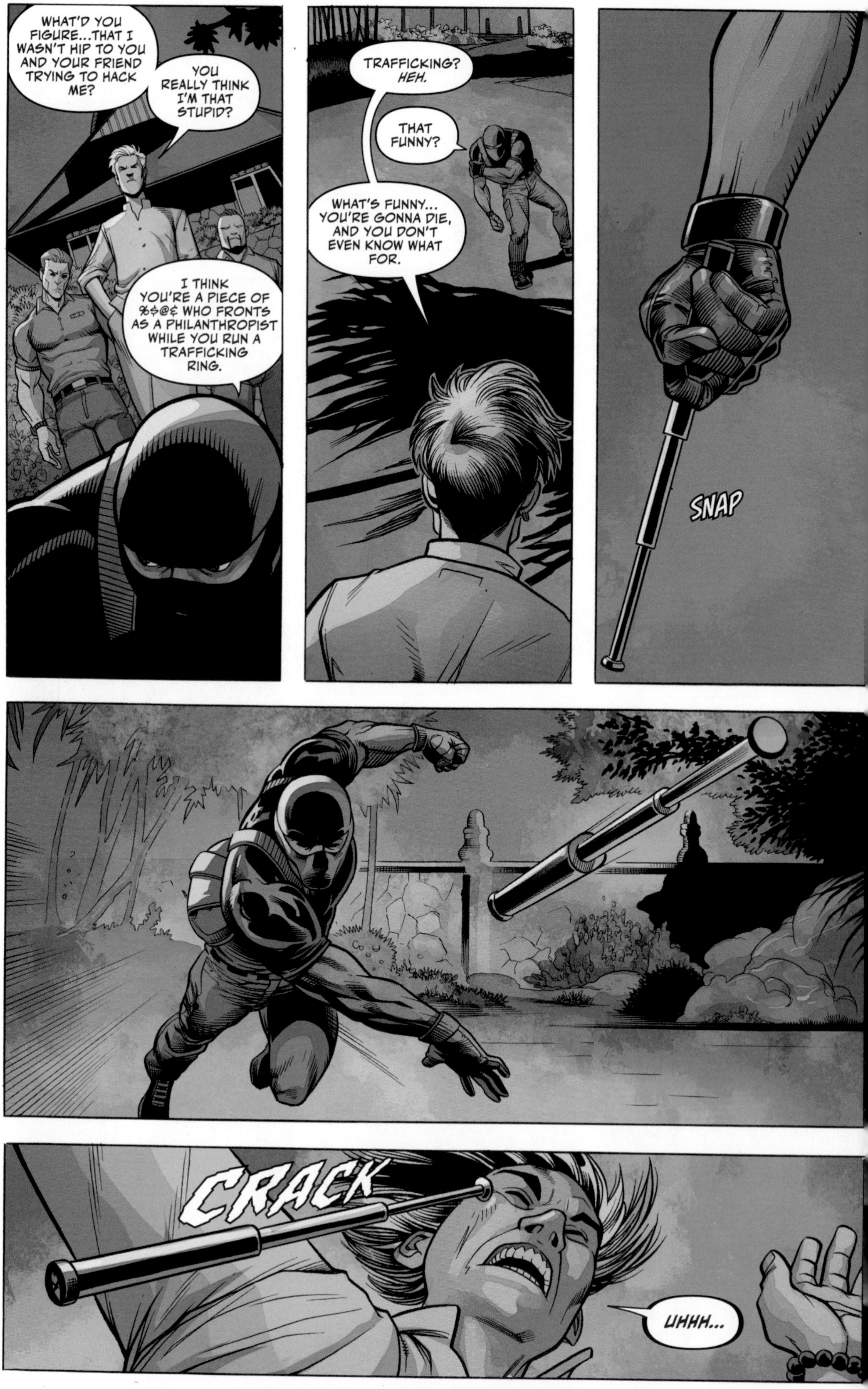
WHAT'D YOU FIGURE...THAT I WASN'T HIP TO YOU AND YOUR FRIEND TRYING TO HACK ME?
YOU REALLY THINK I'M THAT STUPID?
I THINK YOU'RE A PIECE OF %$@& WHO FRONTS AS A PHILANTHROPIST WHILE YOU RUN A TRAFFICKING RING.
TRAFFICKING? HEH.
THAT FUNNY?
WHAT'S FUNNY... YOU'RE GONNA DIE, AND YOU DON'T EVEN KNOW WHAT FOR.
SNAP
CRACK
UHHH...

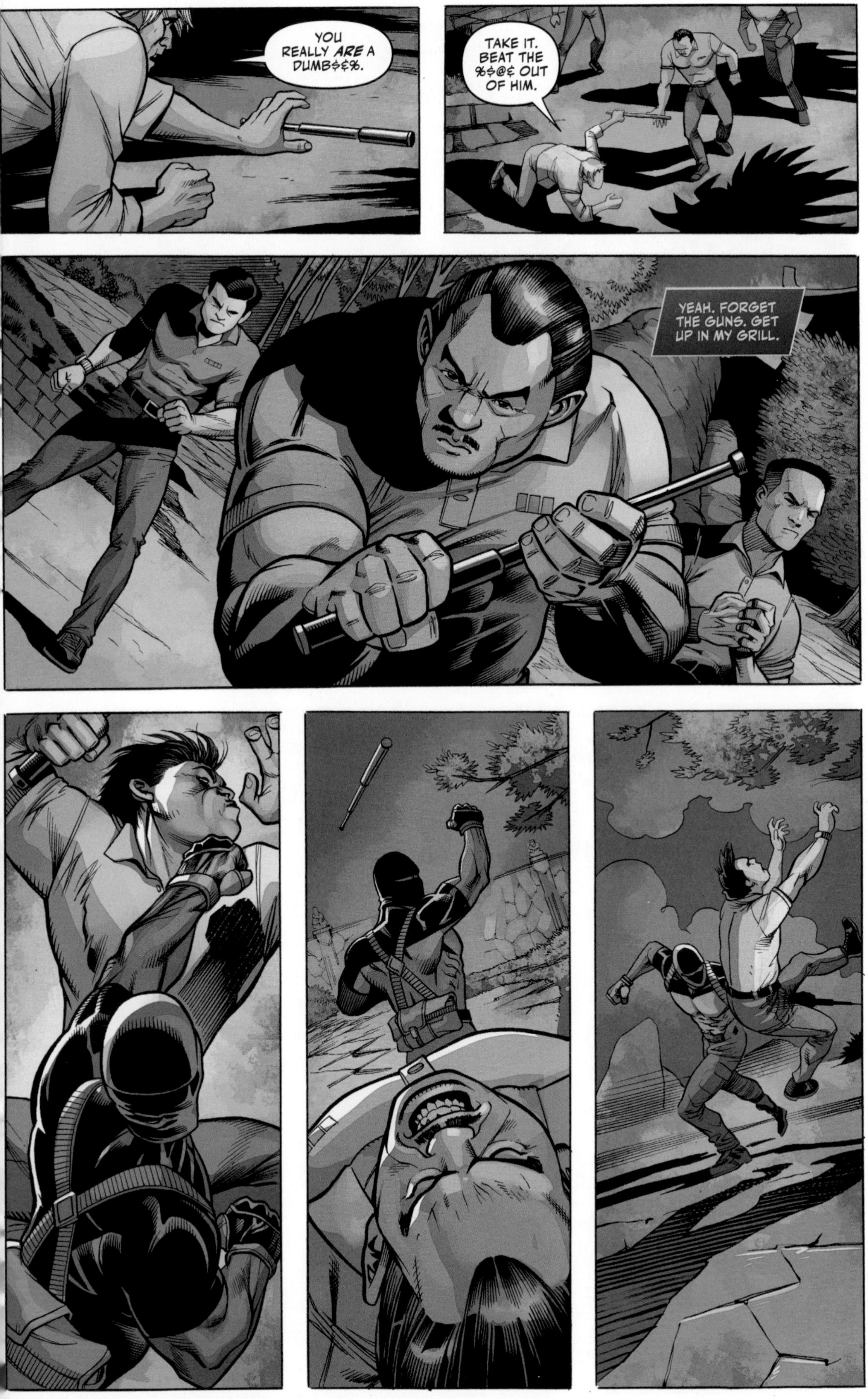
YOU REALLY ARE A DUMB$¢%.
TAKE IT. BEAT THE %$@¢ OUT OF HIM.
YEAH. FORGET THE GUNS. GET UP IN MY GRILL.

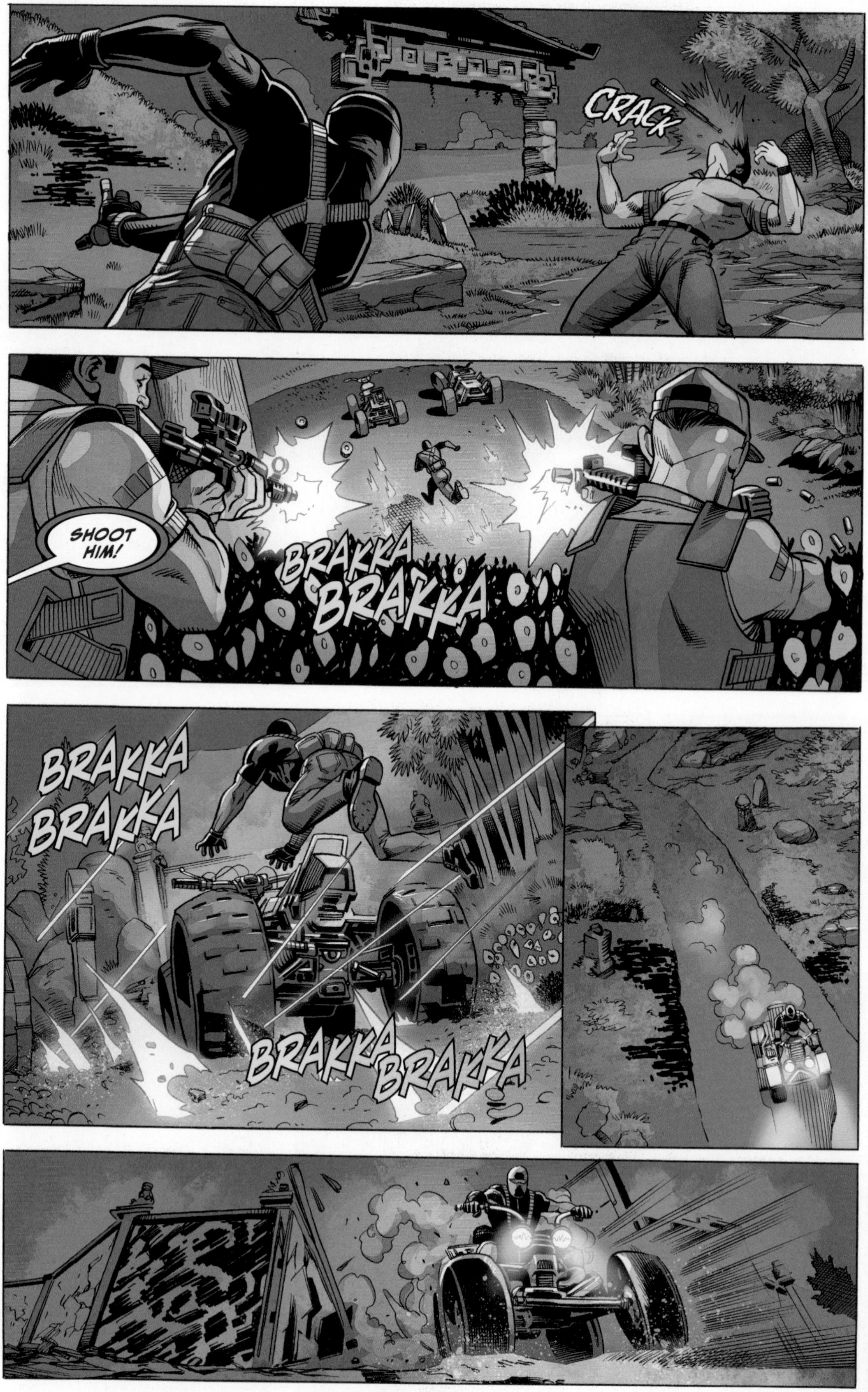
CRACK
SHOOT HIM!
BRAKKA BRAKKA
BRAKKA BRAKKA
BRAKKA BRAKKA

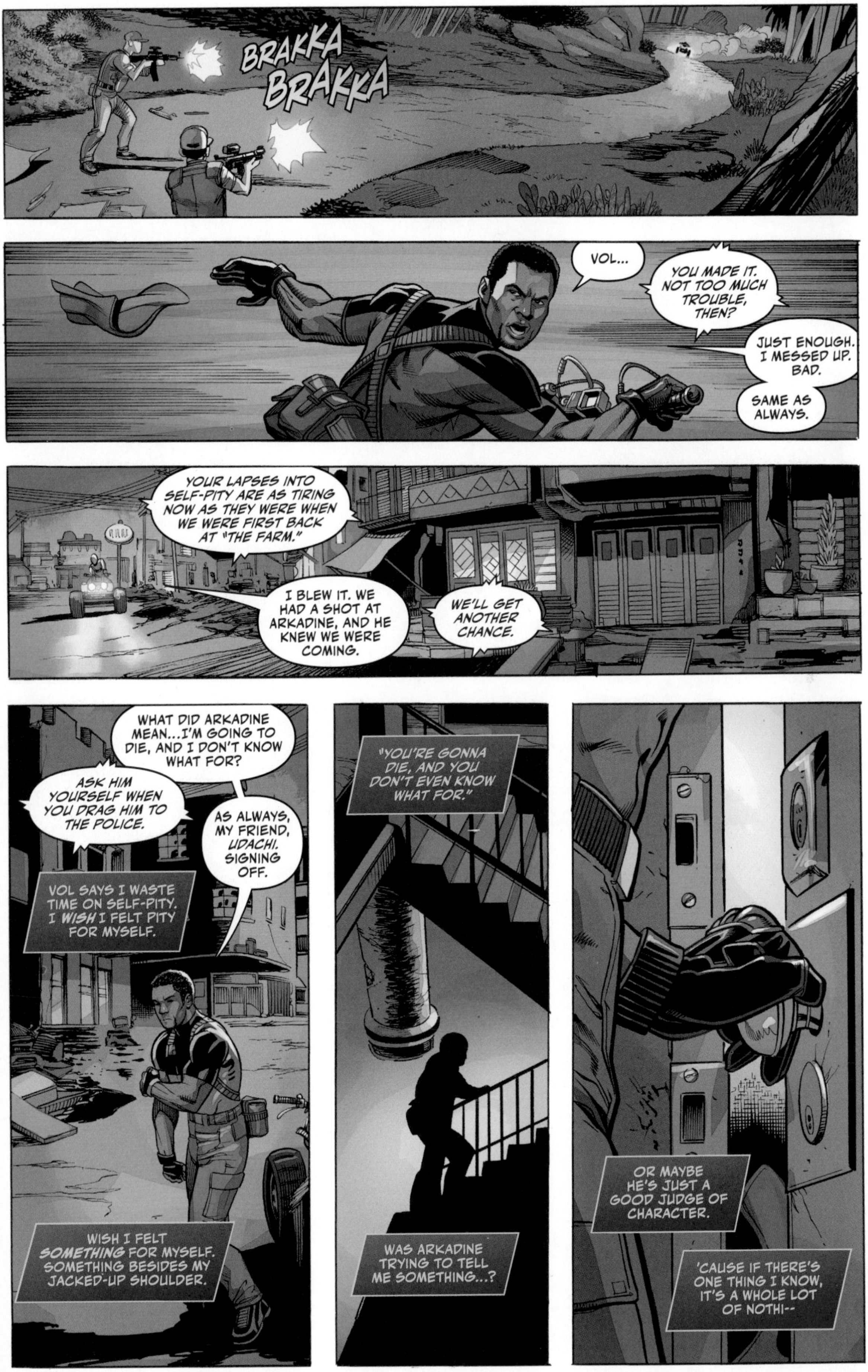
BRAKKA BRAKKA
VOL...
YOU MADE IT. NOT TOO MUCH TROUBLE, THEN?
JUST ENOUGH. I MESSED UP. BAD.
SAME AS ALWAYS.
YOUR LAPSES INTO SELF-PITY ARE AS TIRING NOW AS THEY WERE WHEN WE WERE FIRST BACK AT "THE FARM."
I BLEW IT. WE HAD A SHOT AT ARKADINE, AND HE KNEW WE WERE COMING.
WE'LL GET ANOTHER CHANCE.
WHAT DID ARKADINE MEAN...I'M GOING TO DIE, AND I DON'T KNOW WHAT FOR?
ASK HIM YOURSELF WHEN YOU DRAG HIM TO THE POLICE.
AS ALWAYS, MY FRIEND, UDACHI. SIGNING OFF.
VOL SAYS I WASTE TIME ON SELF-PITY. I WISH I FELT PITY FOR MYSELF.
WISH I FELT SOMETHING FOR MYSELF. SOMETHING BESIDES MY JACKED-UP SHOULDER.
"YOU'RE GONNA DIE, AND YOU DON'T EVEN KNOW WHAT FOR."
WAS ARKADINE TRYING TO TELL ME SOMETHING...?
OR MAYBE HE'S JUST A GOOD JUDGE OF CHARACTER.
'CAUSE IF THERE'S ONE THING I KNOW, IT'S A WHOLE LOT OF NOTHI--

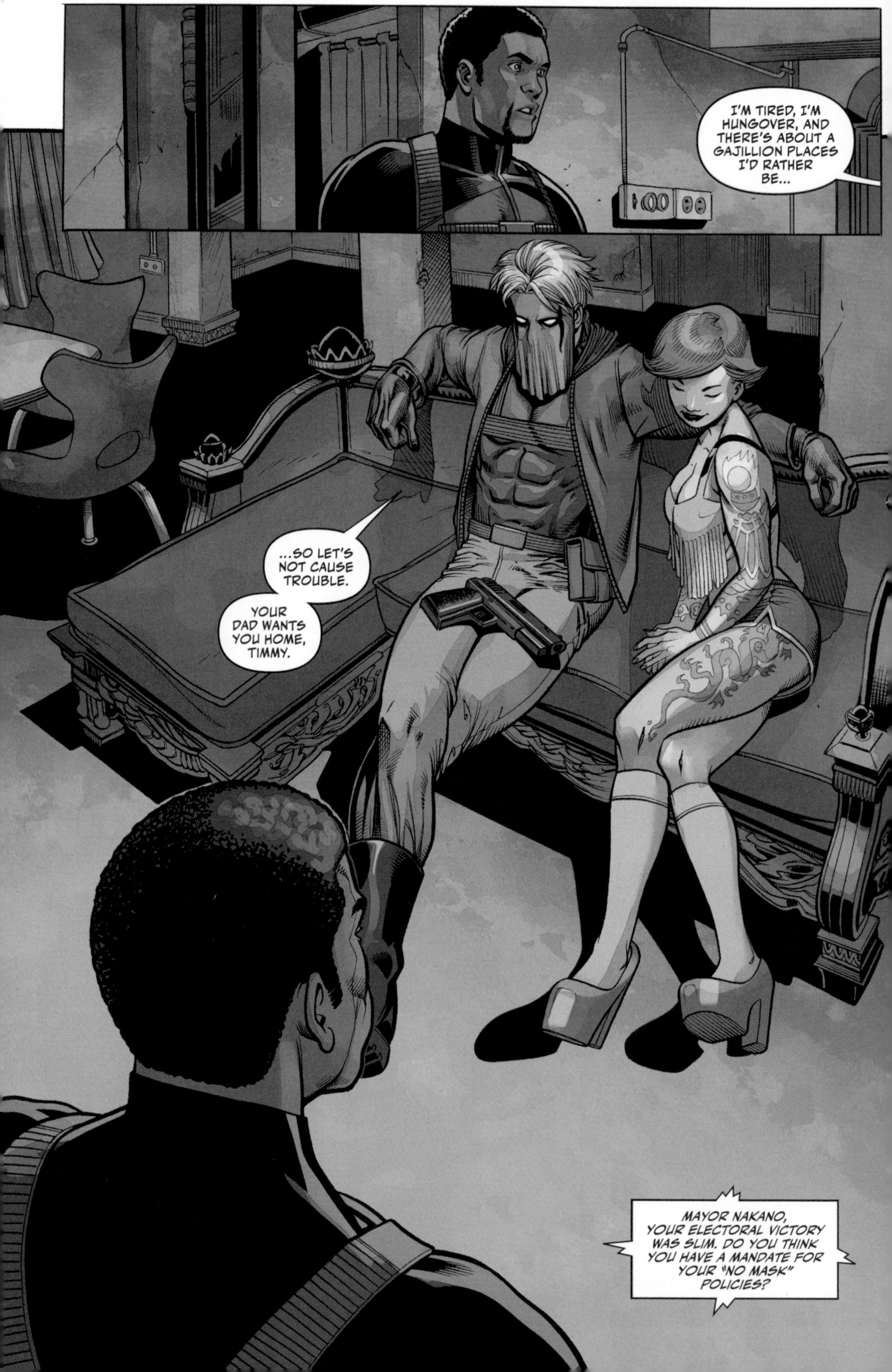
I'M TIRED, I'M HUNGOVER, AND THERE'S ABOUT A GAJILLION PLACES I'D RATHER BE...
...SO LET'S NOT CAUSE TROUBLE.
YOUR DAD WANTS YOU HOME, TIMMY.
MAYOR NAKANO, YOUR ELECTORAL VICTORY WAS SLIM. DO YOU THINK YOU HAVE A MANDATE FOR YOUR "NO MASK" POLICIES?

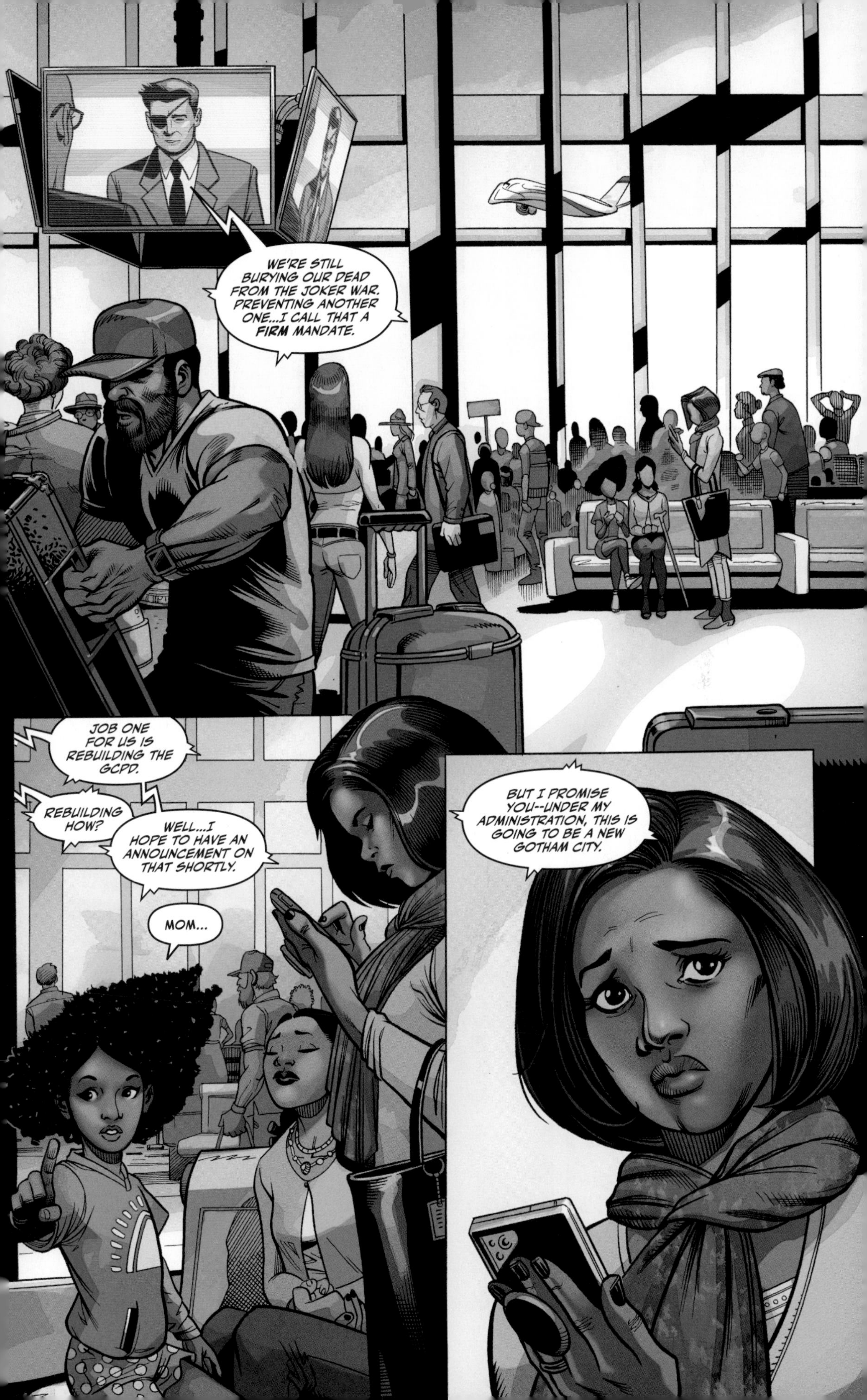
WE'RE STILL BURYING OUR DEAD FROM THE JOKER WAR. PREVENTING ANOTHER ONE...I CALL THAT A FIRM MANDATE.
JOB ONE FOR US IS REBUILDING THE GCPD.
REBUILDING HOW?
WELL...I HOPE TO HAVE AN ANNOUNCEMENT ON THAT SHORTLY.
MOM...
BUT I PROMISE YOU--UNDER MY ADMINISTRATION, THIS IS GOING TO BE A NEW GOTHAM CITY.

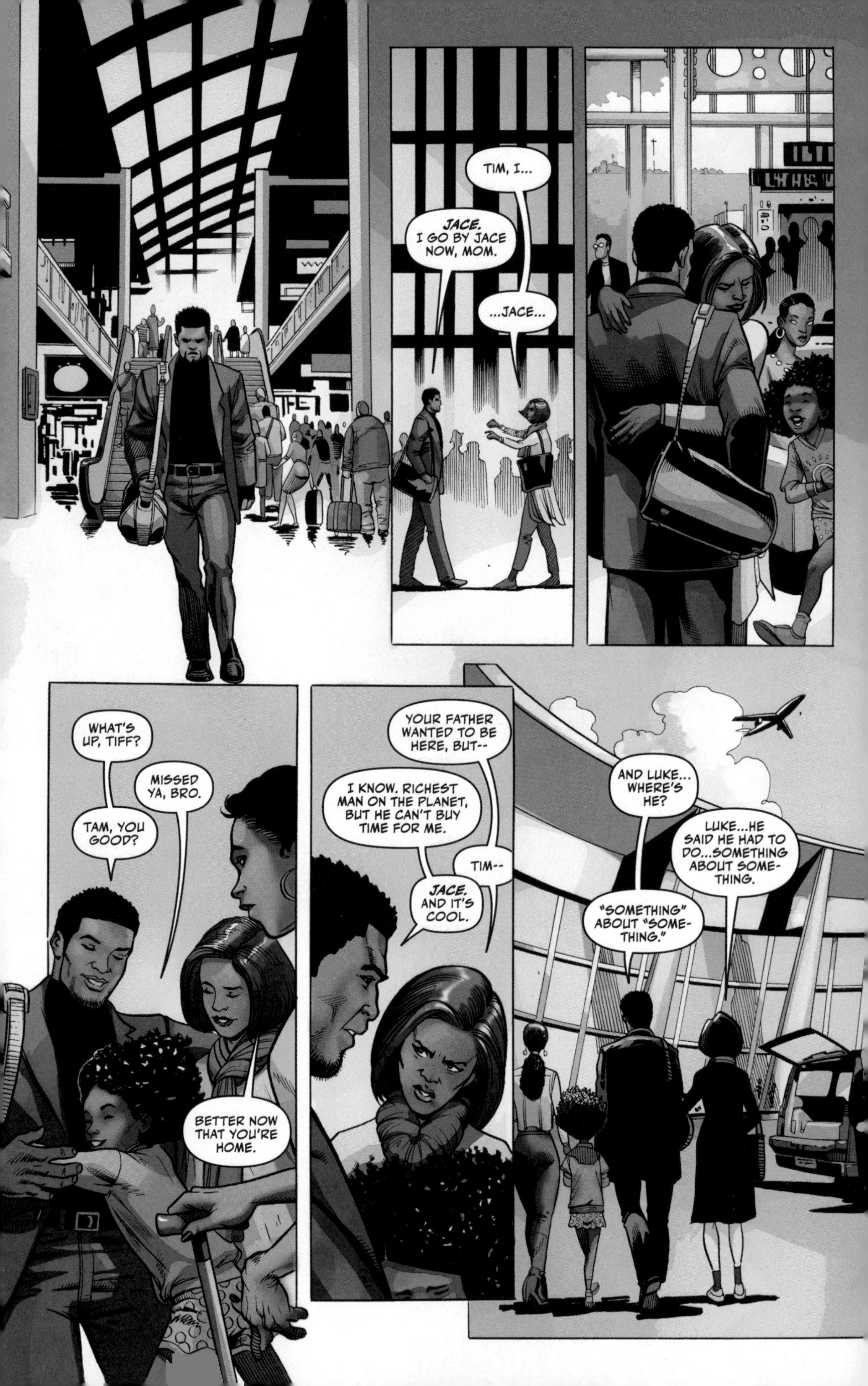
TIM, I...
JACE. I GO BY JACE NOW, MOM.
...JACE...
WHAT'S UP, TIFF?
MISSED YA, BRO.
TAM, YOU GOOD?
BETTER NOW THAT YOU'RE HOME.
YOUR FATHER WANTED TO BE HERE, BUT--
I KNOW. RICHEST MAN ON THE PLANET, BUT HE CAN'T BUY TIME FOR ME.
TIM--
JACE. AND IT'S COOL.
AND LUKE... WHERE'S HE?
LUKE...HE SAID HE HAD TO DO...SOMETHING ABOUT SOME-THING.
"SOMETHING" ABOUT "SOME-THING."

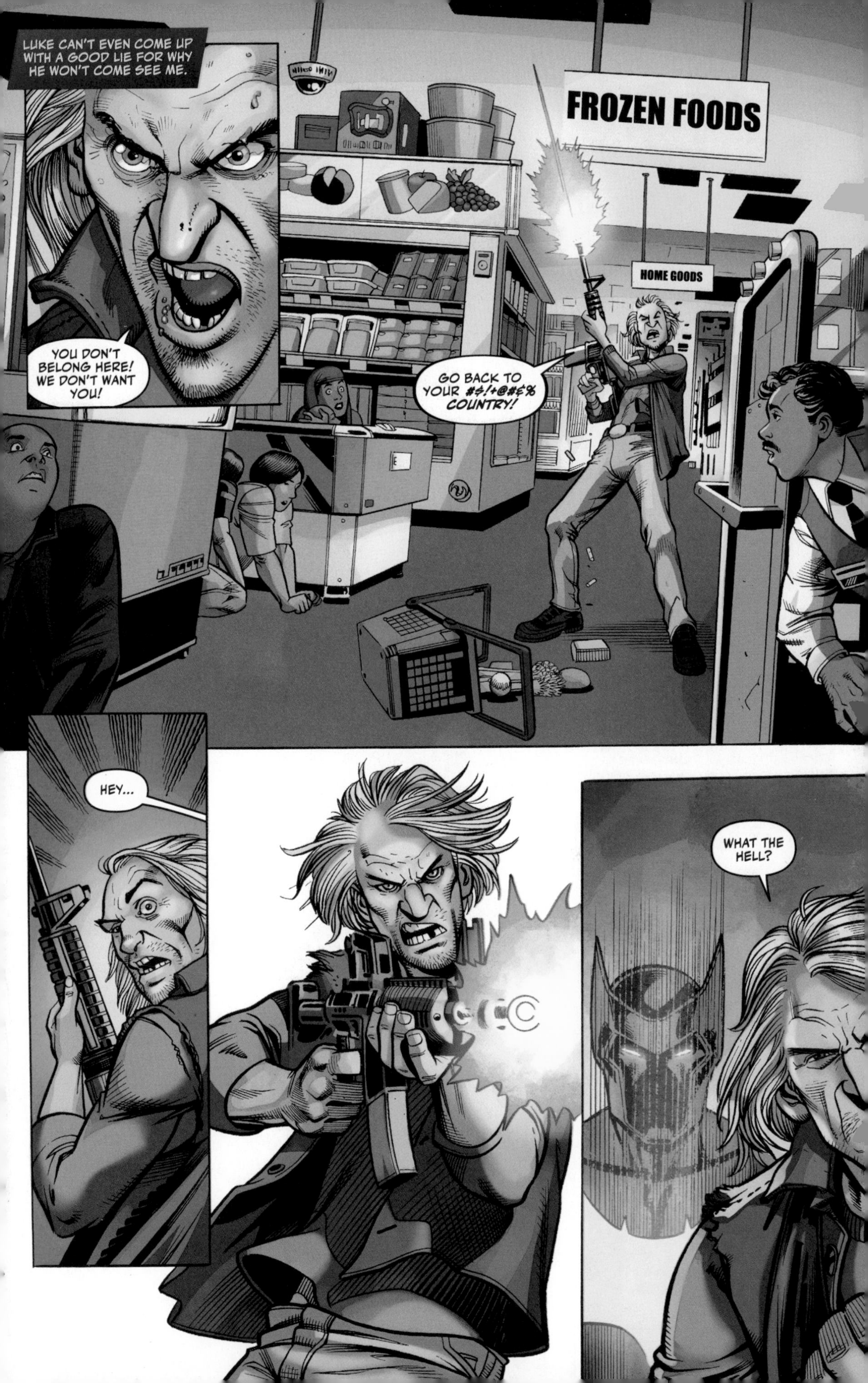
LUKE CAN'T EVEN COME UP WITH A GOOD LIE FOR WHY HE WON'T COME SEE ME.
FROZEN FOODS
HOME GOODS
YOU DON'T BELONG HERE! WE DON'T WANT YOU!
GO BACK TO YOUR #$!+@#£% COUNTRY!
HEY...
WHAT THE HELL?

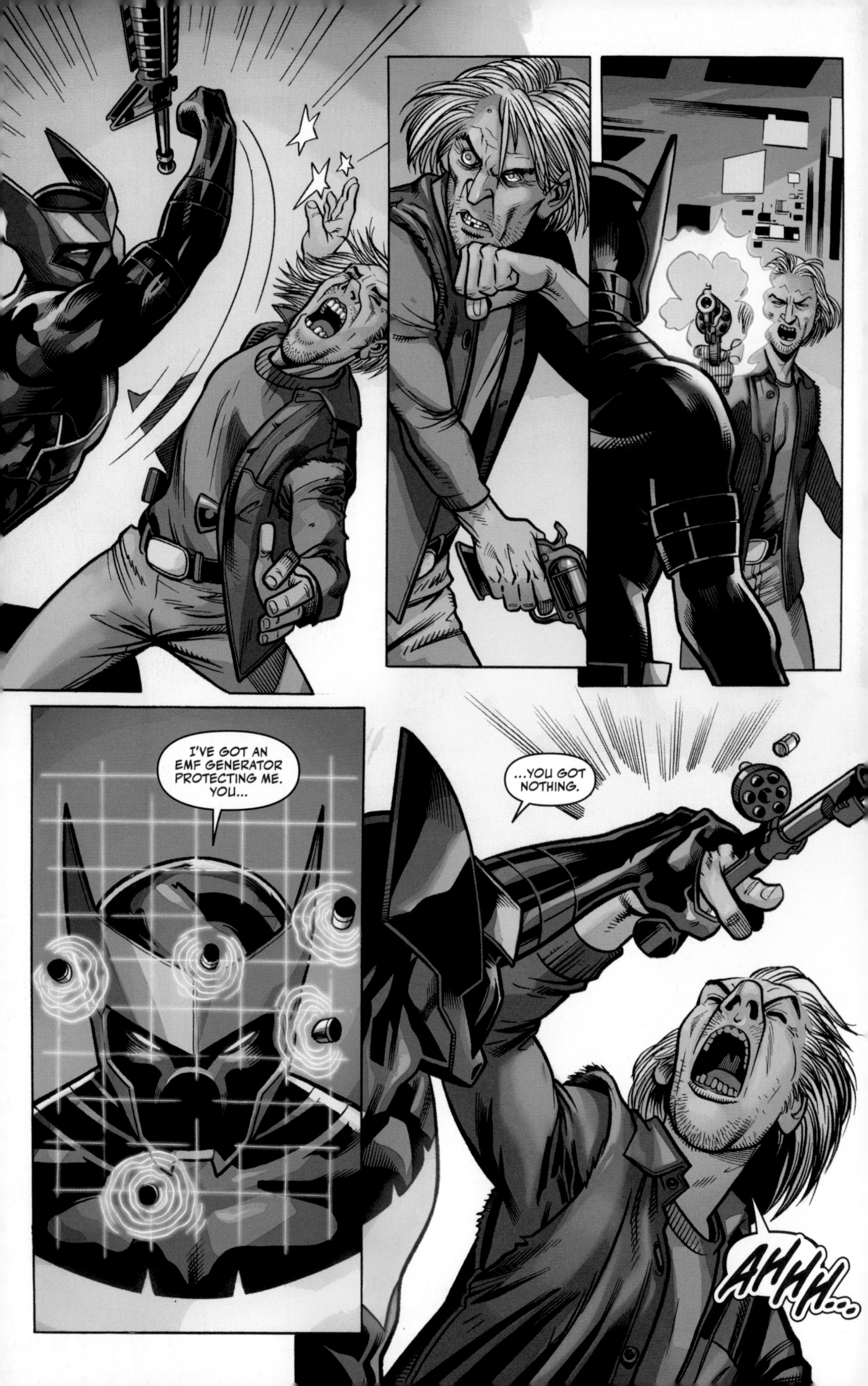
I'VE GOT AN EMF GENERATOR PROTECTING ME. YOU...
...YOU GOT NOTHING.
AHHH...

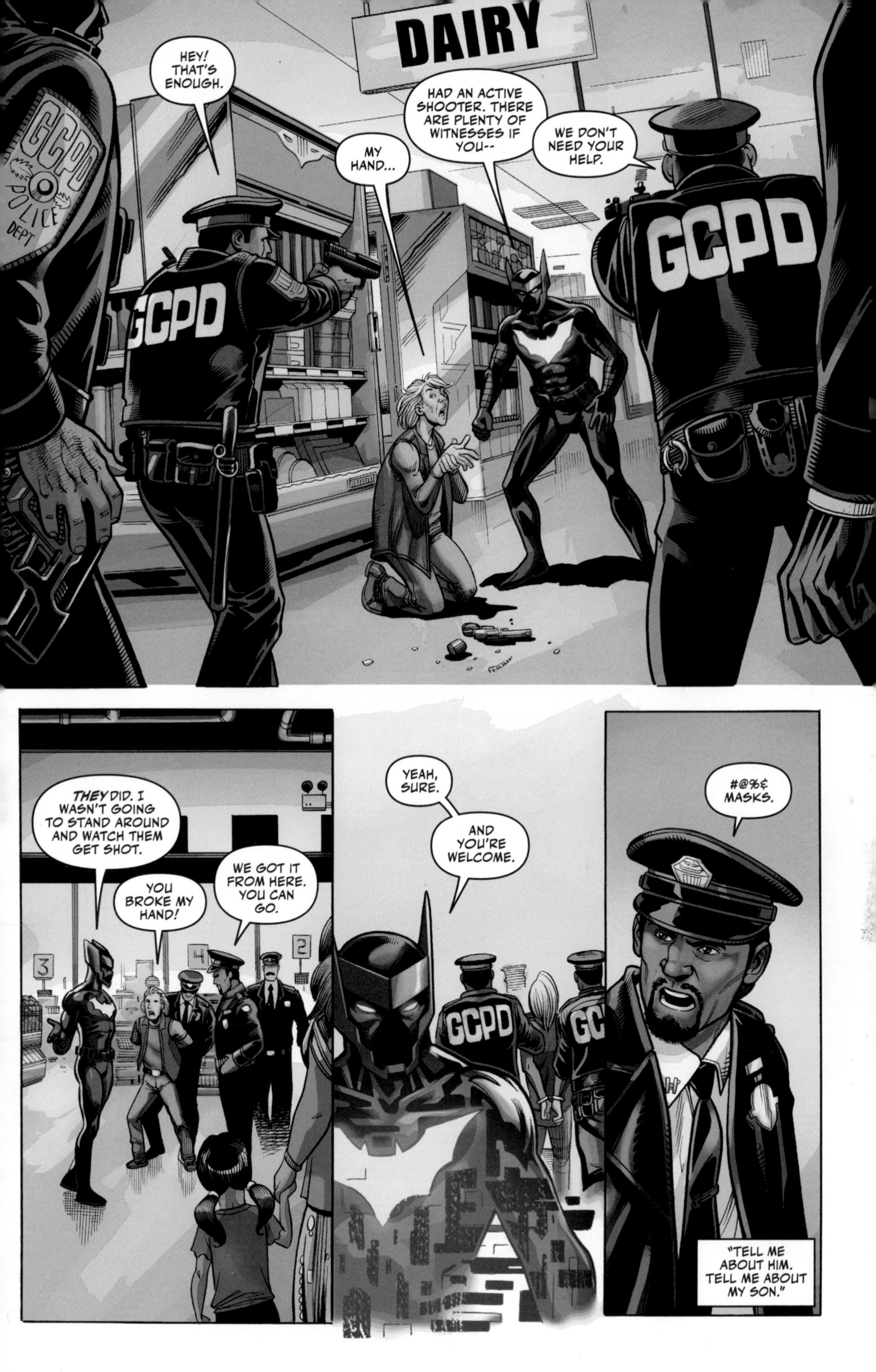
DAIRY
HEY! THAT'S ENOUGH.
MY HAND...
HAD AN ACTIVE SHOOTER. THERE ARE PLENTY OF WITNESSES IF YOU--
WE DON'T NEED YOUR HELP.
GCPD
POLICE DEPT
THEY DID. I WASN'T GOING TO STAND AROUND AND WATCH THEM GET SHOT.
YOU BROKE MY HAND!
WE GOT IT FROM HERE. YOU CAN GO.
YEAH, SURE.
AND YOU'RE WELCOME.
#@%& MASKS.
"TELL ME ABOUT HIM. TELL ME ABOUT MY SON."

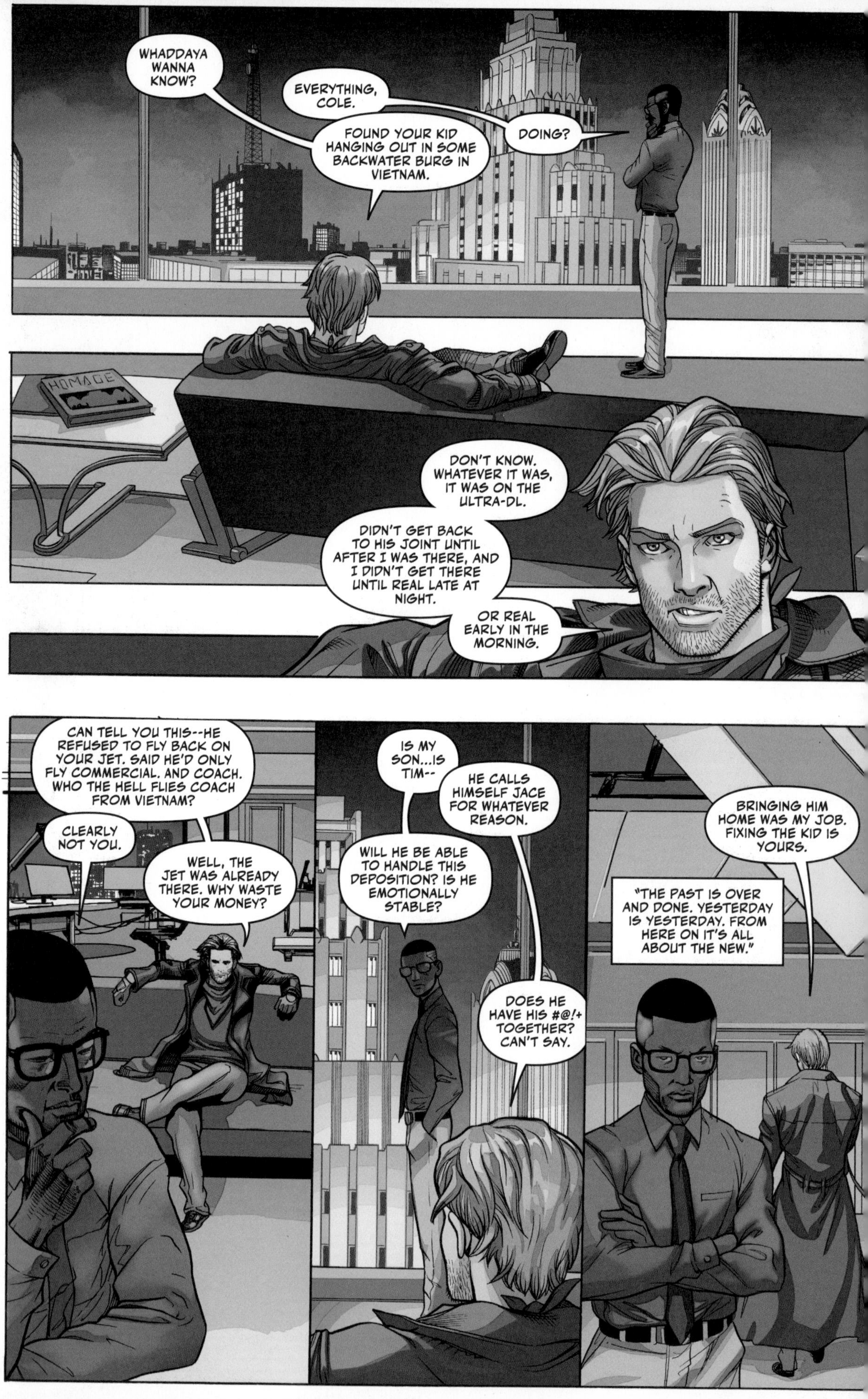
WHADDAYA WANNA KNOW?
EVERYTHING, COLE.
DOING?
FOUND YOUR KID HANGING OUT IN SOME BACKWATER BURG IN VIETNAM.
DON'T KNOW. WHATEVER IT WAS, IT WAS ON THE ULTRA-DL.
DIDN'T GET BACK TO HIS JOINT UNTIL AFTER I WAS THERE, AND I DIDN'T GET THERE UNTIL REAL LATE AT NIGHT.
OR REAL EARLY IN THE MORNING.
CAN TELL YOU THIS--HE REFUSED TO FLY BACK ON YOUR JET. SAID HE'D ONLY FLY COMMERCIAL. AND COACH. WHO THE HELL FLIES COACH FROM VIETNAM?
CLEARLY NOT YOU.
WELL, THE JET WAS ALREADY THERE. WHY WASTE YOUR MONEY?
IS MY SON...IS TIM--
HE CALLS HIMSELF JACE FOR WHATEVER REASON.
WILL HE BE ABLE TO HANDLE THIS DEPOSITION? IS HE EMOTIONALLY STABLE?
DOES HE HAVE HIS #@!+ TOGETHER? CAN'T SAY.
BRINGING HIM HOME WAS MY JOB. FIXING THE KID IS YOURS.
"THE PAST IS OVER AND DONE. YESTERDAY IS YESTERDAY. FROM HERE ON IT'S ALL ABOUT THE NEW."

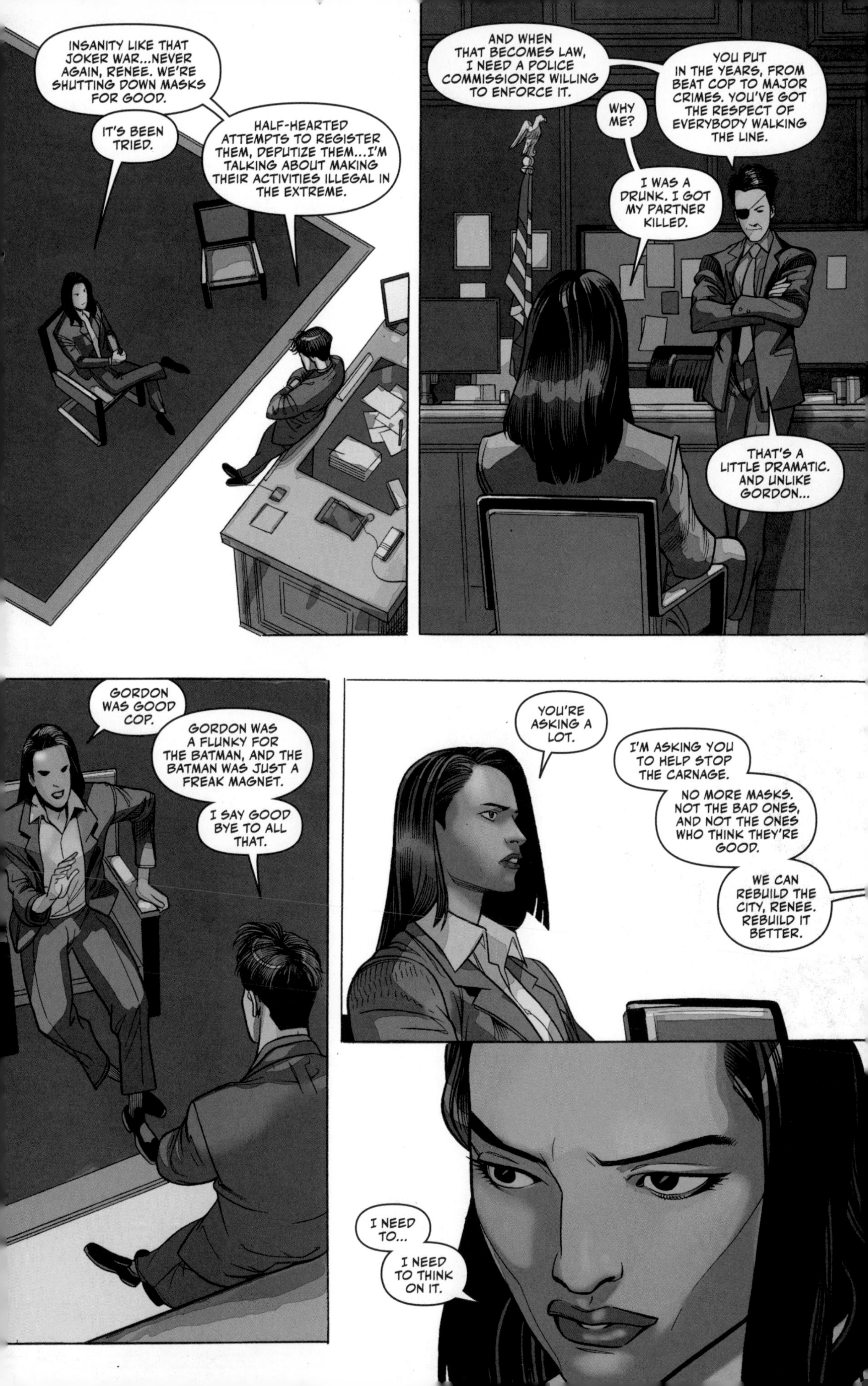
INSANITY LIKE THAT JOKER WAR...NEVER AGAIN, RENEE. WE'RE SHUTTING DOWN MASKS FOR GOOD.
IT'S BEEN TRIED.
HALF-HEARTED ATTEMPTS TO REGISTER THEM, DEPUTIZE THEM...I'M TALKING ABOUT MAKING THEIR ACTIVITIES ILLEGAL IN THE EXTREME.
AND WHEN THAT BECOMES LAW, I NEED A POLICE COMMISSIONER WILLING TO ENFORCE IT.
WHY ME?
YOU PUT IN THE YEARS, FROM BEAT COP TO MAJOR CRIMES. YOU'VE GOT THE RESPECT OF EVERYBODY WALKING THE LINE.
I WAS A DRUNK. I GOT MY PARTNER KILLED.
THAT'S A LITTLE DRAMATIC. AND UNLIKE GORDON...
GORDON WAS GOOD COP.
GORDON WAS A FLUNKY FOR THE BATMAN, AND THE BATMAN WAS JUST A FREAK MAGNET.
I SAY GOOD BYE TO ALL THAT.
YOU'RE ASKING A LOT.
I'M ASKING YOU TO HELP STOP THE CARNAGE.
NO MORE MASKS. NOT THE BAD ONES, AND NOT THE ONES WHO THINK THEY'RE GOOD.
WE CAN REBUILD THE CITY, RENEE. REBUILD IT BETTER.
I NEED TO...
I NEED TO THINK ON IT.

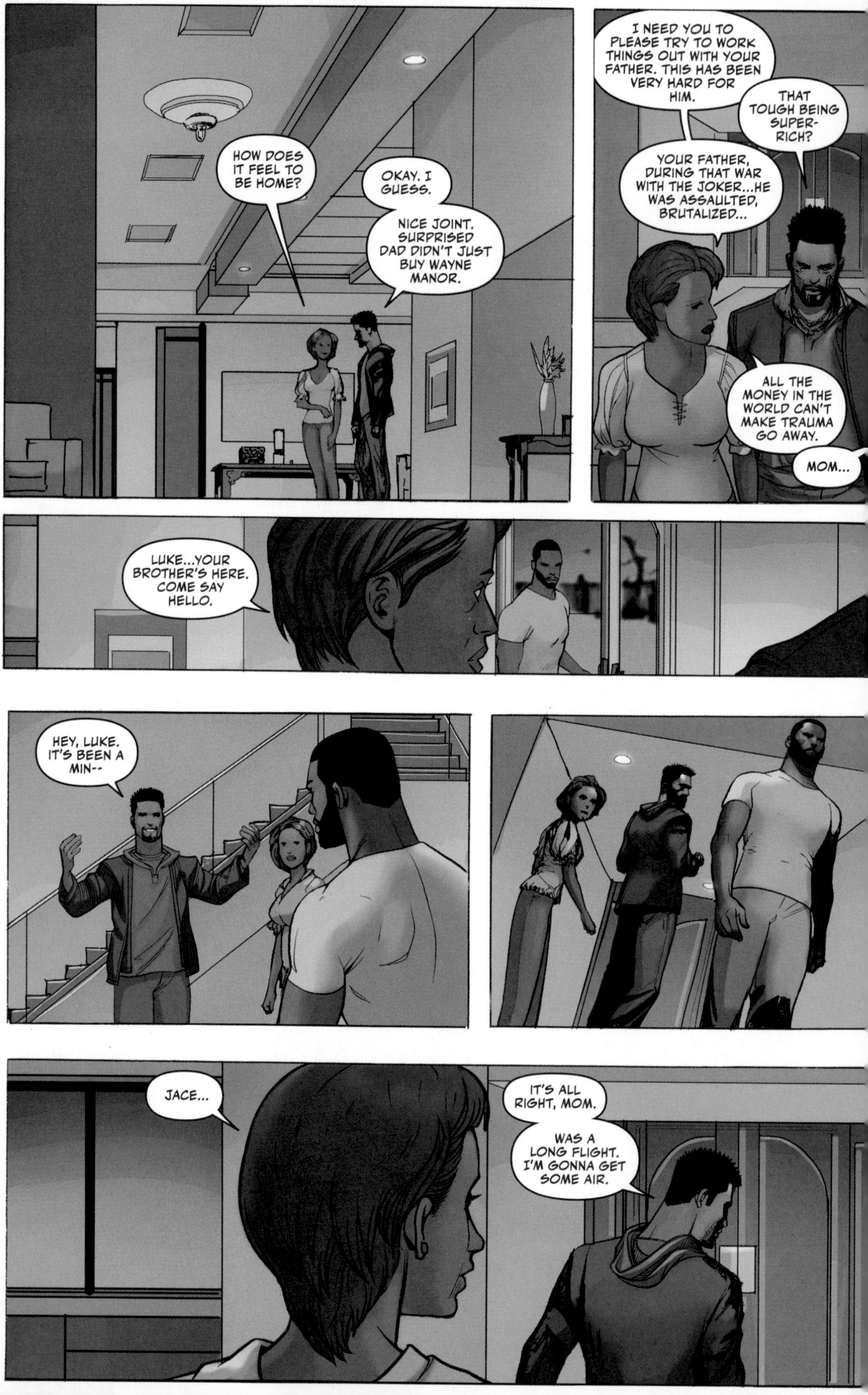
HOW DOES IT FEEL TO BE HOME?
OKAY. I GUESS.
NICE JOINT. SURPRISED DAD DIDN'T JUST BUY WAYNE MANOR.
I NEED YOU TO PLEASE TRY TO WORK THINGS OUT WITH YOUR FATHER. THIS HAS BEEN VERY HARD FOR HIM.
THAT TOUGH BEING SUPER-RICH?
YOUR FATHER, DURING THAT WAR WITH THE JOKER...HE WAS ASSAULTED, BRUTALIZED...
ALL THE MONEY IN THE WORLD CAN'T MAKE TRAUMA GO AWAY.
MOM...
LUKE...YOUR BROTHER'S HERE. COME SAY HELLO.
HEY, LUKE. IT'S BEEN A MIN--
JACE...
IT'S ALL RIGHT, MOM.
WAS A LONG FLIGHT. I'M GONNA GET SOME AIR.

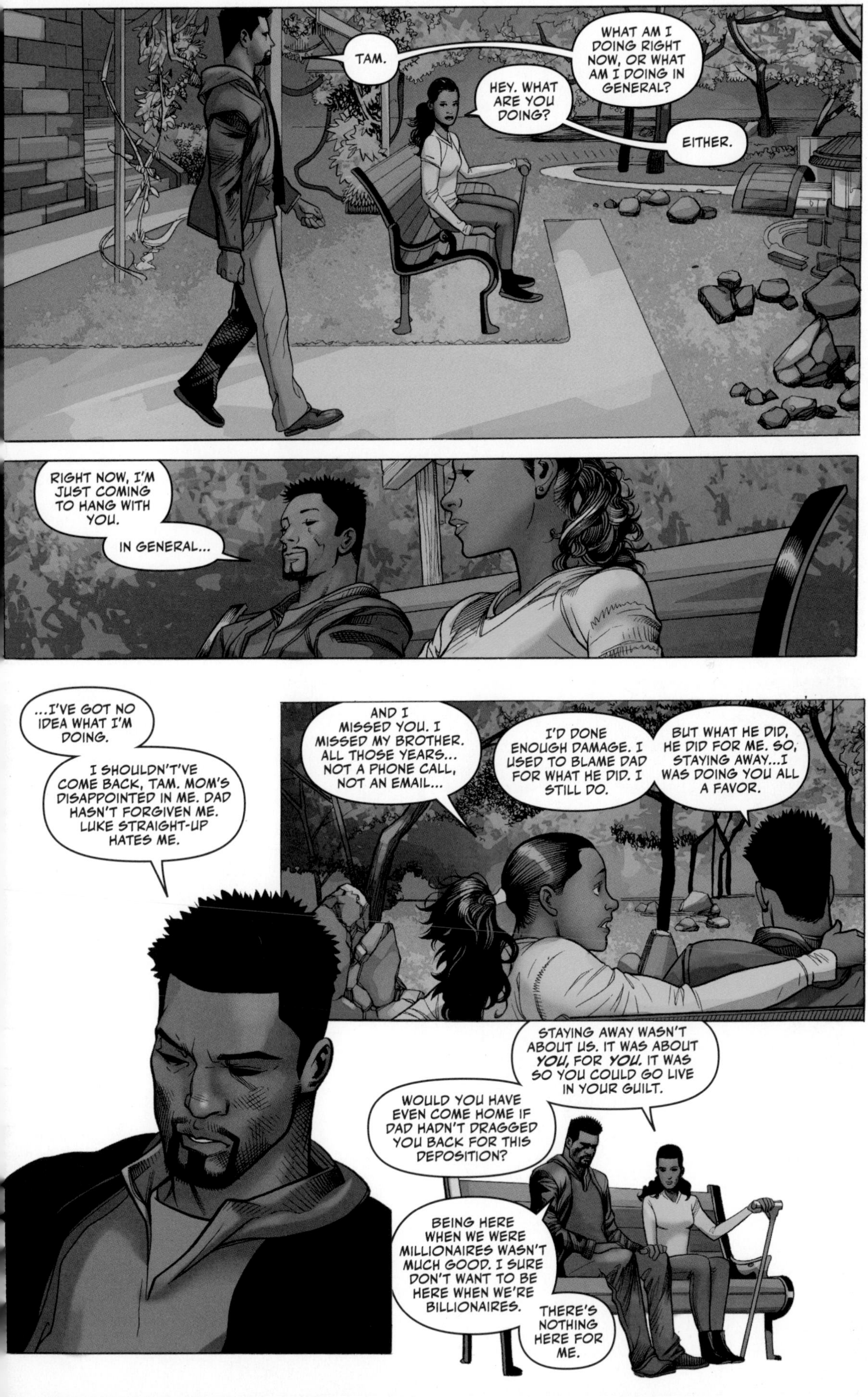
TAM.
HEY. WHAT ARE YOU DOING?
WHAT AM I DOING RIGHT NOW, OR WHAT AM I DOING IN GENERAL?
EITHER.
RIGHT NOW, I'M JUST COMING TO HANG WITH YOU.
IN GENERAL...
...I'VE GOT NO IDEA WHAT I'M DOING.
I SHOULDN'T'VE COME BACK, TAM. MOM'S DISAPPOINTED IN ME. DAD HASN'T FORGIVEN ME. LUKE STRAIGHT-UP HATES ME.
AND I MISSED YOU. I MISSED MY BROTHER. ALL THOSE YEARS... NOT A PHONE CALL, NOT AN EMAIL...
I'D DONE ENOUGH DAMAGE. I USED TO BLAME DAD FOR WHAT HE DID. I STILL DO.
BUT WHAT HE DID, HE DID FOR ME. SO, STAYING AWAY...I WAS DOING YOU ALL A FAVOR.
STAYING AWAY WASN'T ABOUT US. IT WAS ABOUT *YOU*, FOR *YOU*. IT WAS SO YOU COULD GO LIVE IN YOUR GUILT.
WOULD YOU HAVE EVEN COME HOME IF DAD HADN'T DRAGGED YOU BACK FOR THIS DEPOSITION?
BEING HERE WHEN WE WERE MILLIONAIRES WASN'T MUCH GOOD. I SURE DON'T WANT TO BE HERE WHEN WE'RE BILLIONAIRES.
THERE'S NOTHING HERE FOR ME.

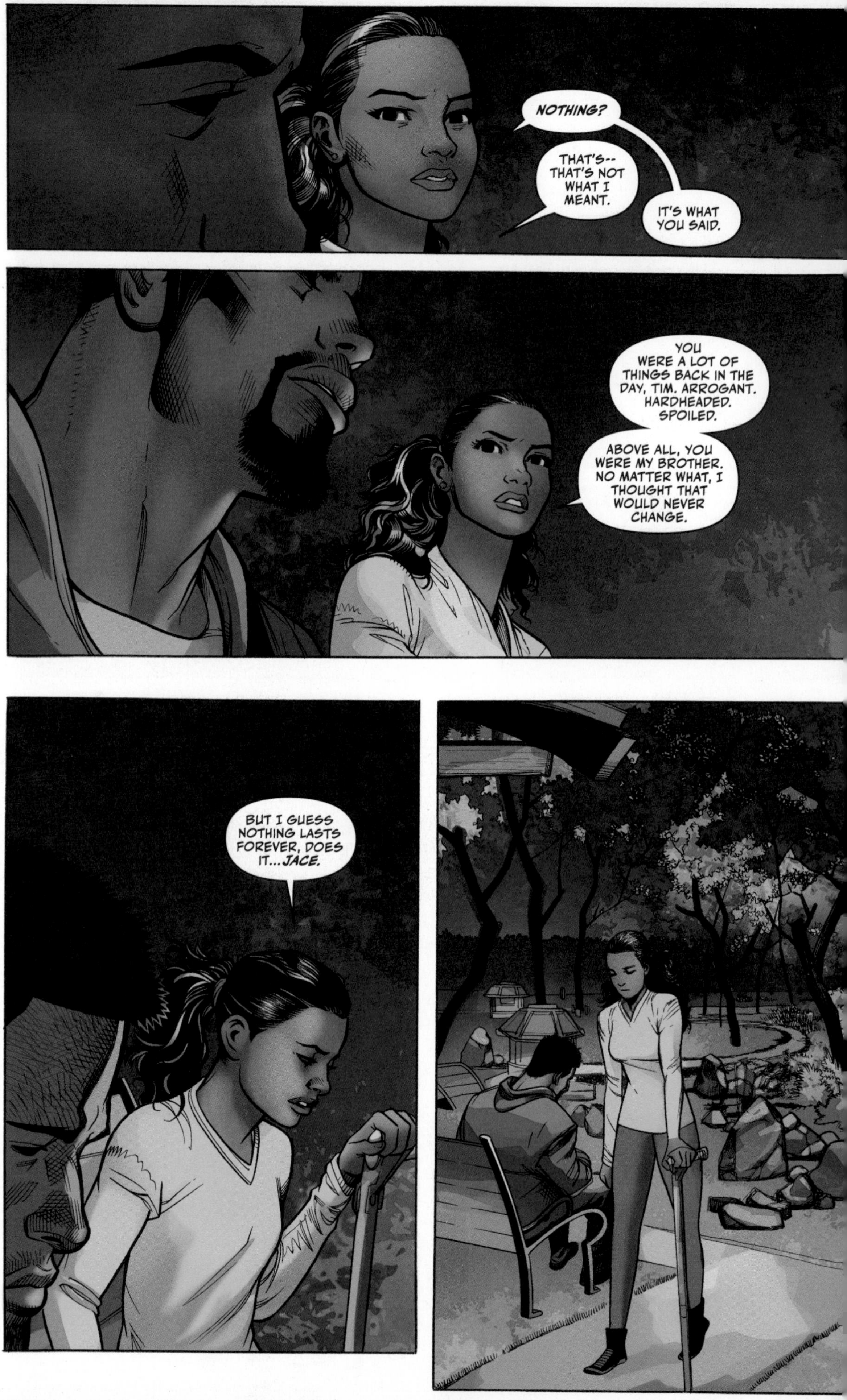
NOTHING?
THAT'S-- THAT'S NOT WHAT I MEANT.
IT'S WHAT YOU SAID.
YOU WERE A LOT OF THINGS BACK IN THE DAY, TIM. ARROGANT. HARDHEADED. SPOILED.
ABOVE ALL, YOU WERE MY BROTHER. NO MATTER WHAT, I THOUGHT THAT WOULD NEVER CHANGE.
BUT I GUESS NOTHING LASTS FOREVER, DOES IT...JACE.

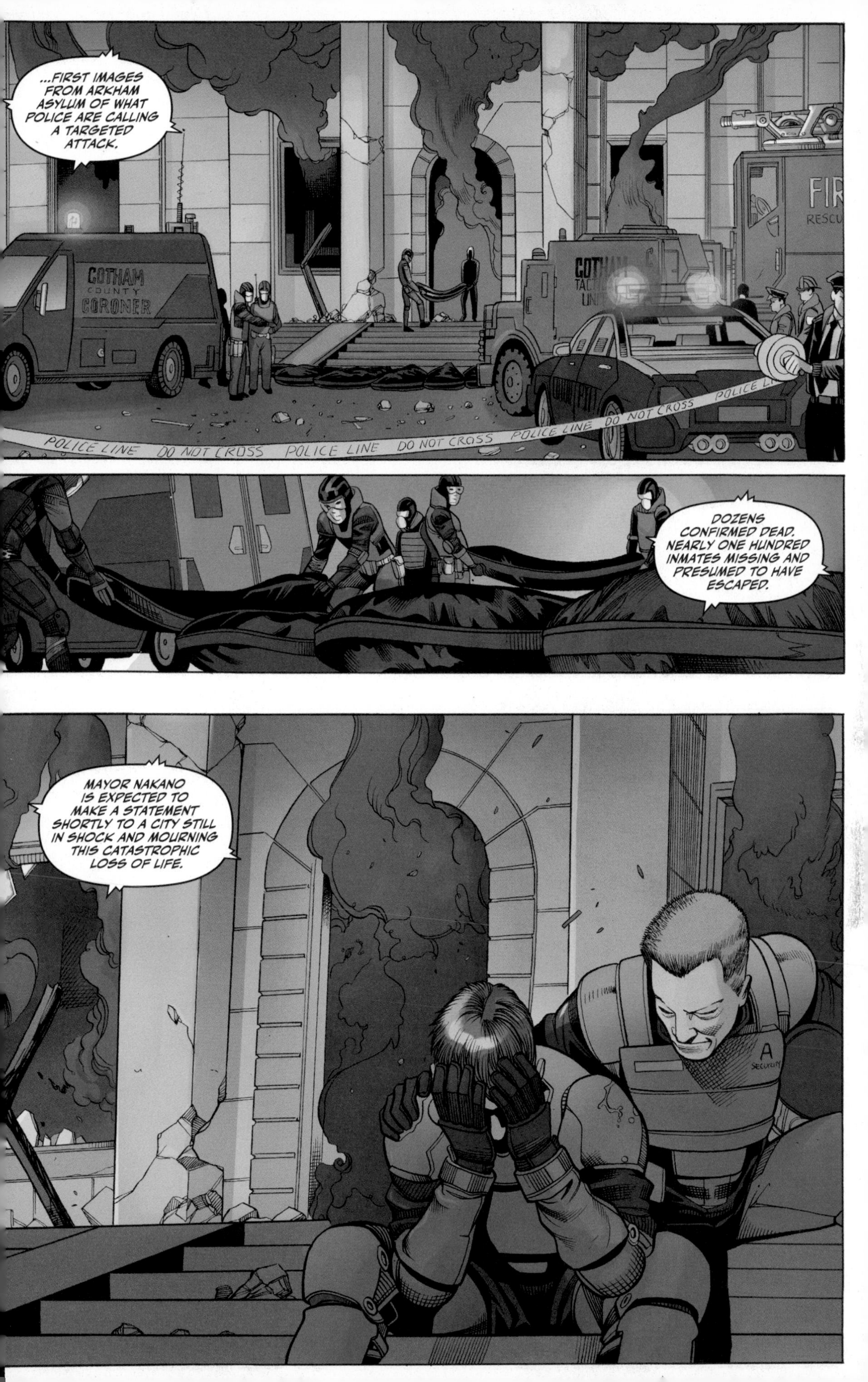
...FIRST IMAGES FROM ARKHAM ASYLUM OF WHAT POLICE ARE CALLING A TARGETED ATTACK.
GOTHAM COUNTY CORONER
GOTHAM TACTICAL UNIT
FIRE RESCUE
POLICE LINE DO NOT CROSS POLICE LINE DO NOT CROSS
POLICE LINE DO NOT CROSS POLICE LINE
DOZENS CONFIRMED DEAD. NEARLY ONE HUNDRED INMATES MISSING AND PRESUMED TO HAVE ESCAPED.
MAYOR NAKANO IS EXPECTED TO MAKE A STATEMENT SHORTLY TO A CITY STILL IN SHOCK AND MOURNING THIS CATASTROPHIC LOSS OF LIFE.
A SECURITY

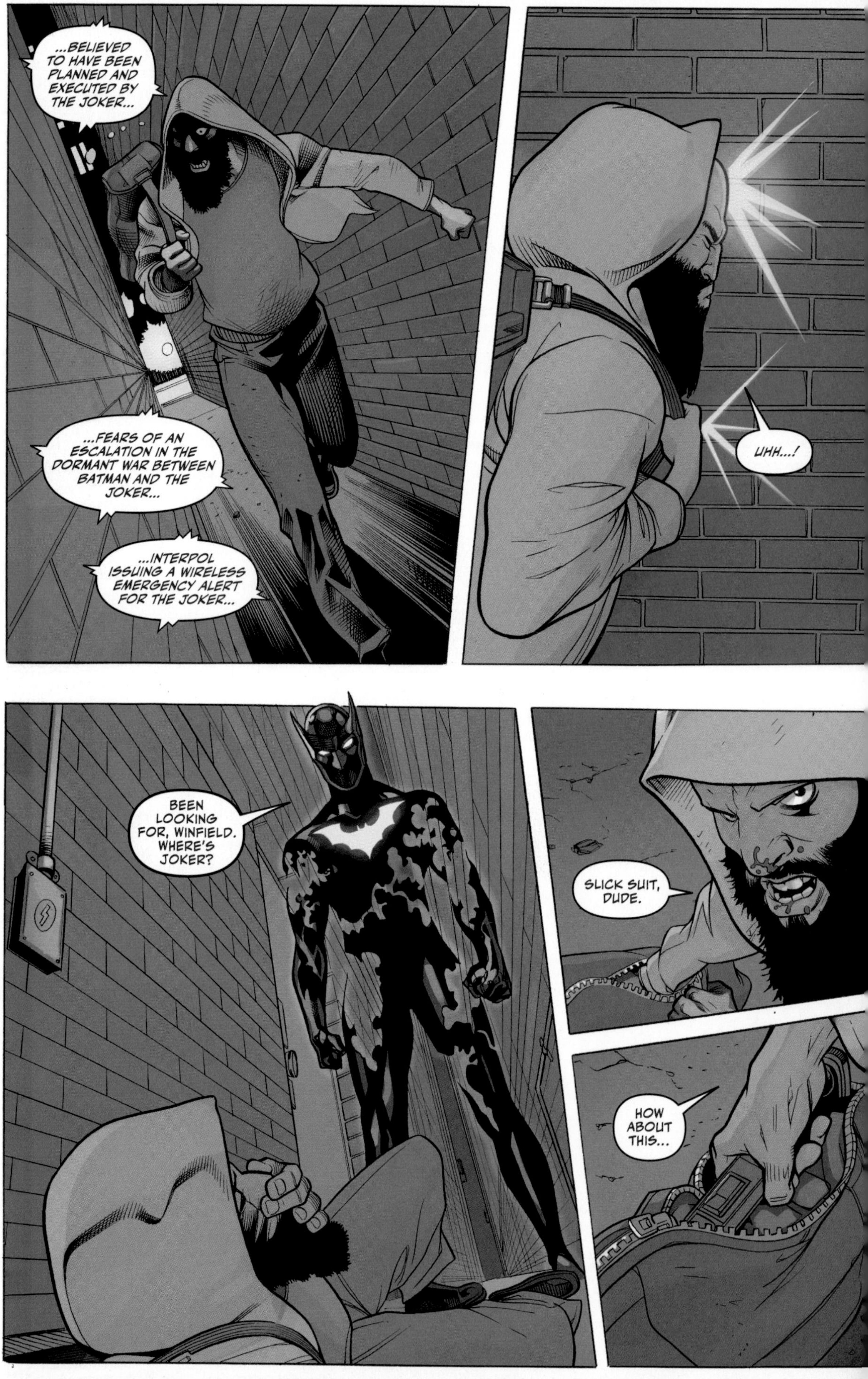
...BELIEVED TO HAVE BEEN PLANNED AND EXECUTED BY THE JOKER...
...FEARS OF AN ESCALATION IN THE DORMANT WAR BETWEEN BATMAN AND THE JOKER...
...INTERPOL ISSUING A WIRELESS EMERGENCY ALERT FOR THE JOKER...
UHH...!
BEEN LOOKING FOR, WINFIELD. WHERE'S JOKER?
SLICK SUIT, DUDE.
HOW ABOUT THIS...

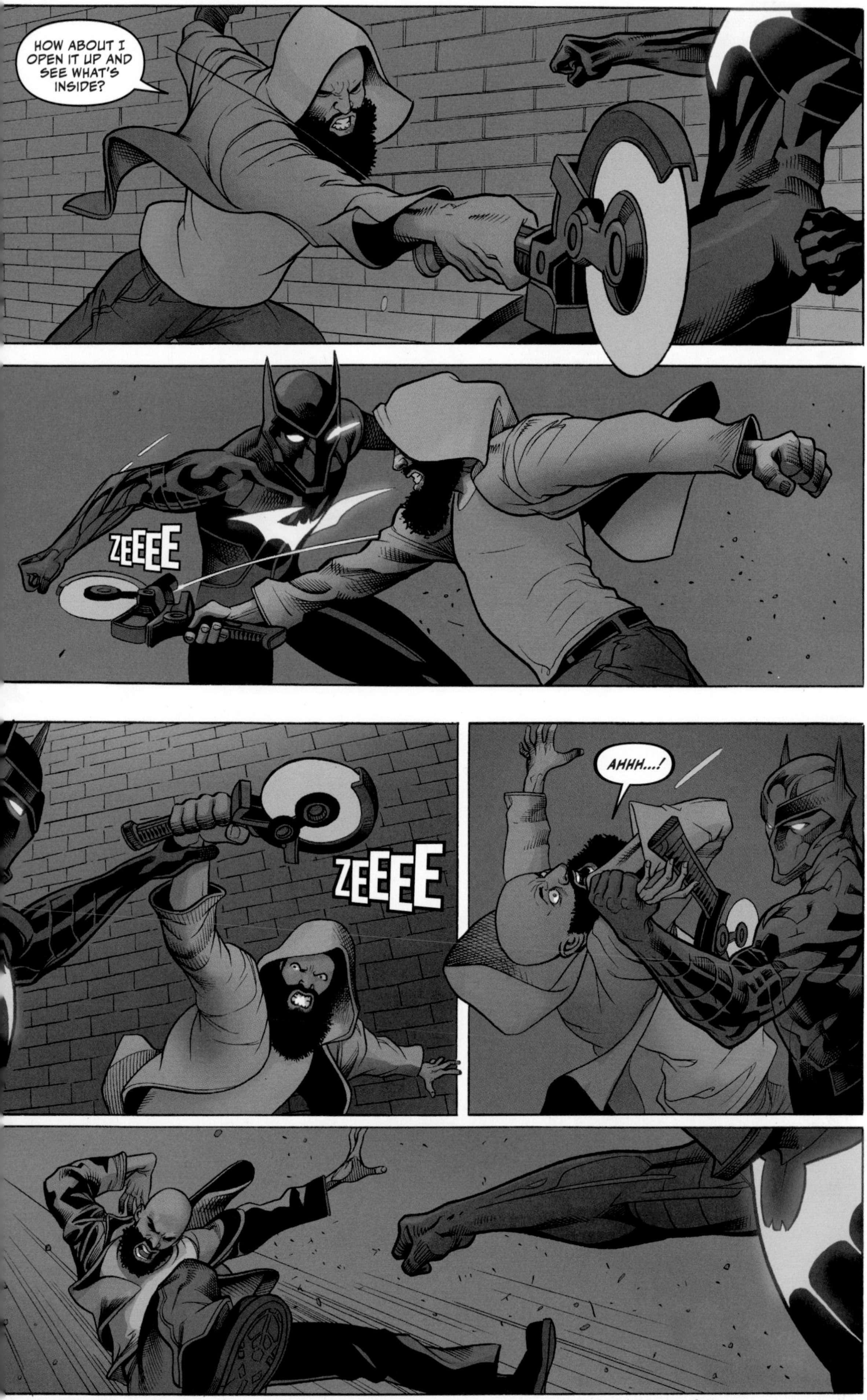
HOW ABOUT I OPEN IT UP AND SEE WHAT'S INSIDE?
ZEEEE
ZEEEE
AHHH...!

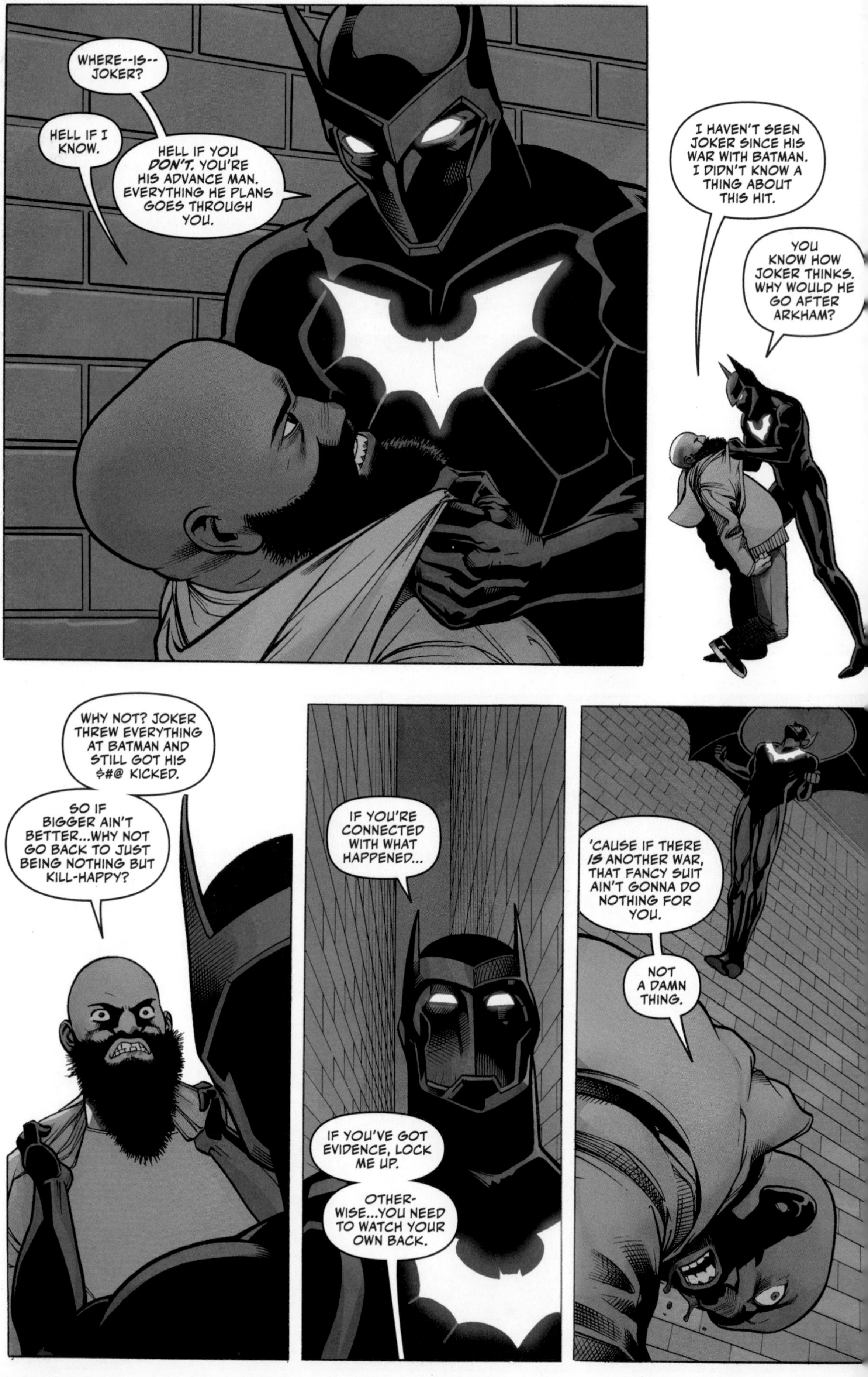
WHERE--IS--JOKER?
HELL IF I KNOW.
HELL IF YOU *DON'T.* YOU'RE HIS ADVANCE MAN. EVERYTHING HE PLANS GOES THROUGH YOU.
I HAVEN'T SEEN JOKER SINCE HIS WAR WITH BATMAN. I DIDN'T KNOW A THING ABOUT THIS HIT.
YOU KNOW HOW JOKER THINKS. WHY WOULD HE GO AFTER ARKHAM?
WHY NOT? JOKER THREW EVERYTHING AT BATMAN AND STILL GOT HIS $#@ KICKED.
SO IF BIGGER AIN'T BETTER...WHY NOT GO BACK TO JUST BEING NOTHING BUT KILL-HAPPY?
IF YOU'RE CONNECTED WITH WHAT HAPPENED...
IF YOU'VE GOT EVIDENCE, LOCK ME UP.
OTHER-WISE...YOU NEED TO WATCH YOUR OWN BACK.
'CAUSE IF THERE *IS* ANOTHER WAR, THAT FANCY SUIT AIN'T GONNA DO NOTHING FOR YOU.
NOT A DAMN THING.

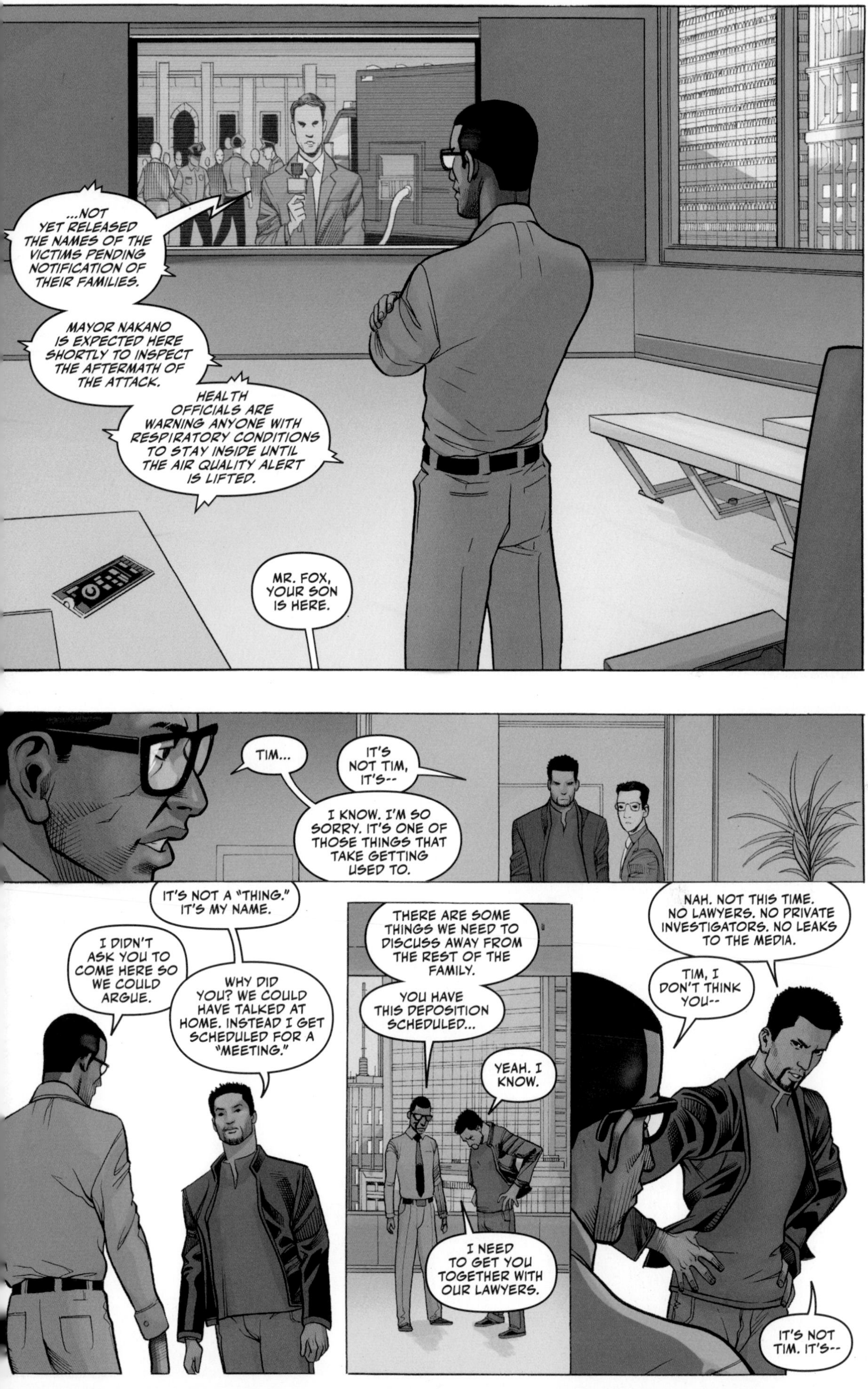
...NOT YET RELEASED THE NAMES OF THE VICTIMS PENDING NOTIFICATION OF THEIR FAMILIES.
MAYOR NAKANO IS EXPECTED HERE SHORTLY TO INSPECT THE AFTERMATH OF THE ATTACK.
HEALTH OFFICIALS ARE WARNING ANYONE WITH RESPIRATORY CONDITIONS TO STAY INSIDE UNTIL THE AIR QUALITY ALERT IS LIFTED.
MR. FOX, YOUR SON IS HERE.
TIM...
IT'S NOT TIM, IT'S--
I KNOW. I'M SO SORRY. IT'S ONE OF THOSE THINGS THAT TAKE GETTING USED TO.
IT'S NOT A "THING." IT'S MY NAME.
I DIDN'T ASK YOU TO COME HERE SO WE COULD ARGUE.
WHY DID YOU? WE COULD HAVE TALKED AT HOME. INSTEAD I GET SCHEDULED FOR A "MEETING."
THERE ARE SOME THINGS WE NEED TO DISCUSS AWAY FROM THE REST OF THE FAMILY.
YOU HAVE THIS DEPOSITION SCHEDULED...
YEAH. I KNOW.
I NEED TO GET YOU TOGETHER WITH OUR LAWYERS.
NAH. NOT THIS TIME. NO LAWYERS. NO PRIVATE INVESTIGATORS. NO LEAKS TO THE MEDIA.
TIM, I DON'T THINK YOU--
IT'S NOT TIM. IT'S--

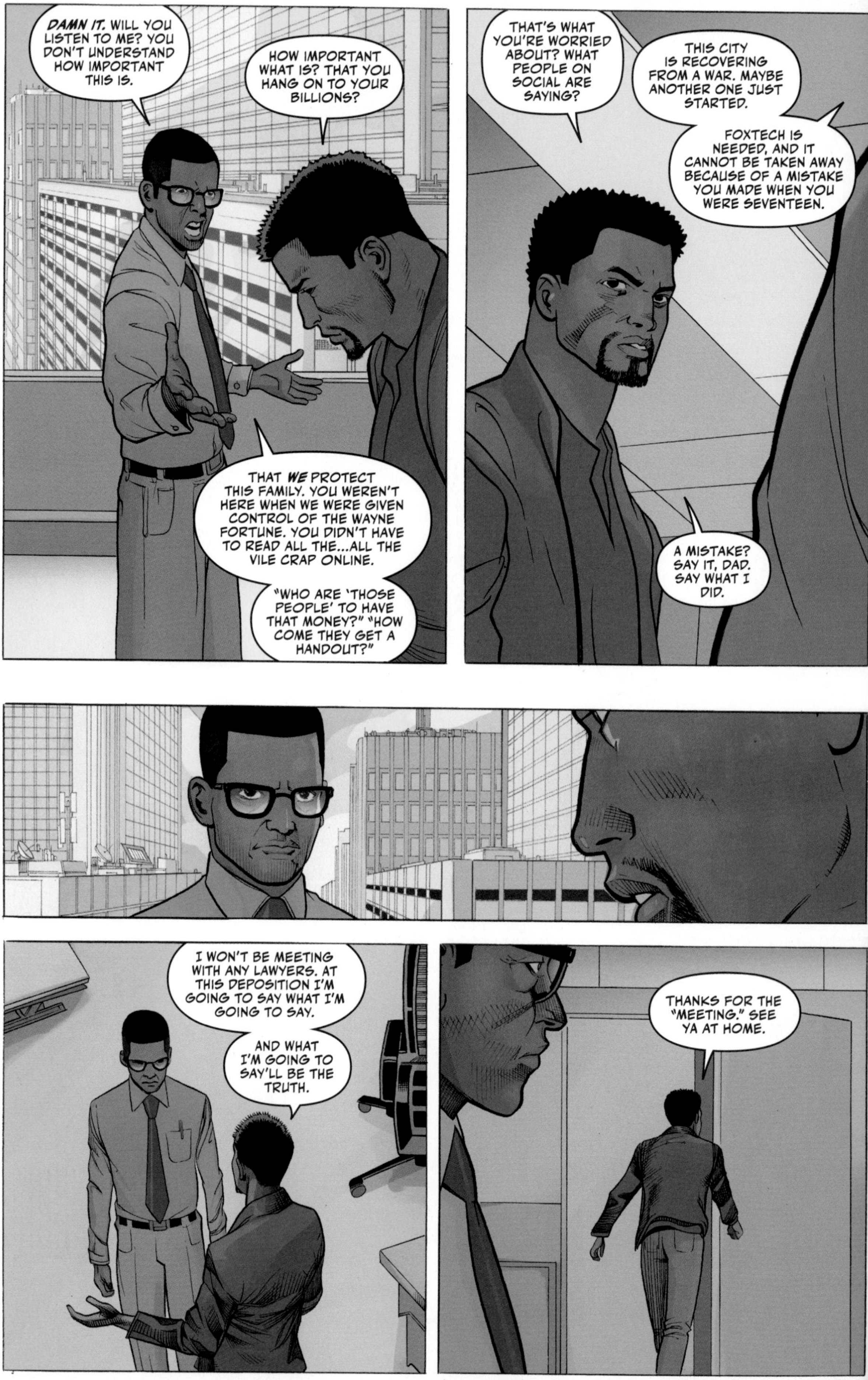
DAMN IT. WILL YOU LISTEN TO ME? YOU DON'T UNDERSTAND HOW IMPORTANT THIS IS.
HOW IMPORTANT WHAT IS? THAT YOU HANG ON TO YOUR BILLIONS?
THAT WE PROTECT THIS FAMILY. YOU WEREN'T HERE WHEN WE WERE GIVEN CONTROL OF THE WAYNE FORTUNE. YOU DIDN'T HAVE TO READ ALL THE...ALL THE VILE CRAP ONLINE.
"WHO ARE 'THOSE PEOPLE' TO HAVE THAT MONEY?" "HOW COME THEY GET A HANDOUT?"
THAT'S WHAT YOU'RE WORRIED ABOUT? WHAT PEOPLE ON SOCIAL ARE SAYING?
THIS CITY IS RECOVERING FROM A WAR. MAYBE ANOTHER ONE JUST STARTED.
FOXTECH IS NEEDED, AND IT CANNOT BE TAKEN AWAY BECAUSE OF A MISTAKE YOU MADE WHEN YOU WERE SEVENTEEN.
A MISTAKE? SAY IT, DAD. SAY WHAT I DID.
I WON'T BE MEETING WITH ANY LAWYERS. AT THIS DEPOSITION I'M GOING TO SAY WHAT I'M GOING TO SAY.
AND WHAT I'M GOING TO SAY'LL BE THE TRUTH.
THANKS FOR THE "MEETING." SEE YA AT HOME.

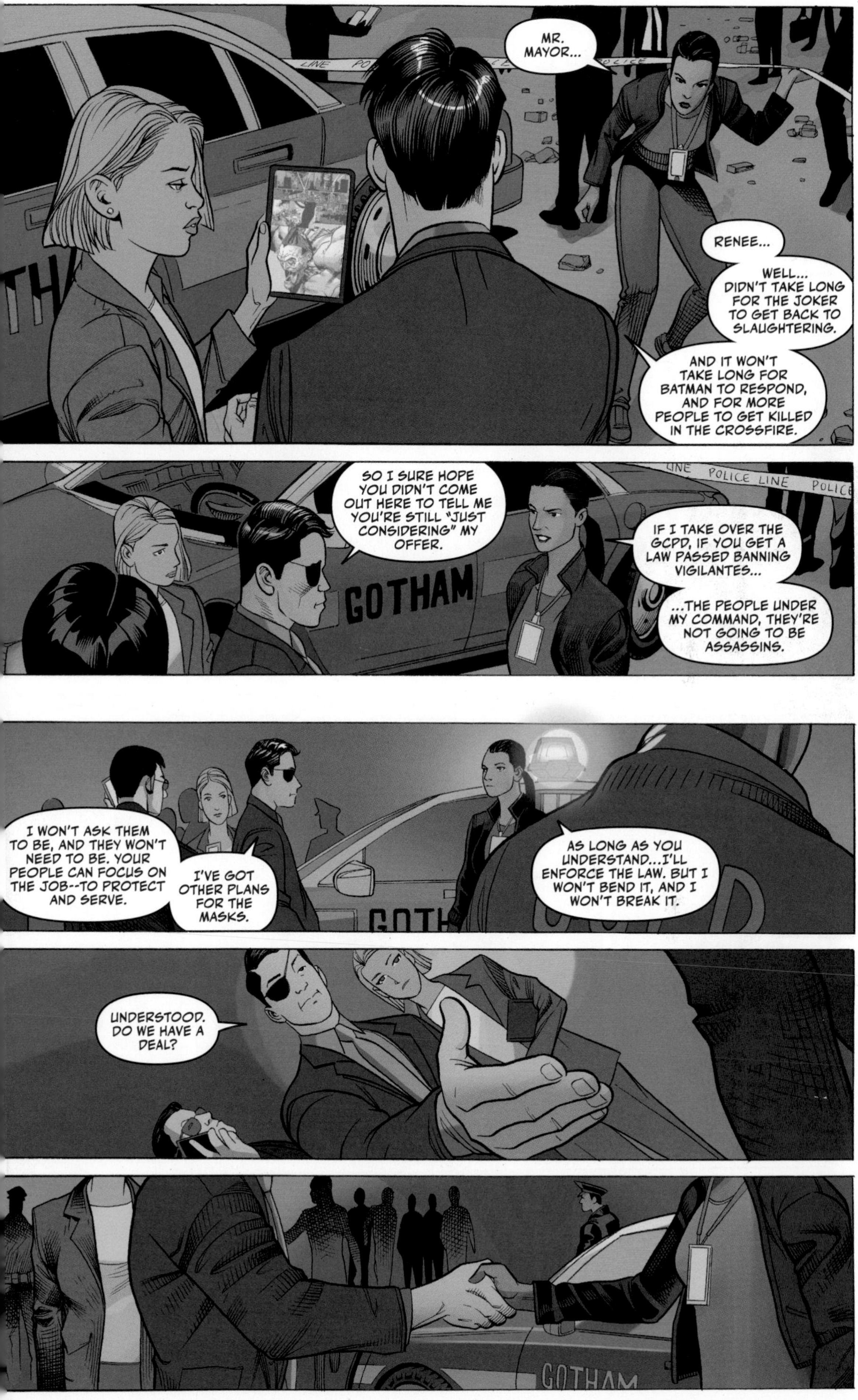

MR. MAYOR...
RENEE...
WELL... DIDN'T TAKE LONG FOR THE JOKER TO GET BACK TO SLAUGHTERING.
AND IT WON'T TAKE LONG FOR BATMAN TO RESPOND, AND FOR MORE PEOPLE TO GET KILLED IN THE CROSSFIRE.
POLICE LINE POLICE
GOTHAM
SO I SURE HOPE YOU DIDN'T COME OUT HERE TO TELL ME YOU'RE STILL "JUST CONSIDERING" MY OFFER.
IF I TAKE OVER THE GCPD, IF YOU GET A LAW PASSED BANNING VIGILANTES...
...THE PEOPLE UNDER MY COMMAND, THEY'RE NOT GOING TO BE ASSASSINS.
I WON'T ASK THEM TO BE, AND THEY WON'T NEED TO BE. YOUR PEOPLE CAN FOCUS ON THE JOB--TO PROTECT AND SERVE.
I'VE GOT OTHER PLANS FOR THE MASKS.
AS LONG AS YOU UNDERSTAND...I'LL ENFORCE THE LAW. BUT I WON'T BEND IT, AND I WON'T BREAK IT.
UNDERSTOOD. DO WE HAVE A DEAL?
GOTHAM

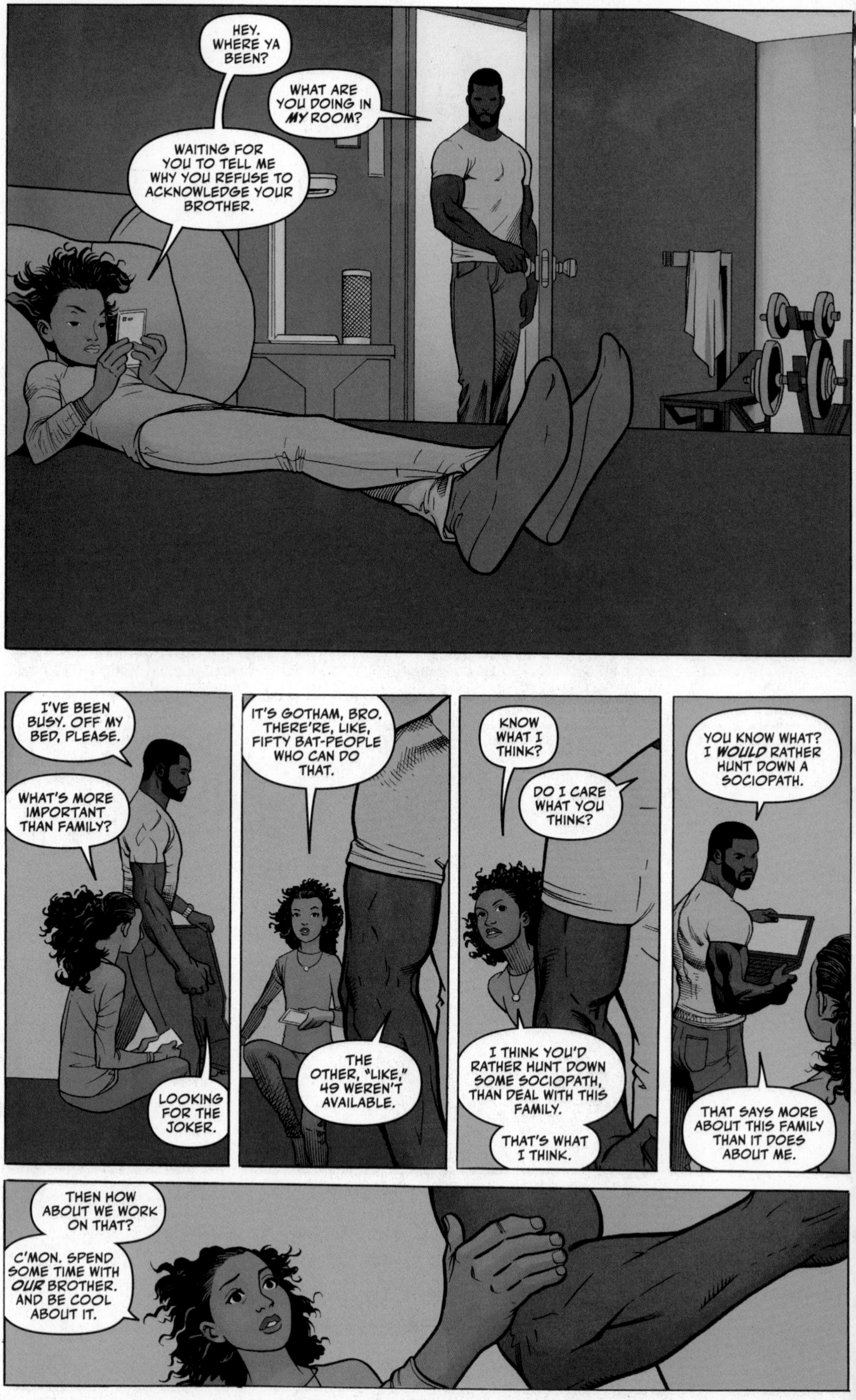
HEY. WHERE YA BEEN?
WHAT ARE YOU DOING IN MY ROOM?
WAITING FOR YOU TO TELL ME WHY YOU REFUSE TO ACKNOWLEDGE YOUR BROTHER.
I'VE BEEN BUSY. OFF MY BED, PLEASE.
WHAT'S MORE IMPORTANT THAN FAMILY?
LOOKING FOR THE JOKER.
IT'S GOTHAM, BRO. THERE'RE, LIKE, FIFTY BAT-PEOPLE WHO CAN DO THAT.
THE OTHER, "LIKE," 49 WEREN'T AVAILABLE.
KNOW WHAT I THINK?
DO I CARE WHAT YOU THINK?
I THINK YOU'D RATHER HUNT DOWN SOME SOCIOPATH, THAN DEAL WITH THIS FAMILY.
THAT'S WHAT I THINK.
YOU KNOW WHAT? I WOULD RATHER HUNT DOWN A SOCIOPATH.
THAT SAYS MORE ABOUT THIS FAMILY THAN IT DOES ABOUT ME.
THEN HOW ABOUT WE WORK ON THAT?
C'MON. SPEND SOME TIME WITH OUR BROTHER. AND BE COOL ABOUT IT.

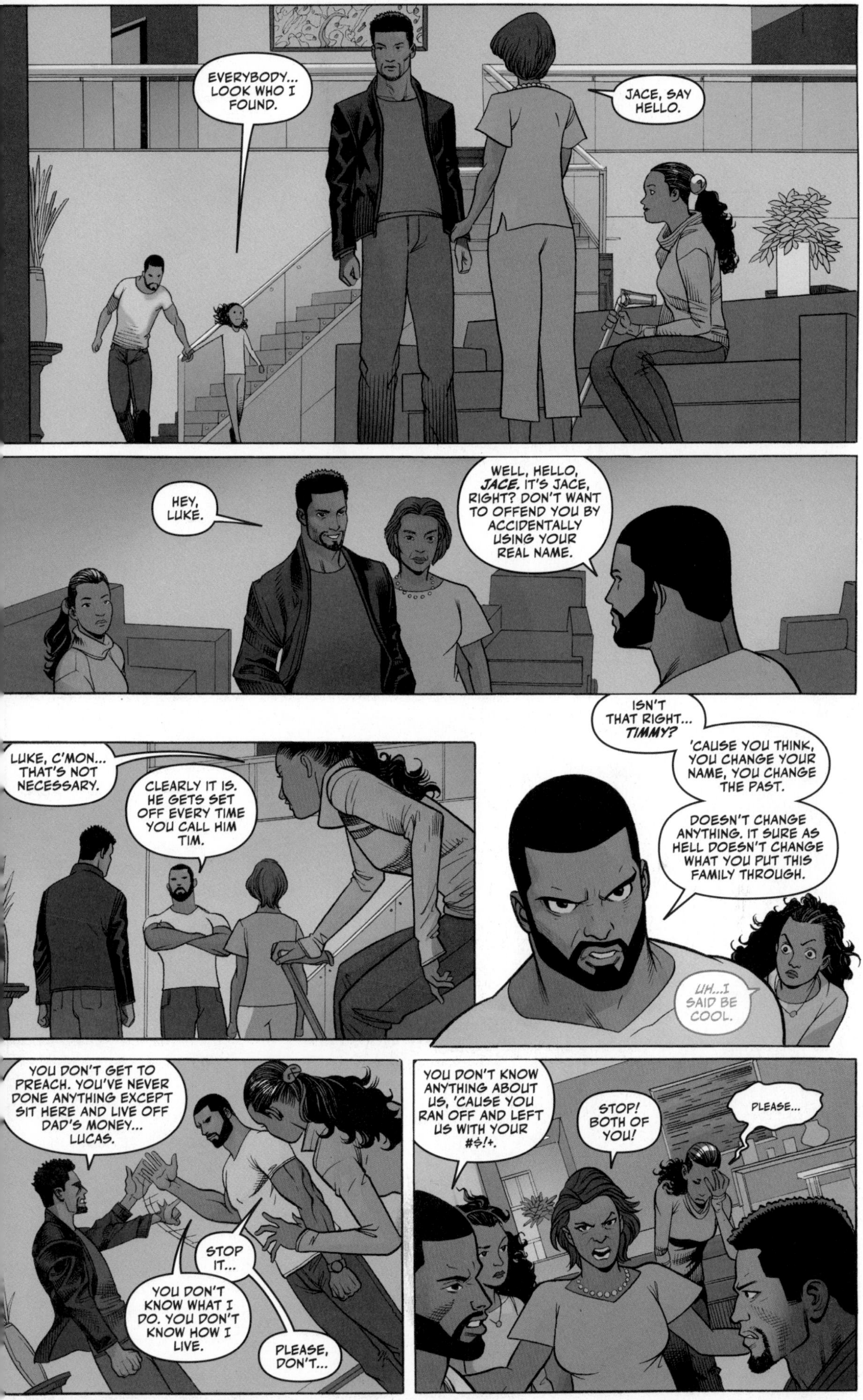
EVERYBODY... LOOK WHO I FOUND.
JACE, SAY HELLO.
HEY, LUKE.
WELL, HELLO, JACE. IT'S JACE, RIGHT? DON'T WANT TO OFFEND YOU BY ACCIDENTALLY USING YOUR REAL NAME.
ISN'T THAT RIGHT... TIMMY?
LUKE, C'MON... THAT'S NOT NECESSARY.
CLEARLY IT IS. HE GETS SET OFF EVERY TIME YOU CALL HIM TIM.
'CAUSE YOU THINK, YOU CHANGE YOUR NAME, YOU CHANGE THE PAST.
DOESN'T CHANGE ANYTHING. IT SURE AS HELL DOESN'T CHANGE WHAT YOU PUT THIS FAMILY THROUGH.
UH...I SAID BE COOL.
YOU DON'T GET TO PREACH. YOU'VE NEVER DONE ANYTHING EXCEPT SIT HERE AND LIVE OFF DAD'S MONEY... LUCAS.
STOP IT...
YOU DON'T KNOW WHAT I DO. YOU DON'T KNOW HOW I LIVE.
PLEASE, DON'T...
YOU DON'T KNOW ANYTHING ABOUT US, 'CAUSE YOU RAN OFF AND LEFT US WITH YOUR #$!+.
STOP! BOTH OF YOU!
PLEASE...

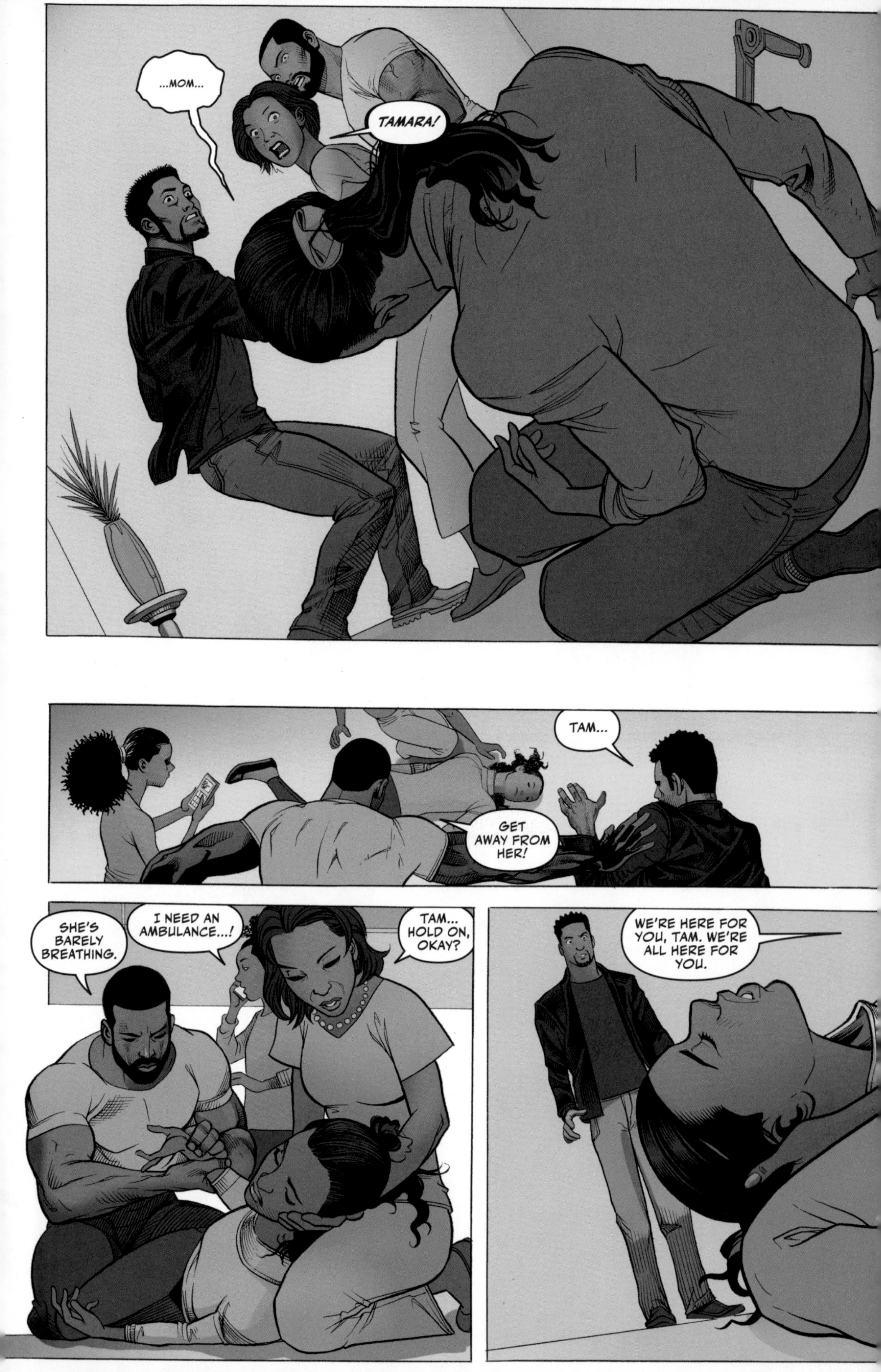
...MOM...
TAMARA!
TAM...
GET AWAY FROM HER!
SHE'S BARELY BREATHING.
I NEED AN AMBULANCE...!
TAM... HOLD ON, OKAY?
WE'RE HERE FOR YOU, TAM. WE'RE ALL HERE FOR YOU.

THE NEXT BATMAN: SECOND SON #2
Cover Art by **DOUG BRAITHWAITE**

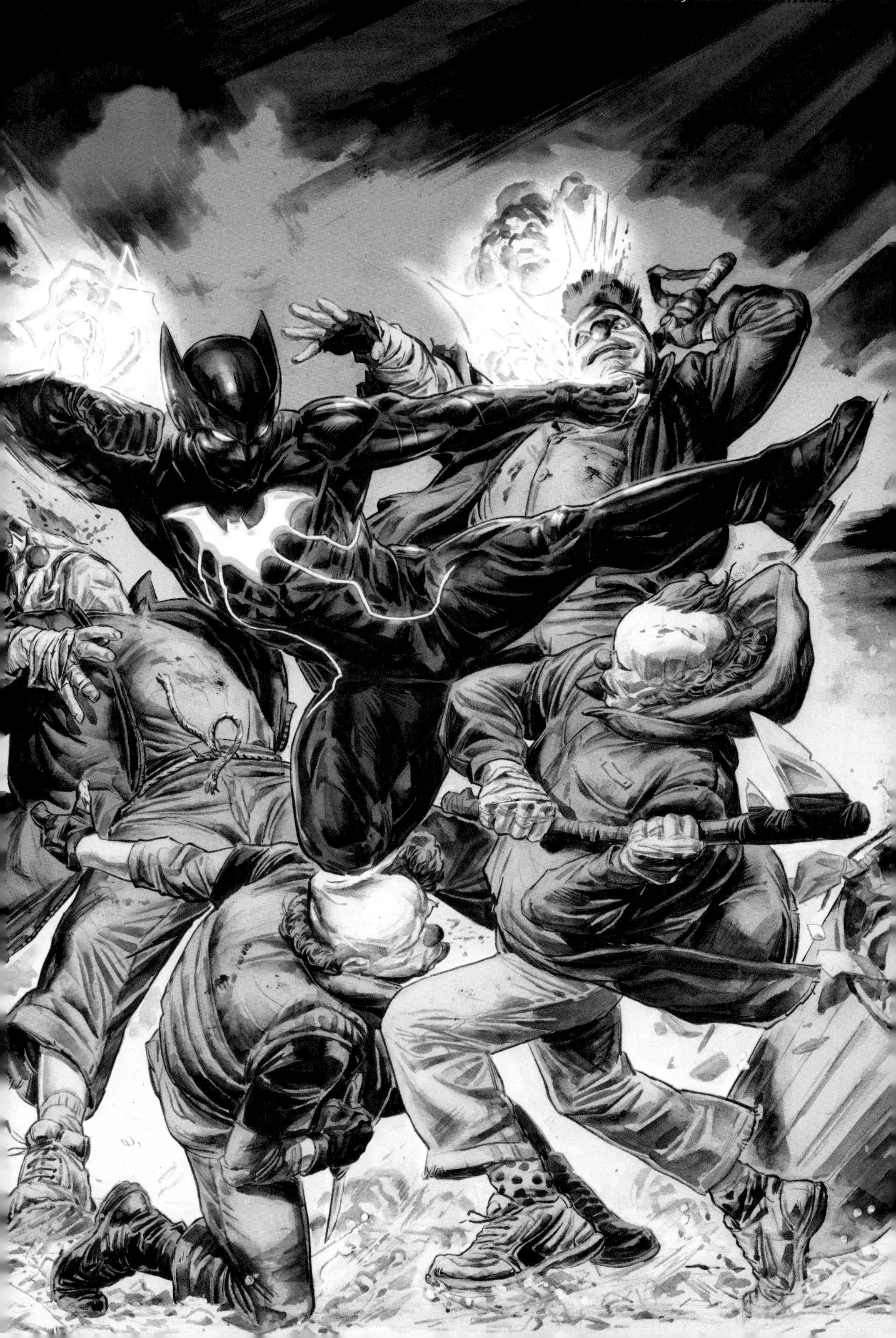

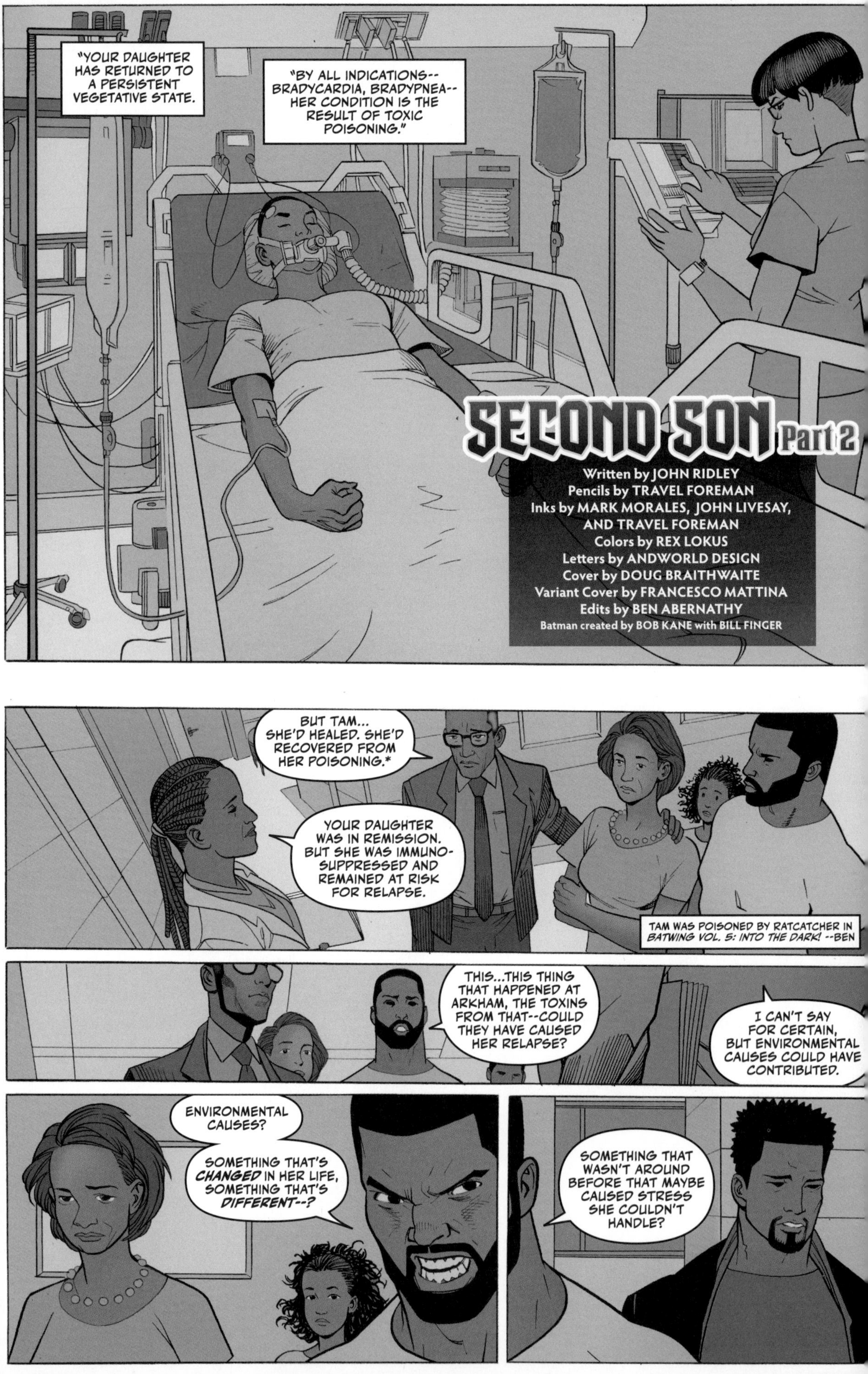

"YOUR DAUGHTER HAS RETURNED TO A PERSISTENT VEGETATIVE STATE.
"BY ALL INDICATIONS--BRADYCARDIA, BRADYPNEA--HER CONDITION IS THE RESULT OF TOXIC POISONING."
SECOND SON Part 2
Written by JOHN RIDLEY
Pencils by TRAVEL FOREMAN
Inks by MARK MORALES, JOHN LIVESAY, AND TRAVEL FOREMAN
Colors by REX LOKUS
Letters by ANDWORLD DESIGN
Cover by DOUG BRAITHWAITE
Variant Cover by FRANCESCO MATTINA
Edits by BEN ABERNATHY
Batman created by BOB KANE with BILL FINGER
BUT TAM... SHE'D HEALED. SHE'D RECOVERED FROM HER POISONING.*
YOUR DAUGHTER WAS IN REMISSION. BUT SHE WAS IMMUNO-SUPPRESSED AND REMAINED AT RISK FOR RELAPSE.
TAM WAS POISONED BY RATCATCHER IN *BATWING VOL. 5: INTO THE DARK!* --BEN
THIS...THIS THING THAT HAPPENED AT ARKHAM, THE TOXINS FROM THAT--COULD THEY HAVE CAUSED HER RELAPSE?
I CAN'T SAY FOR CERTAIN, BUT ENVIRONMENTAL CAUSES COULD HAVE CONTRIBUTED.
ENVIRONMENTAL CAUSES?
SOMETHING THAT'S *CHANGED* IN HER LIFE, SOMETHING THAT'S *DIFFERENT*--?
SOMETHING THAT WASN'T AROUND BEFORE THAT MAYBE CAUSED STRESS SHE COULDN'T HANDLE?

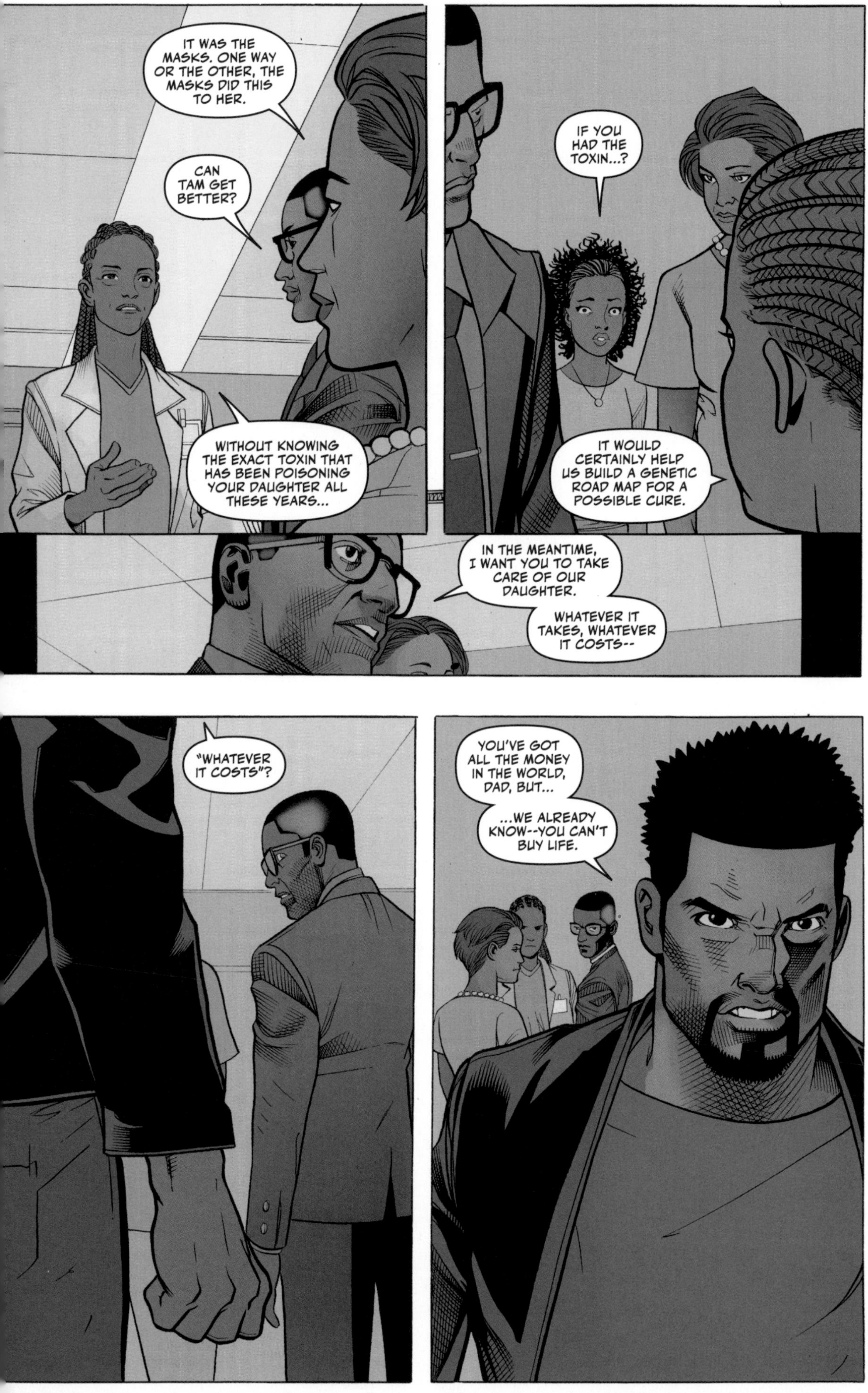
IT WAS THE MASKS. ONE WAY OR THE OTHER, THE MASKS DID THIS TO HER.
CAN TAM GET BETTER?
WITHOUT KNOWING THE EXACT TOXIN THAT HAS BEEN POISONING YOUR DAUGHTER ALL THESE YEARS...
IF YOU HAD THE TOXIN...?
IT WOULD CERTAINLY HELP US BUILD A GENETIC ROAD MAP FOR A POSSIBLE CURE.
IN THE MEANTIME, I WANT YOU TO TAKE CARE OF OUR DAUGHTER.
WHATEVER IT TAKES, WHATEVER IT COSTS--
"WHATEVER IT COSTS"?
YOU'VE GOT ALL THE MONEY IN THE WORLD, DAD, BUT...
...WE ALREADY KNOW--YOU CAN'T BUY LIFE.

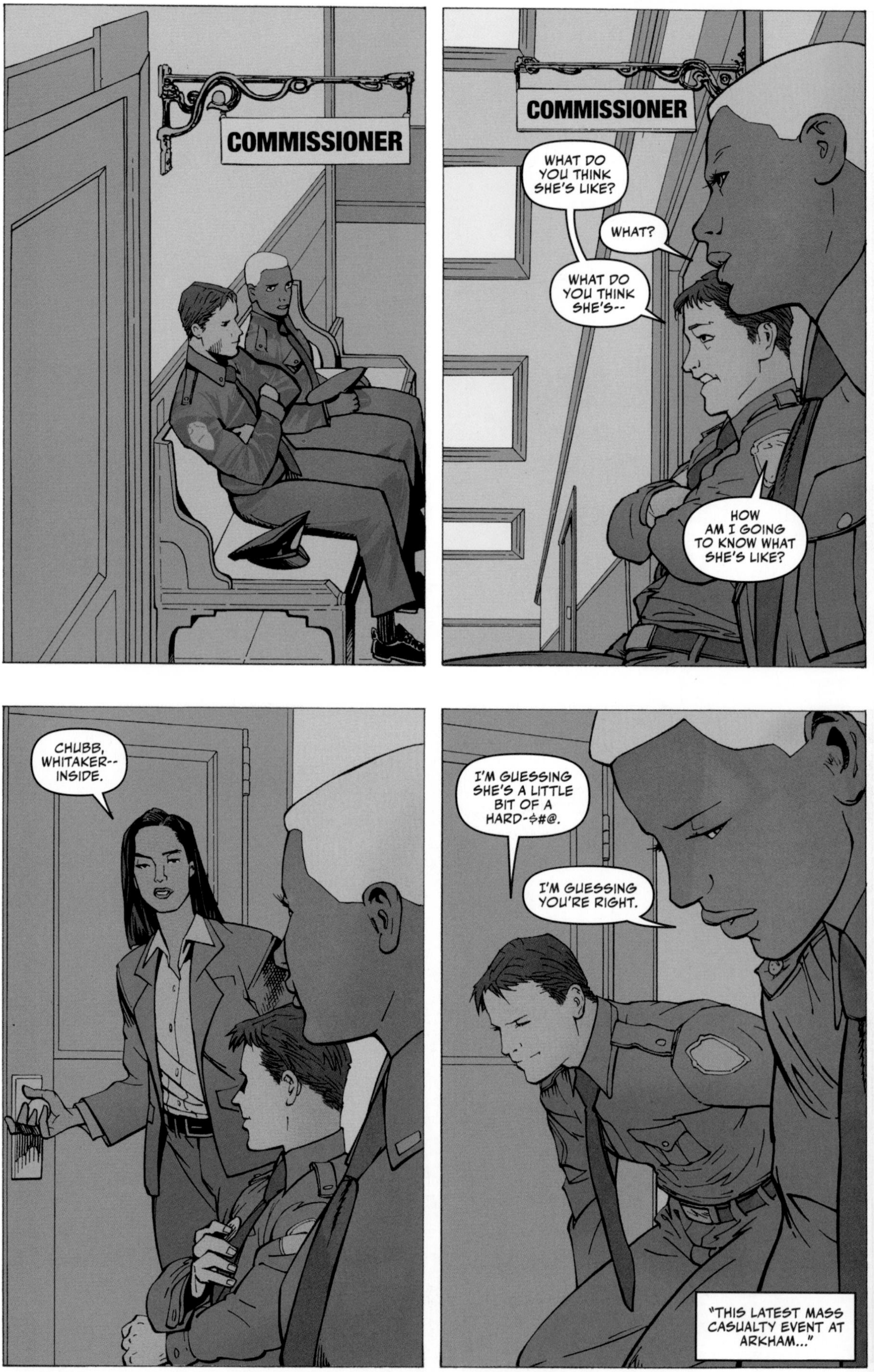
COMMISSIONER
COMMISSIONER
WHAT DO YOU THINK SHE'S LIKE?
WHAT?
WHAT DO YOU THINK SHE'S--
HOW AM I GOING TO KNOW WHAT SHE'S LIKE?
CHUBB, WHITAKER--INSIDE.
I'M GUESSING SHE'S A LITTLE BIT OF A HARD-$#@.
I'M GUESSING YOU'RE RIGHT.
"THIS LATEST MASS CASUALTY EVENT AT ARKHAM..."

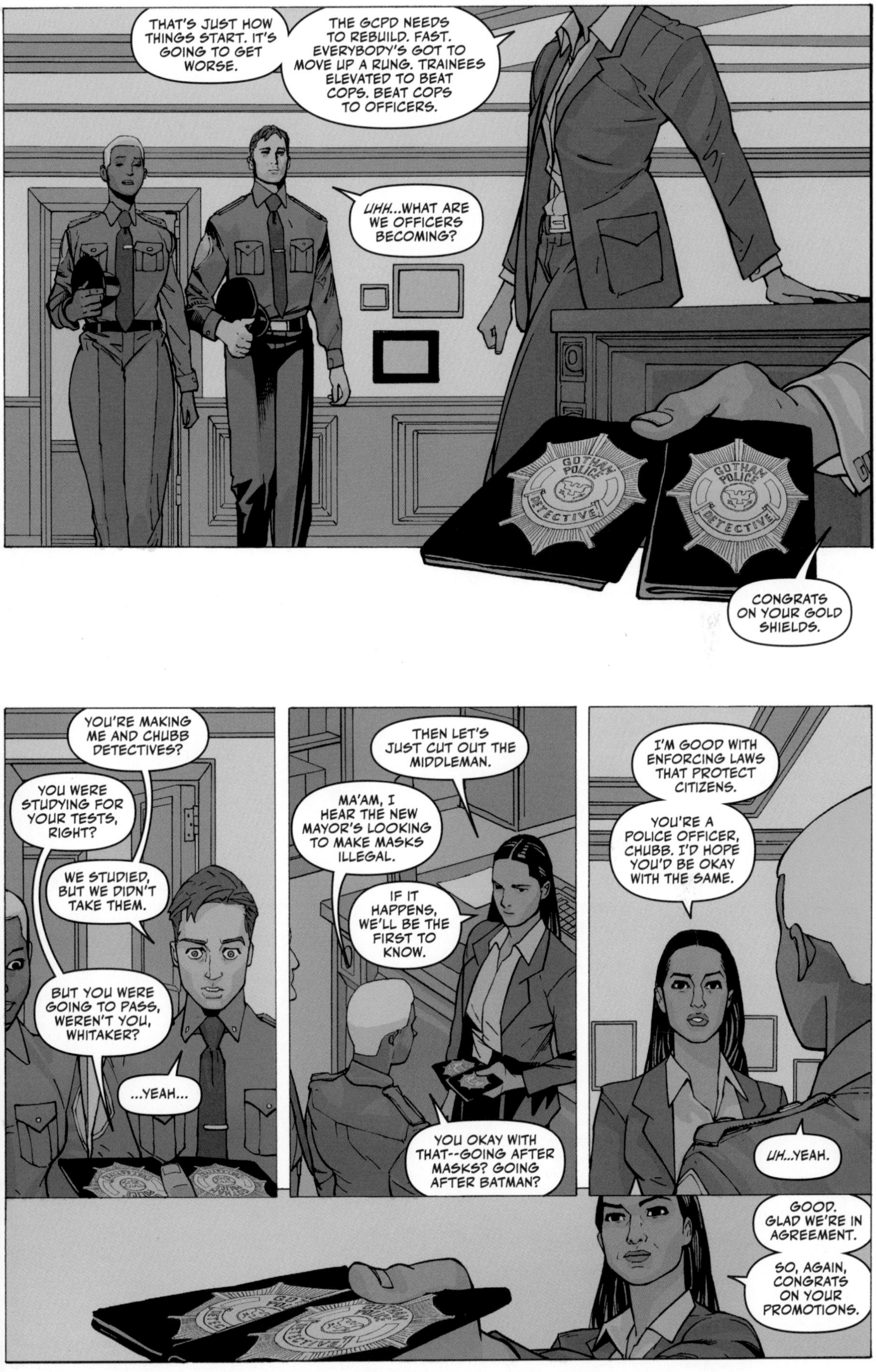
THAT'S JUST HOW THINGS START. IT'S GOING TO GET WORSE.
THE GCPD NEEDS TO REBUILD. FAST. EVERYBODY'S GOT TO MOVE UP A RUNG. TRAINEES ELEVATED TO BEAT COPS. BEAT COPS TO OFFICERS.
UHH...WHAT ARE WE OFFICERS BECOMING?
GOTHAM POLICE DETECTIVE
GOTHAM POLICE DETECTIVE
CONGRATS ON YOUR GOLD SHIELDS.
YOU'RE MAKING ME AND CHUBB DETECTIVES?
YOU WERE STUDYING FOR YOUR TESTS, RIGHT?
WE STUDIED, BUT WE DIDN'T TAKE THEM.
BUT YOU WERE GOING TO PASS, WEREN'T YOU, WHITAKER?
...YEAH...
THEN LET'S JUST CUT OUT THE MIDDLEMAN.
MA'AM, I HEAR THE NEW MAYOR'S LOOKING TO MAKE MASKS ILLEGAL.
IF IT HAPPENS, WE'LL BE THE FIRST TO KNOW.
YOU OKAY WITH THAT--GOING AFTER MASKS? GOING AFTER BATMAN?
I'M GOOD WITH ENFORCING LAWS THAT PROTECT CITIZENS.
YOU'RE A POLICE OFFICER, CHUBB. I'D HOPE YOU'D BE OKAY WITH THE SAME.
UH...YEAH.
GOOD. GLAD WE'RE IN AGREEMENT.
SO, AGAIN, CONGRATS ON YOUR PROMOTIONS.

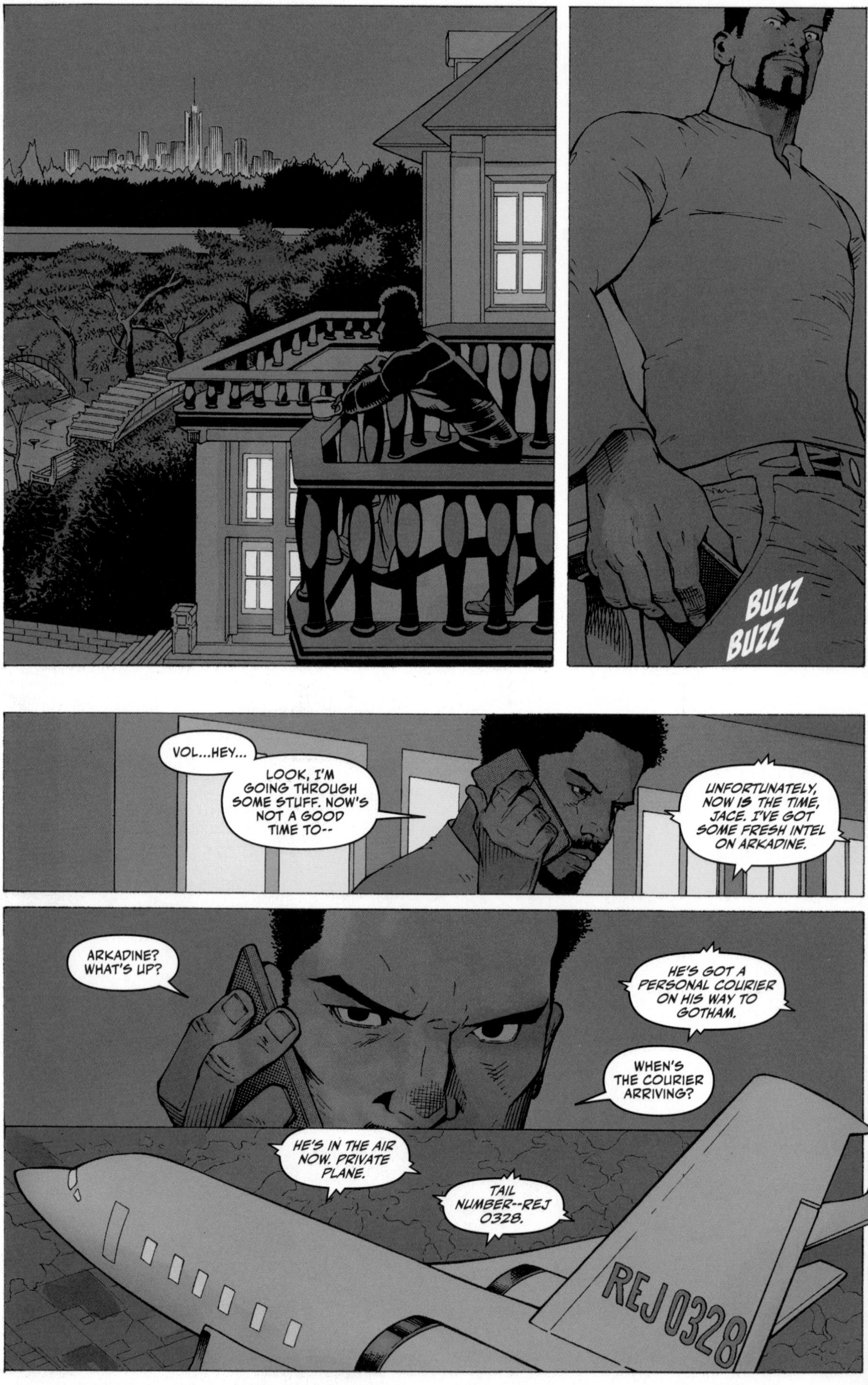
BUZZ
BUZZ
VOL...HEY...
LOOK, I'M GOING THROUGH SOME STUFF. NOW'S NOT A GOOD TIME TO--
UNFORTUNATELY, NOW IS THE TIME, JACE. I'VE GOT SOME FRESH INTEL ON ARKADINE.
ARKADINE? WHAT'S UP?
HE'S GOT A PERSONAL COURIER ON HIS WAY TO GOTHAM.
WHEN'S THE COURIER ARRIVING?
HE'S IN THE AIR NOW. PRIVATE PLANE.
TAIL NUMBER--REJ 0328.
REJ 0328

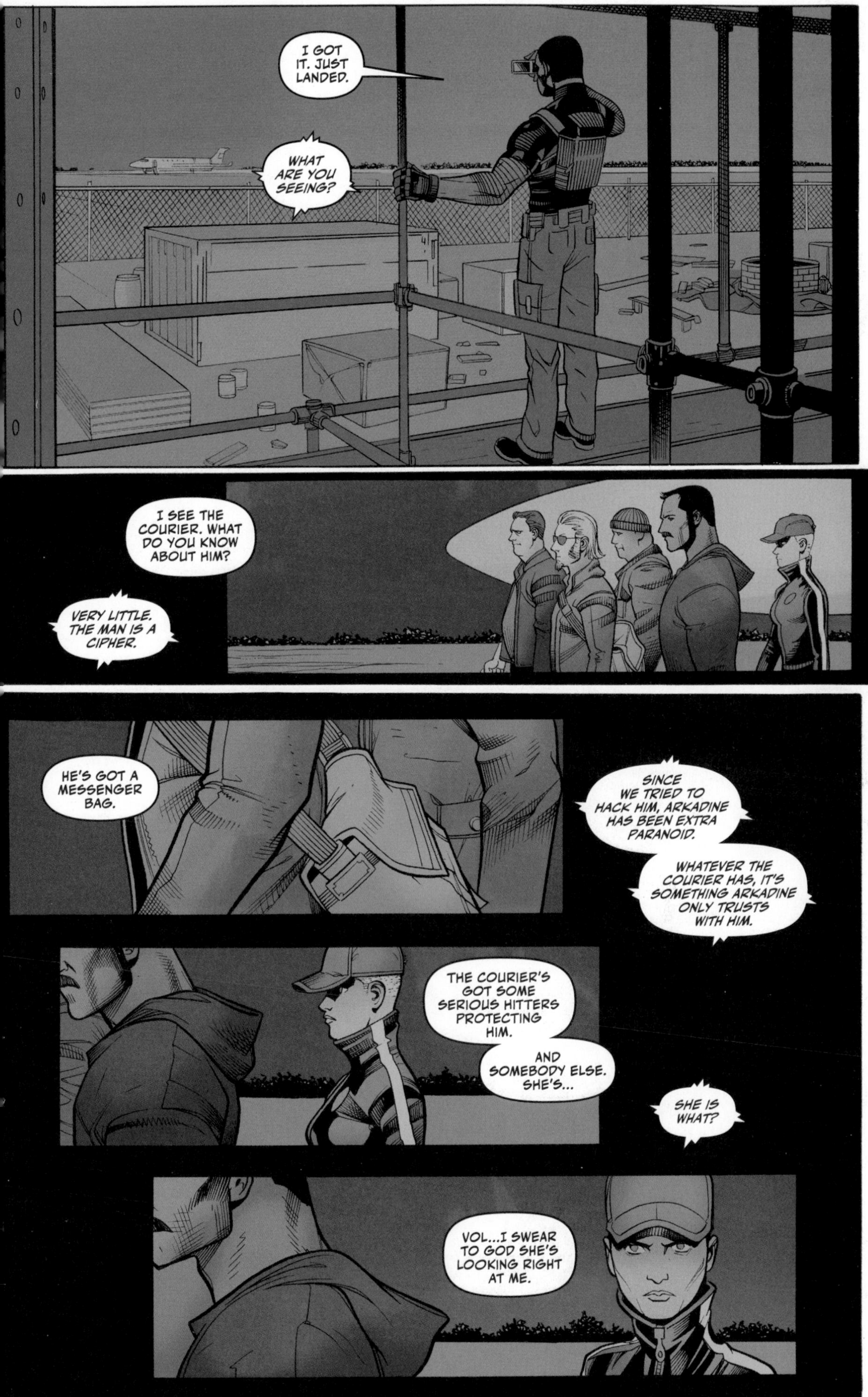
I GOT IT. JUST LANDED.
WHAT ARE YOU SEEING?
I SEE THE COURIER. WHAT DO YOU KNOW ABOUT HIM?
VERY LITTLE. THE MAN IS A CIPHER.
HE'S GOT A MESSENGER BAG.
SINCE WE TRIED TO HACK HIM, ARKADINE HAS BEEN EXTRA PARANOID.
WHATEVER THE COURIER HAS, IT'S SOMETHING ARKADINE ONLY TRUSTS WITH HIM.
THE COURIER'S GOT SOME SERIOUS HITTERS PROTECTING HIM.
AND SOMEBODY ELSE. SHE'S...
SHE IS WHAT?
VOL...I SWEAR TO GOD SHE'S LOOKING RIGHT AT ME.

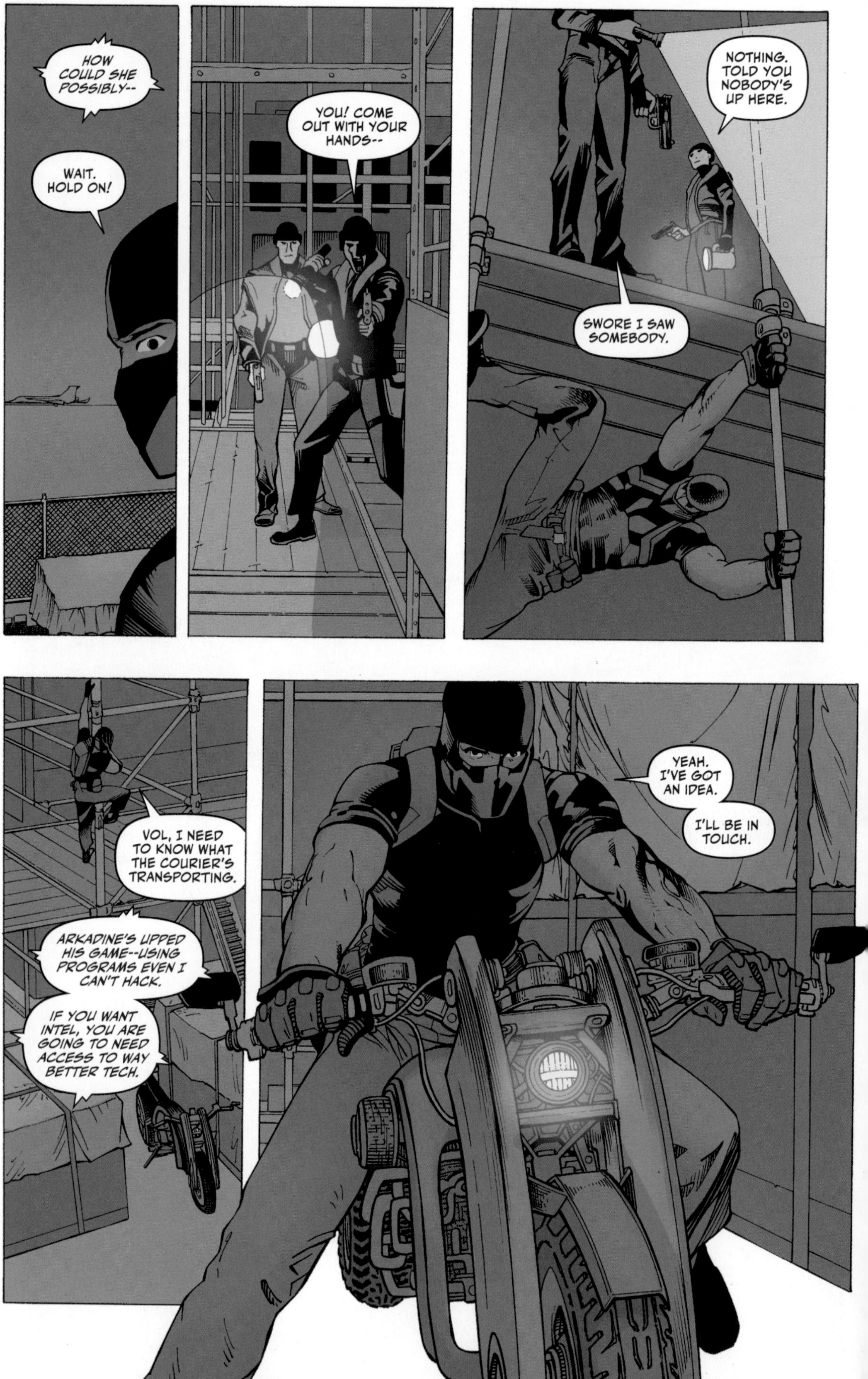
HOW COULD SHE POSSIBLY--
WAIT. HOLD ON!
YOU! COME OUT WITH YOUR HANDS--
NOTHING. TOLD YOU NOBODY'S UP HERE.
SWORE I SAW SOMEBODY.
VOL, I NEED TO KNOW WHAT THE COURIER'S TRANSPORTING.
ARKADINE'S UPPED HIS GAME--USING PROGRAMS EVEN I CAN'T HACK.
IF YOU WANT INTEL, YOU ARE GOING TO NEED ACCESS TO WAY BETTER TECH.
YEAH. I'VE GOT AN IDEA.
I'LL BE IN TOUCH.

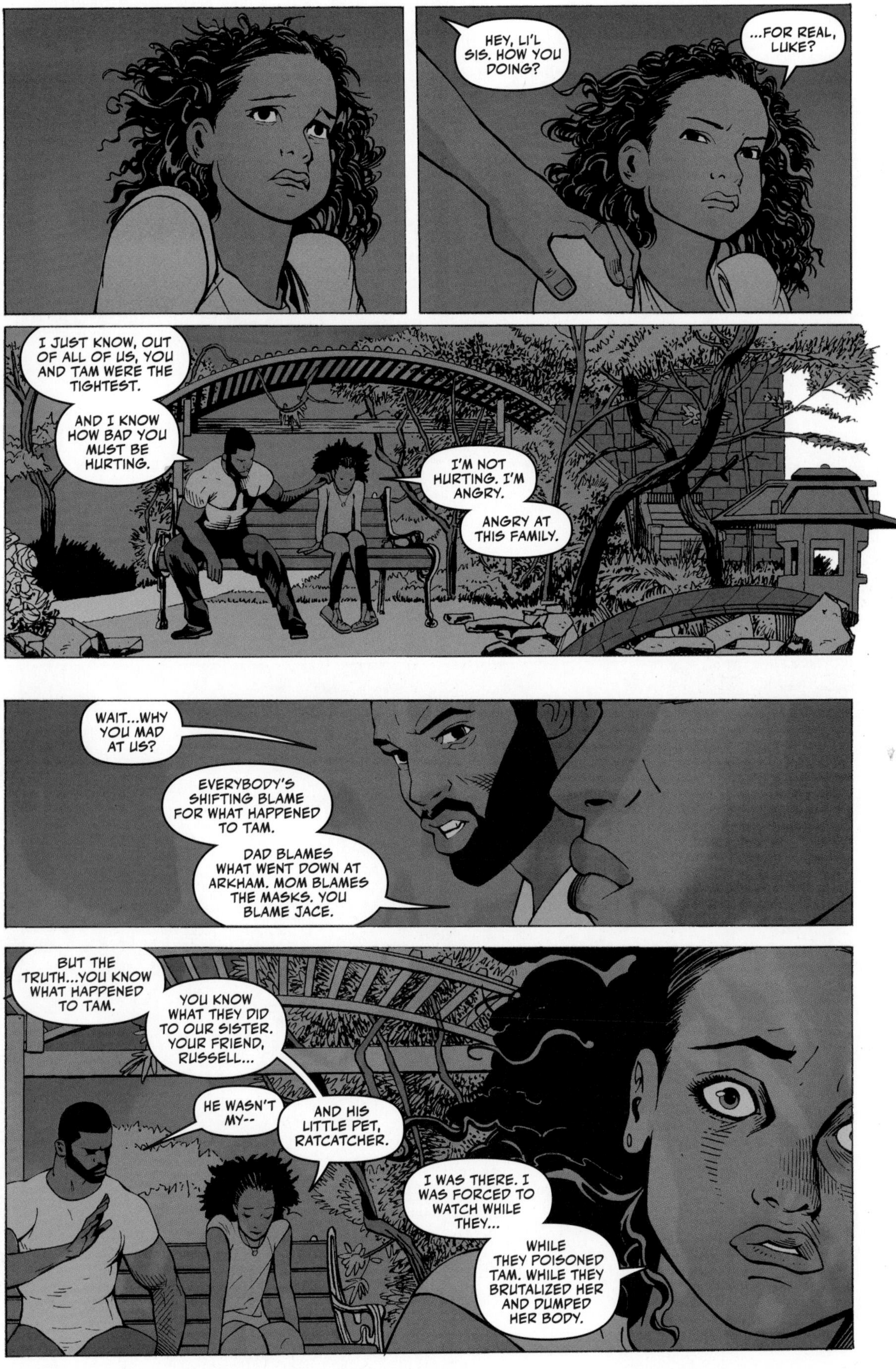
HEY, LI'L SIS. HOW YOU DOING?
...FOR REAL, LUKE?
I JUST KNOW, OUT OF ALL OF US, YOU AND TAM WERE THE TIGHTEST.
AND I KNOW HOW BAD YOU MUST BE HURTING.
I'M NOT HURTING. I'M ANGRY.
ANGRY AT THIS FAMILY.
WAIT...WHY YOU MAD AT US?
EVERYBODY'S SHIFTING BLAME FOR WHAT HAPPENED TO TAM.
DAD BLAMES WHAT WENT DOWN AT ARKHAM. MOM BLAMES THE MASKS. YOU BLAME JACE.
BUT THE TRUTH...YOU KNOW WHAT HAPPENED TO TAM.
YOU KNOW WHAT THEY DID TO OUR SISTER. YOUR FRIEND, RUSSELL...
HE WASN'T MY--
AND HIS LITTLE PET, RATCATCHER.
I WAS THERE. I WAS FORCED TO WATCH WHILE THEY...
WHILE THEY POISONED TAM. WHILE THEY BRUTALIZED HER AND DUMPED HER BODY.

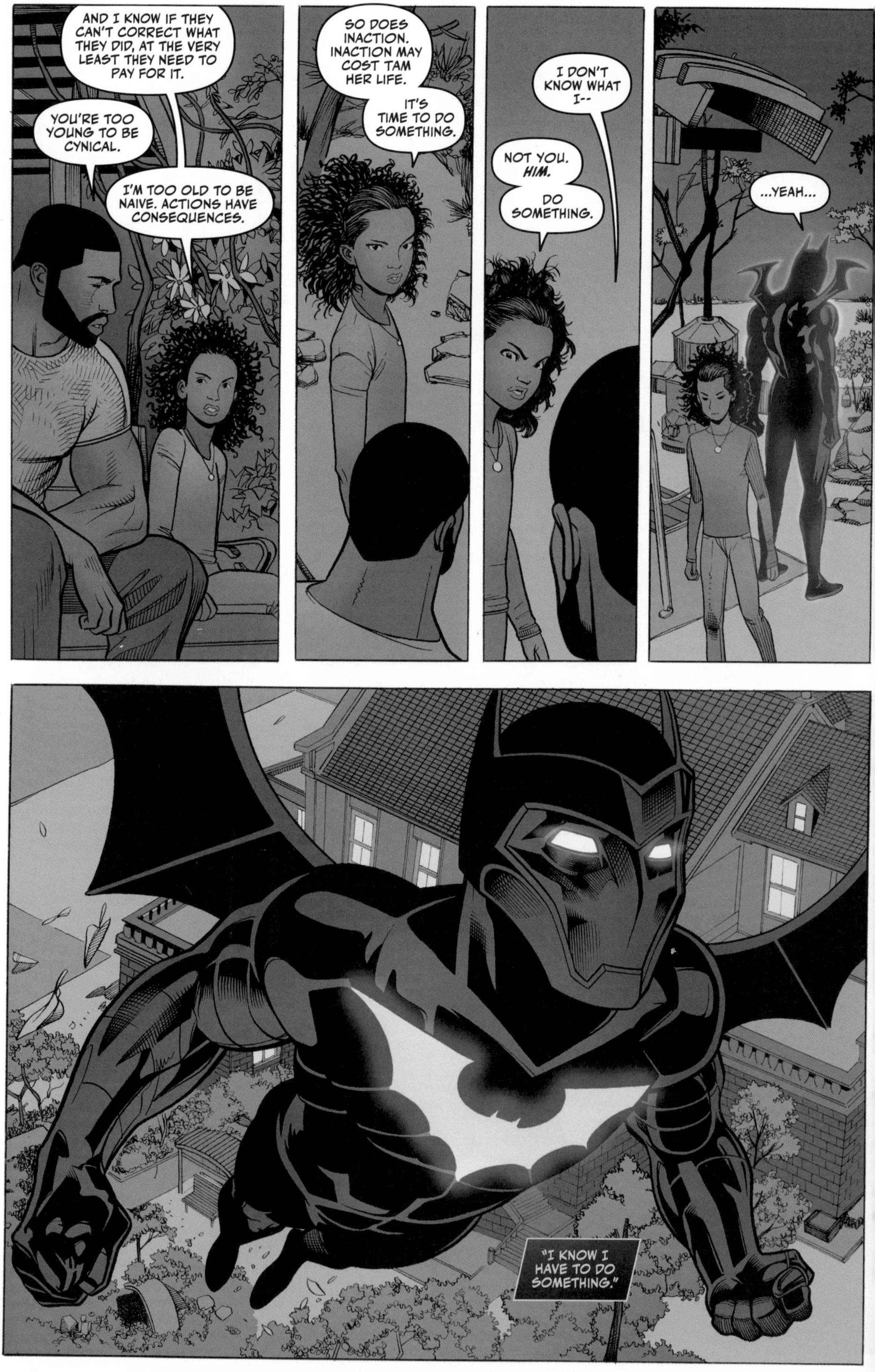
AND I KNOW IF THEY CAN'T CORRECT WHAT THEY DID, AT THE VERY LEAST THEY NEED TO PAY FOR IT.
YOU'RE TOO YOUNG TO BE CYNICAL.
I'M TOO OLD TO BE NAIVE. ACTIONS HAVE CONSEQUENCES.
SO DOES INACTION. INACTION MAY COST TAM HER LIFE.
IT'S TIME TO DO SOMETHING.
I DON'T KNOW WHAT I--
NOT YOU. *HIM.*
DO SOMETHING.
...YEAH...
"I KNOW I HAVE TO DO SOMETHING."

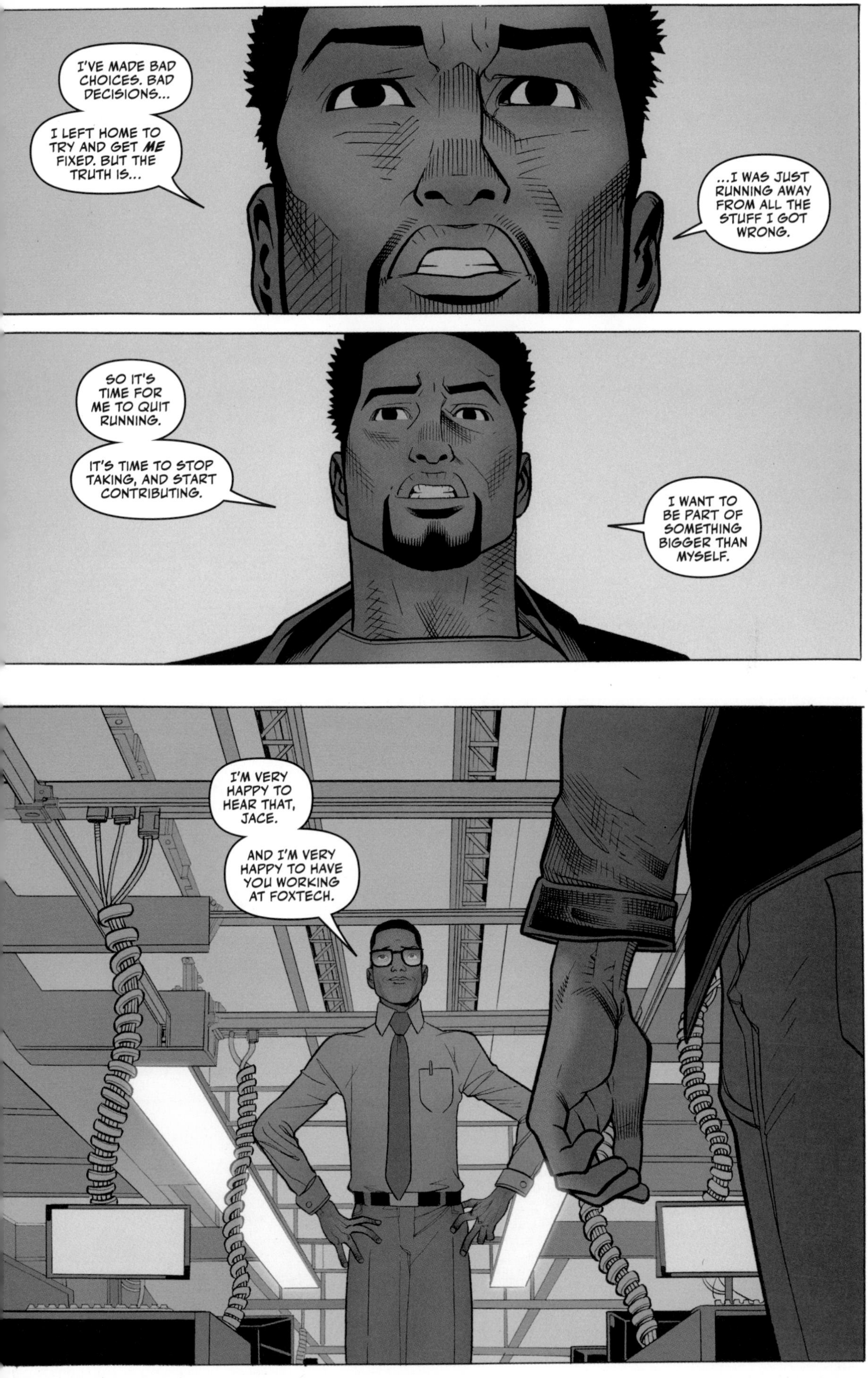
I'VE MADE BAD CHOICES. BAD DECISIONS...
I LEFT HOME TO TRY AND GET ME FIXED. BUT THE TRUTH IS...
...I WAS JUST RUNNING AWAY FROM ALL THE STUFF I GOT WRONG.
SO IT'S TIME FOR ME TO QUIT RUNNING.
IT'S TIME TO STOP TAKING, AND START CONTRIBUTING.
I WANT TO BE PART OF SOMETHING BIGGER THAN MYSELF.
I'M VERY HAPPY TO HEAR THAT, JACE.
AND I'M VERY HAPPY TO HAVE YOU WORKING AT FOXTECH.

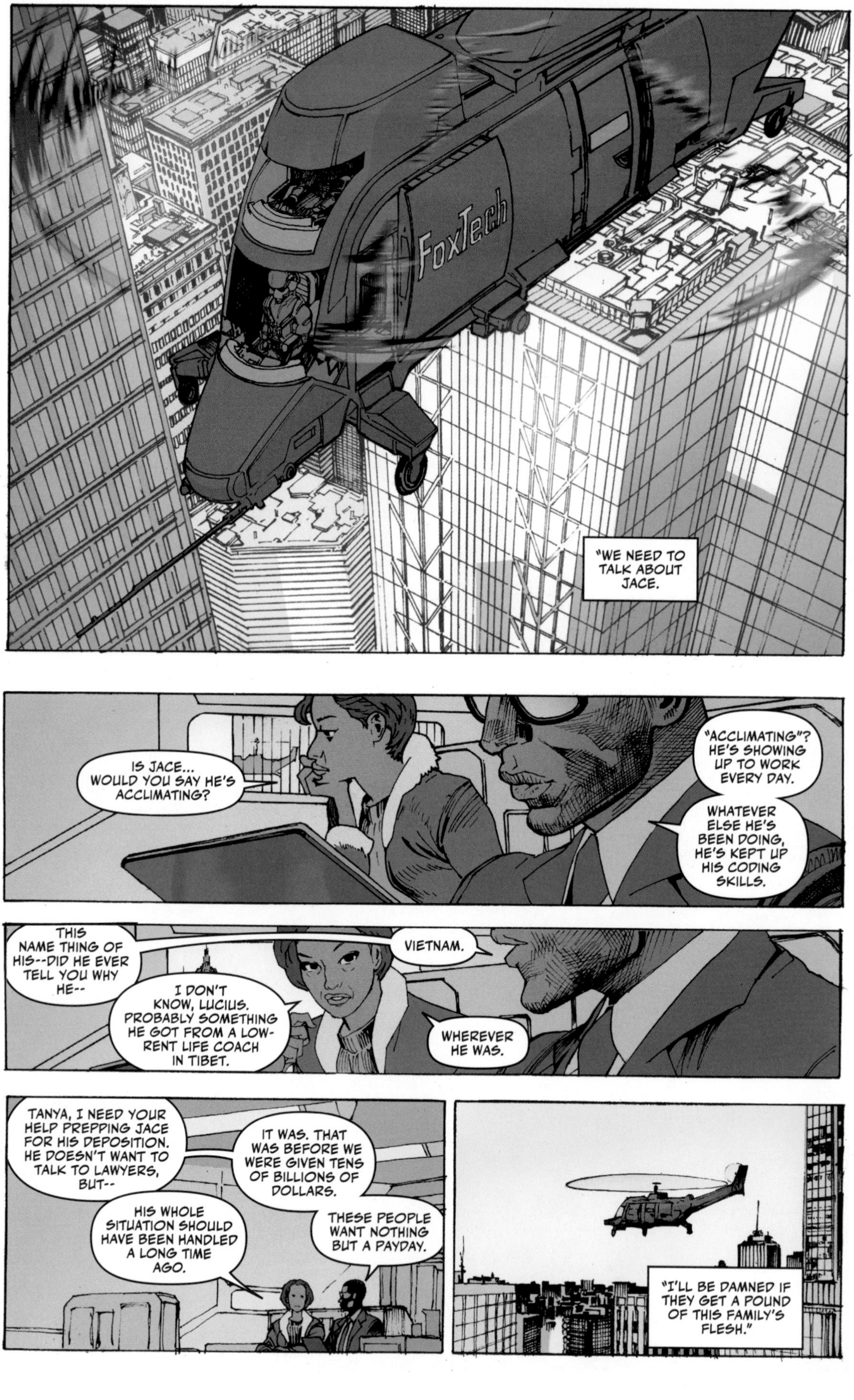
FoxTech
"WE NEED TO TALK ABOUT JACE.
IS JACE... WOULD YOU SAY HE'S ACCLIMATING?
"ACCLIMATING"? HE'S SHOWING UP TO WORK EVERY DAY.
WHATEVER ELSE HE'S BEEN DOING, HE'S KEPT UP HIS CODING SKILLS.
THIS NAME THING OF HIS--DID HE EVER TELL YOU WHY HE--
VIETNAM.
I DON'T KNOW, LUCIUS. PROBABLY SOMETHING HE GOT FROM A LOW-RENT LIFE COACH IN TIBET.
WHEREVER HE WAS.
TANYA, I NEED YOUR HELP PREPPING JACE FOR HIS DEPOSITION. HE DOESN'T WANT TO TALK TO LAWYERS, BUT--
IT WAS. THAT WAS BEFORE WE WERE GIVEN TENS OF BILLIONS OF DOLLARS.
HIS WHOLE SITUATION SHOULD HAVE BEEN HANDLED A LONG TIME AGO.
THESE PEOPLE WANT NOTHING BUT A PAYDAY.
"I'LL BE DAMNED IF THEY GET A POUND OF THIS FAMILY'S FLESH."

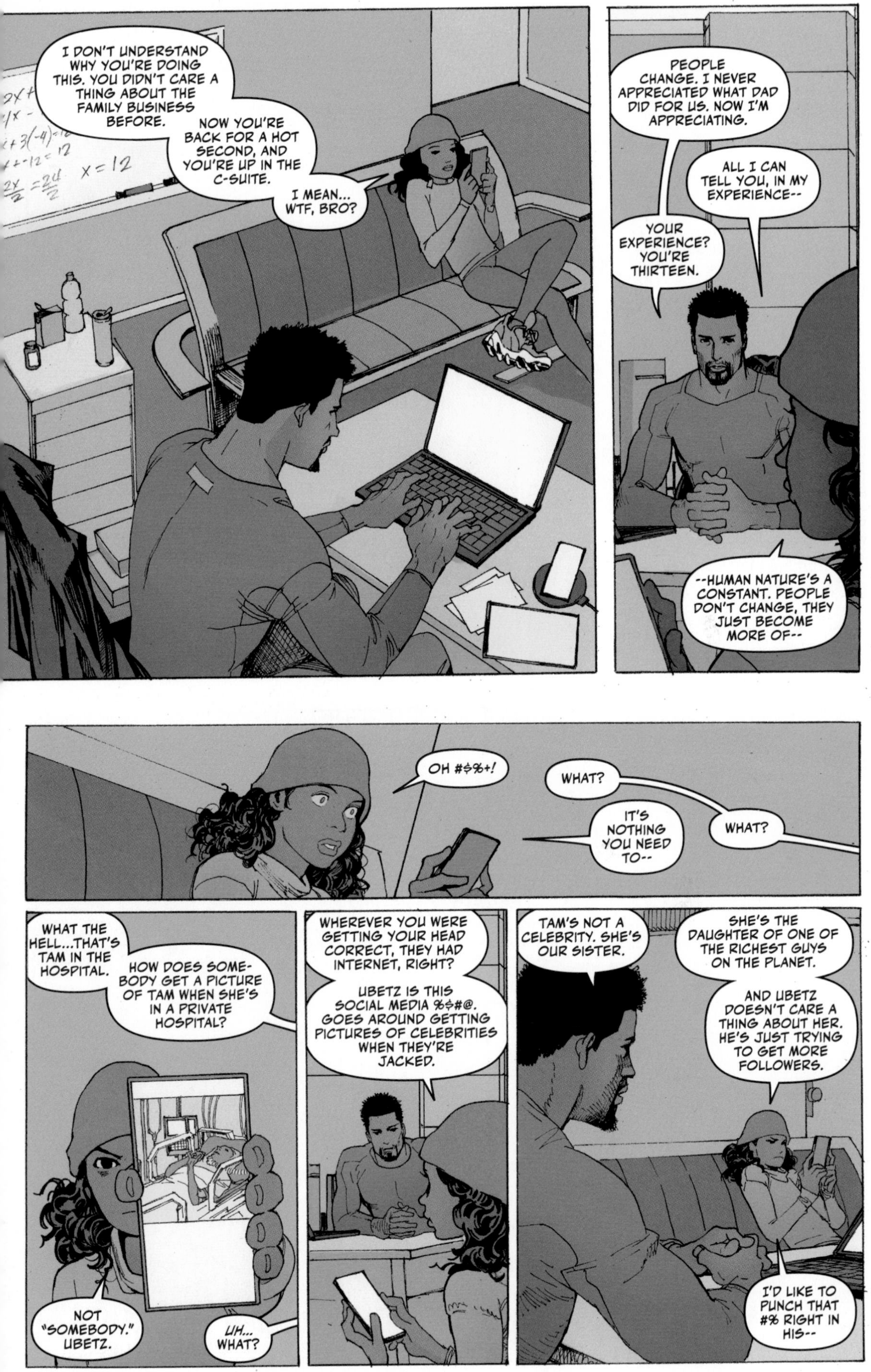
I DON'T UNDERSTAND WHY YOU'RE DOING THIS. YOU DIDN'T CARE A THING ABOUT THE FAMILY BUSINESS BEFORE.
NOW YOU'RE BACK FOR A HOT SECOND, AND YOU'RE UP IN THE C-SUITE.
I MEAN... WTF, BRO?
PEOPLE CHANGE. I NEVER APPRECIATED WHAT DAD DID FOR US. NOW I'M APPRECIATING.
ALL I CAN TELL YOU, IN MY EXPERIENCE--
YOUR EXPERIENCE? YOU'RE THIRTEEN.
--HUMAN NATURE'S A CONSTANT. PEOPLE DON'T CHANGE, THEY JUST BECOME MORE OF--
OH #$%+!
WHAT?
IT'S NOTHING YOU NEED TO--
WHAT?
WHAT THE HELL...THAT'S TAM IN THE HOSPITAL.
HOW DOES SOMEBODY GET A PICTURE OF TAM WHEN SHE'S IN A PRIVATE HOSPITAL?
NOT "SOMEBODY." UBETZ.
UH... WHAT?
WHEREVER YOU WERE GETTING YOUR HEAD CORRECT, THEY HAD INTERNET, RIGHT?
UBETZ IS THIS SOCIAL MEDIA %$#@. GOES AROUND GETTING PICTURES OF CELEBRITIES WHEN THEY'RE JACKED.
TAM'S NOT A CELEBRITY. SHE'S OUR SISTER.
SHE'S THE DAUGHTER OF ONE OF THE RICHEST GUYS ON THE PLANET.
AND UBETZ DOESN'T CARE A THING ABOUT HER. HE'S JUST TRYING TO GET MORE FOLLOWERS.
I'D LIKE TO PUNCH THAT #% RIGHT IN HIS--

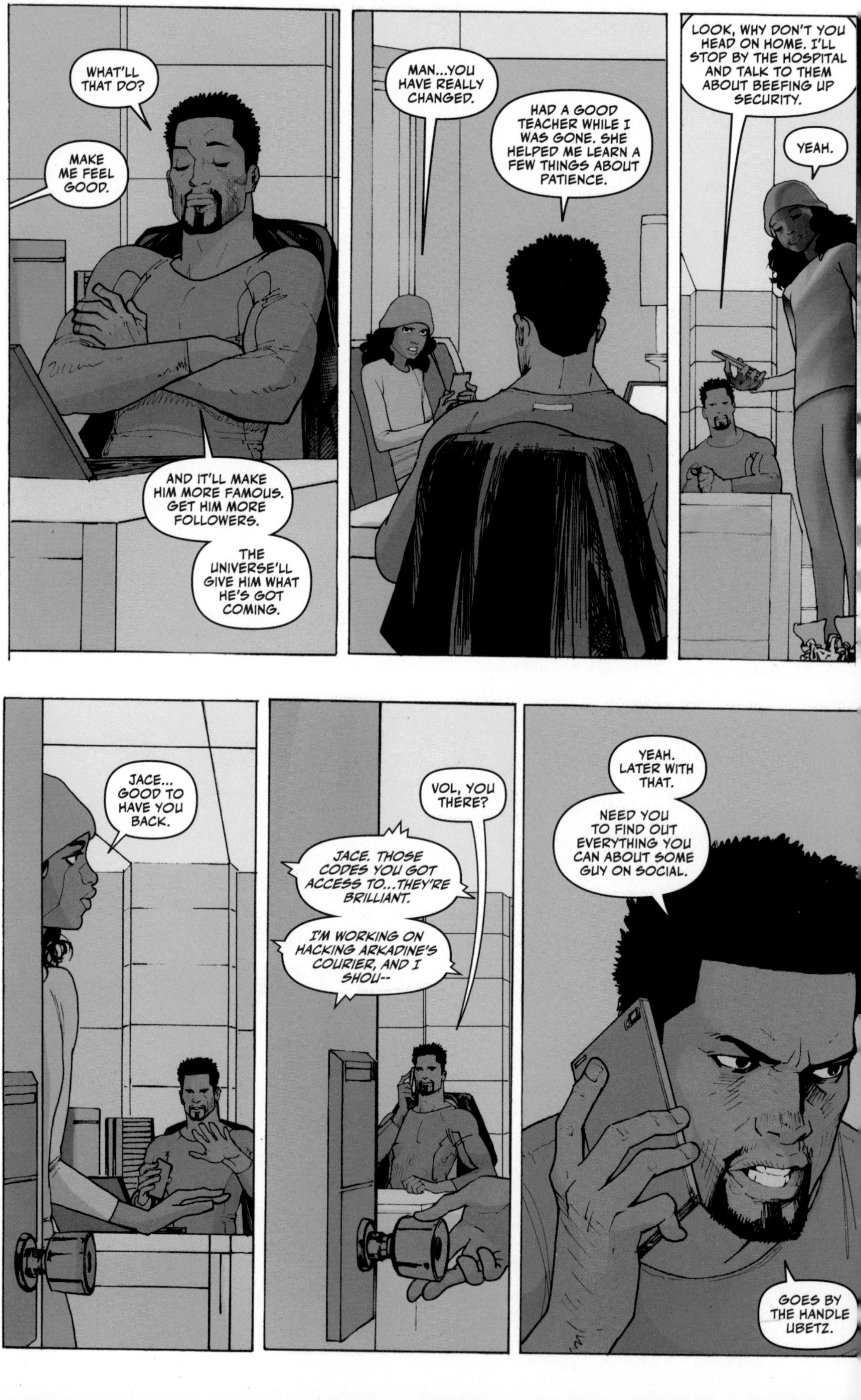
WHAT'LL THAT DO?
MAKE ME FEEL GOOD.
AND IT'LL MAKE HIM MORE FAMOUS. GET HIM MORE FOLLOWERS.
THE UNIVERSE'LL GIVE HIM WHAT HE'S GOT COMING.
MAN...YOU HAVE REALLY CHANGED.
HAD A GOOD TEACHER WHILE I WAS GONE. SHE HELPED ME LEARN A FEW THINGS ABOUT PATIENCE.
LOOK, WHY DON'T YOU HEAD ON HOME. I'LL STOP BY THE HOSPITAL AND TALK TO THEM ABOUT BEEFING UP SECURITY.
YEAH.
JACE... GOOD TO HAVE YOU BACK.
VOL, YOU THERE?
JACE. THOSE CODES YOU GOT ACCESS TO...THEY'RE BRILLIANT.
I'M WORKING ON HACKING ARKADINE'S COURIER, AND I SHOU--
YEAH. LATER WITH THAT.
NEED YOU TO FIND OUT EVERYTHING YOU CAN ABOUT SOME GUY ON SOCIAL.
GOES BY THE HANDLE UBETZ.

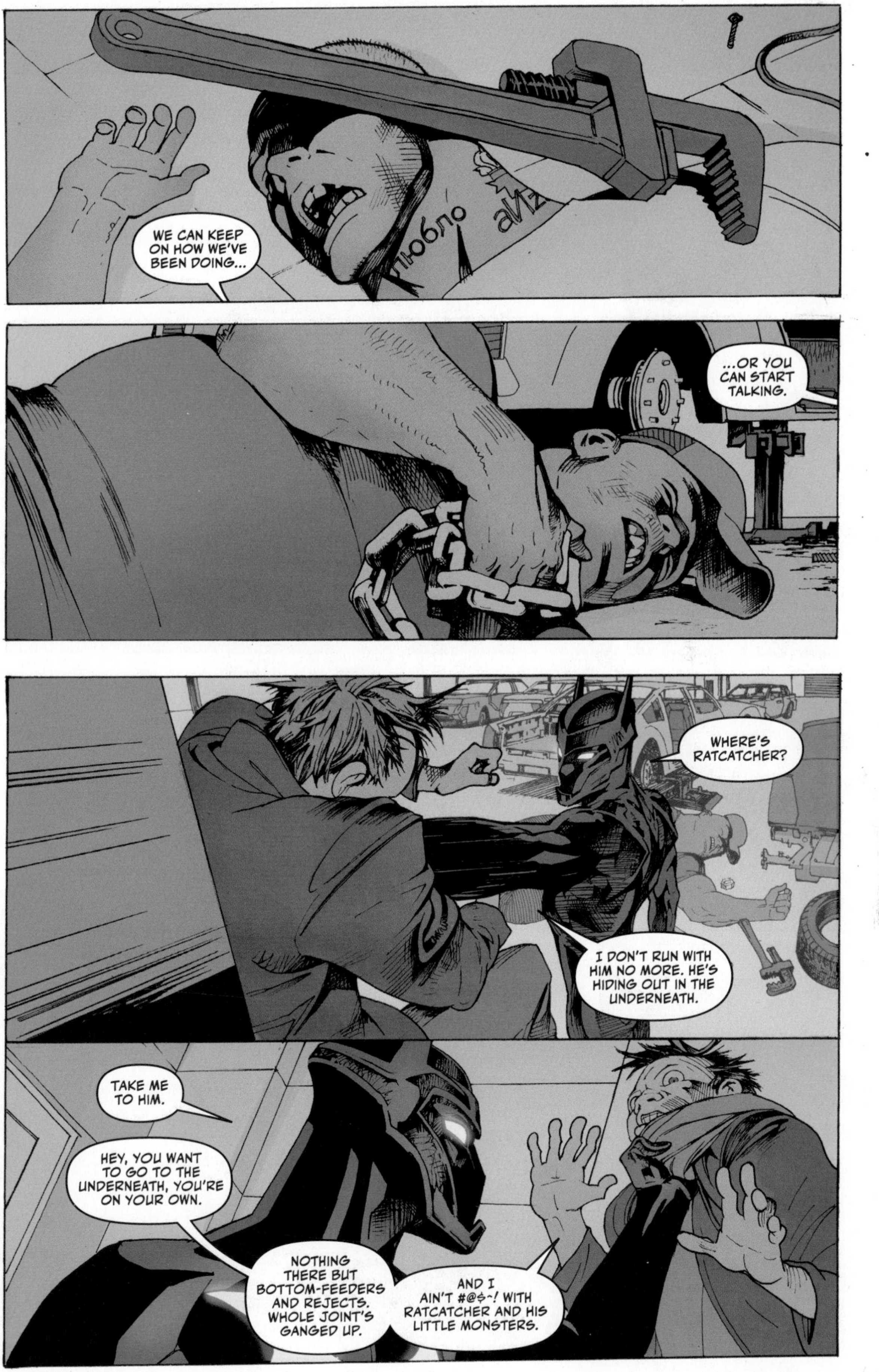
WE CAN KEEP ON HOW WE'VE BEEN DOING...
...OR YOU CAN START TALKING.
WHERE'S RATCATCHER?
I DON'T RUN WITH HIM NO MORE. HE'S HIDING OUT IN THE UNDERNEATH.
TAKE ME TO HIM.
HEY, YOU WANT TO GO TO THE UNDERNEATH, YOU'RE ON YOUR OWN.
NOTHING THERE BUT BOTTOM-FEEDERS AND REJECTS. WHOLE JOINT'S GANGED UP.
AND I AIN'T #@$~! WITH RATCATCHER AND HIS LITTLE MONSTERS.

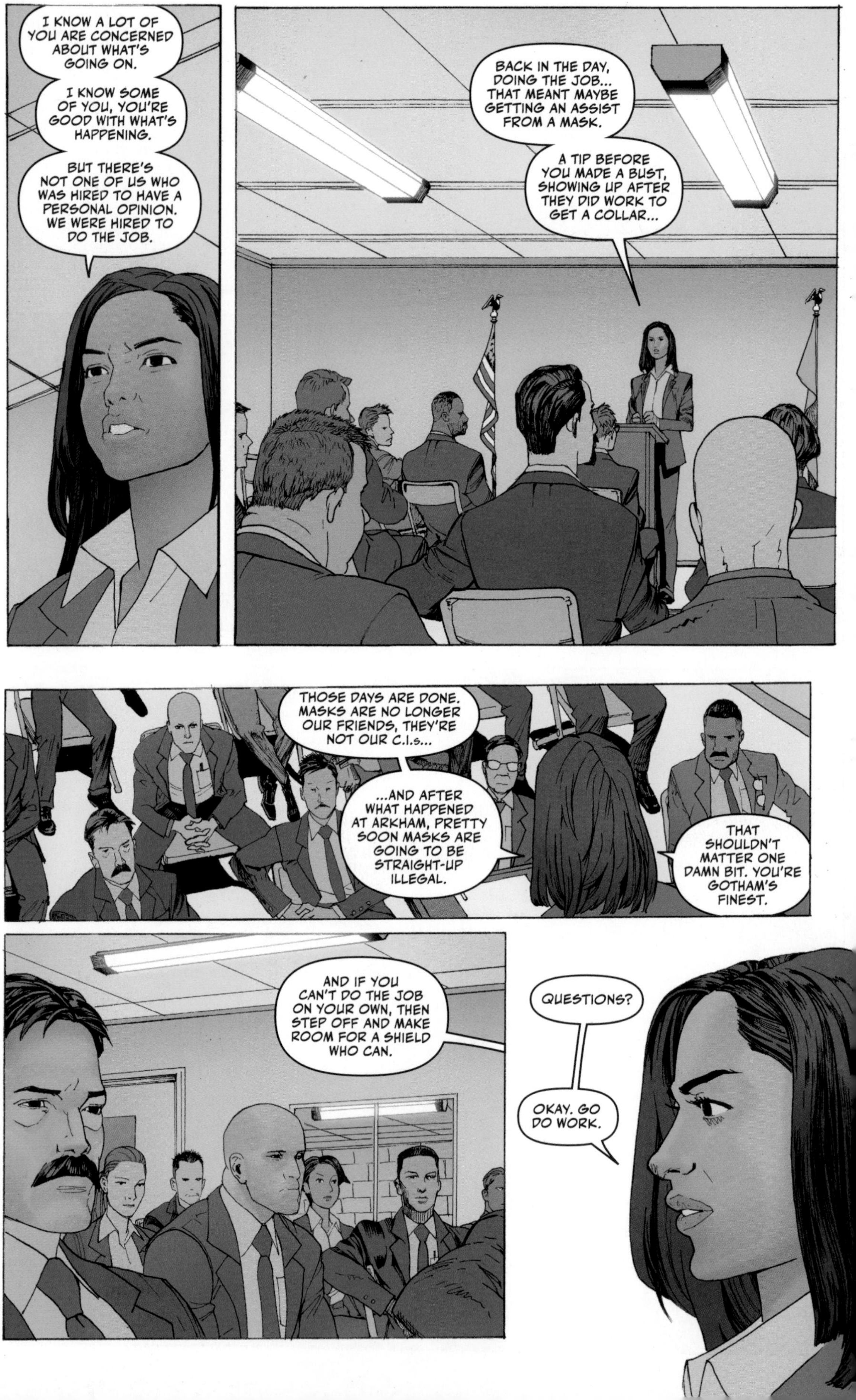
I KNOW A LOT OF YOU ARE CONCERNED ABOUT WHAT'S GOING ON.
I KNOW SOME OF YOU, YOU'RE GOOD WITH WHAT'S HAPPENING.
BUT THERE'S NOT ONE OF US WHO WAS HIRED TO HAVE A PERSONAL OPINION. WE WERE HIRED TO DO THE JOB.
BACK IN THE DAY, DOING THE JOB... THAT MEANT MAYBE GETTING AN ASSIST FROM A MASK.
A TIP BEFORE YOU MADE A BUST, SHOWING UP AFTER THEY DID WORK TO GET A COLLAR...
THOSE DAYS ARE DONE. MASKS ARE NO LONGER OUR FRIENDS, THEY'RE NOT OUR C.I.s...
...AND AFTER WHAT HAPPENED AT ARKHAM, PRETTY SOON MASKS ARE GOING TO BE STRAIGHT-UP ILLEGAL.
THAT SHOULDN'T MATTER ONE DAMN BIT. YOU'RE GOTHAM'S FINEST.
AND IF YOU CAN'T DO THE JOB ON YOUR OWN, THEN STEP OFF AND MAKE ROOM FOR A SHIELD WHO CAN.
QUESTIONS?
OKAY. GO DO WORK.

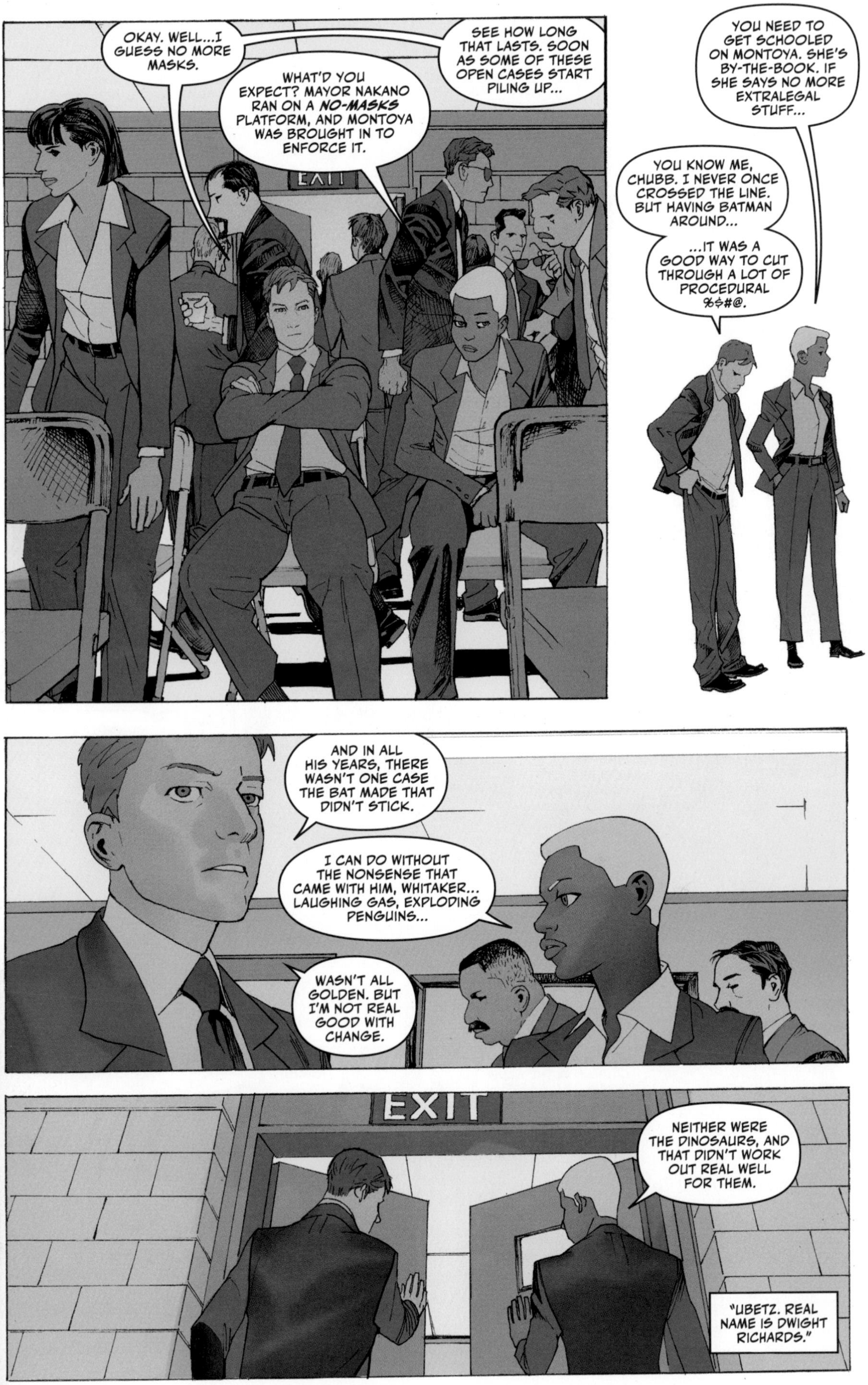

OKAY. WELL...I GUESS NO MORE MASKS.
WHAT'D YOU EXPECT? MAYOR NAKANO RAN ON A *NO-MASKS* PLATFORM, AND MONTOYA WAS BROUGHT IN TO ENFORCE IT.
SEE HOW LONG THAT LASTS. SOON AS SOME OF THESE OPEN CASES START PILING UP...
EXIT
YOU NEED TO GET SCHOOLED ON MONTOYA. SHE'S BY-THE-BOOK. IF SHE SAYS NO MORE EXTRALEGAL STUFF...
YOU KNOW ME, CHUBB. I NEVER ONCE CROSSED THE LINE. BUT HAVING BATMAN AROUND...
...IT WAS A GOOD WAY TO CUT THROUGH A LOT OF PROCEDURAL %$#@.
AND IN ALL HIS YEARS, THERE WASN'T ONE CASE THE BAT MADE THAT DIDN'T STICK.
I CAN DO WITHOUT THE NONSENSE THAT CAME WITH HIM, WHITAKER... LAUGHING GAS, EXPLODING PENGUINS...
WASN'T ALL GOLDEN. BUT I'M NOT REAL GOOD WITH CHANGE.
EXIT
NEITHER WERE THE DINOSAURS, AND THAT DIDN'T WORK OUT REAL WELL FOR THEM.
"UBETZ. REAL NAME IS DWIGHT RICHARDS."

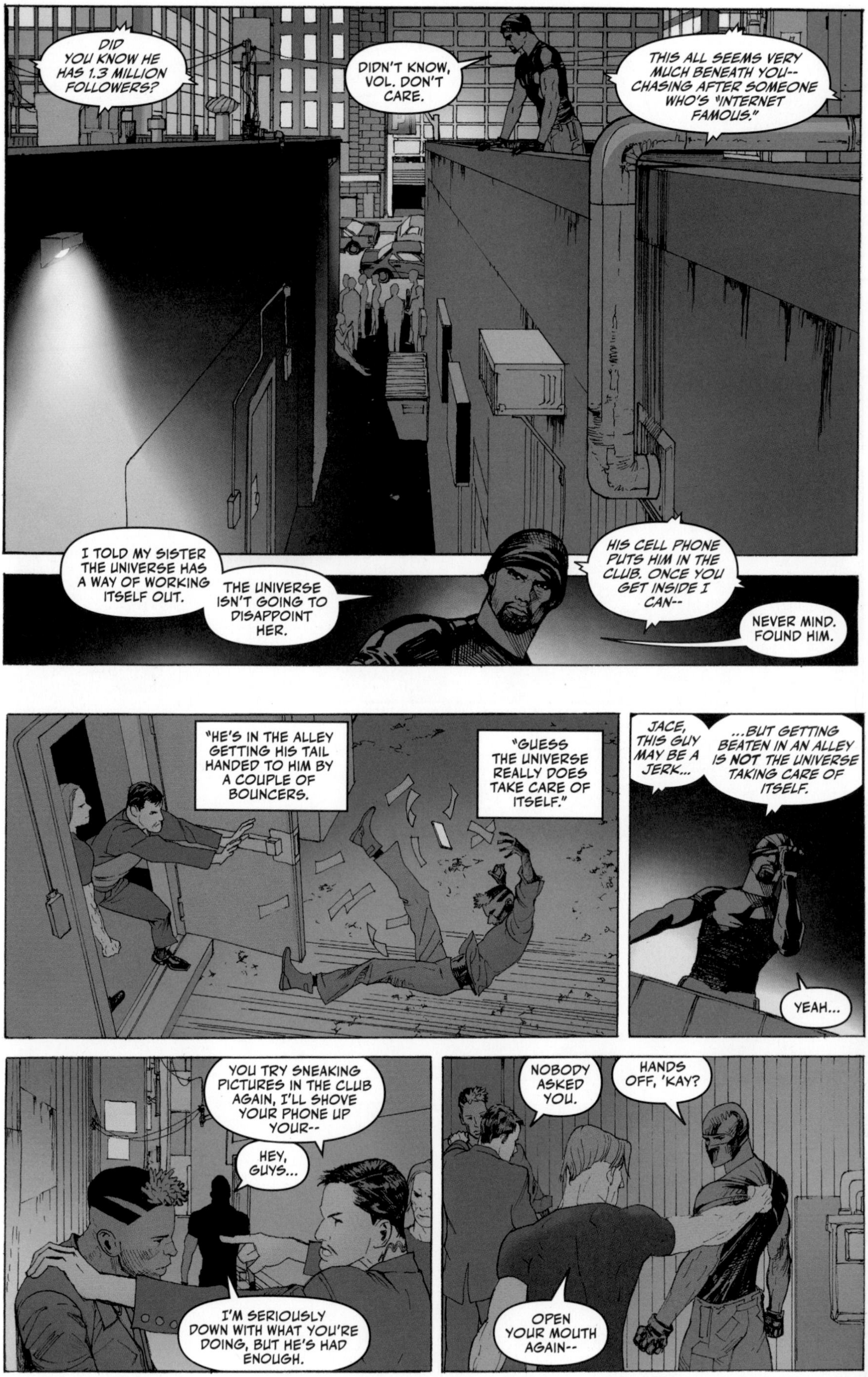
DID YOU KNOW HE HAS 1.3 MILLION FOLLOWERS?
DIDN'T KNOW, VOL. DON'T CARE.
THIS ALL SEEMS VERY MUCH BENEATH YOU-- CHASING AFTER SOMEONE WHO'S "INTERNET FAMOUS."
I TOLD MY SISTER THE UNIVERSE HAS A WAY OF WORKING ITSELF OUT.
THE UNIVERSE ISN'T GOING TO DISAPPOINT HER.
HIS CELL PHONE PUTS HIM IN THE CLUB. ONCE YOU GET INSIDE I CAN--
NEVER MIND. FOUND HIM.
"HE'S IN THE ALLEY GETTING HIS TAIL HANDED TO HIM BY A COUPLE OF BOUNCERS.
"GUESS THE UNIVERSE REALLY DOES TAKE CARE OF ITSELF."
JACE, THIS GUY MAY BE A JERK...
...BUT GETTING BEATEN IN AN ALLEY IS NOT THE UNIVERSE TAKING CARE OF ITSELF.
YEAH...
YOU TRY SNEAKING PICTURES IN THE CLUB AGAIN, I'LL SHOVE YOUR PHONE UP YOUR--
HEY, GUYS...
I'M SERIOUSLY DOWN WITH WHAT YOU'RE DOING, BUT HE'S HAD ENOUGH.
NOBODY ASKED YOU.
HANDS OFF, 'KAY?
OPEN YOUR MOUTH AGAIN--

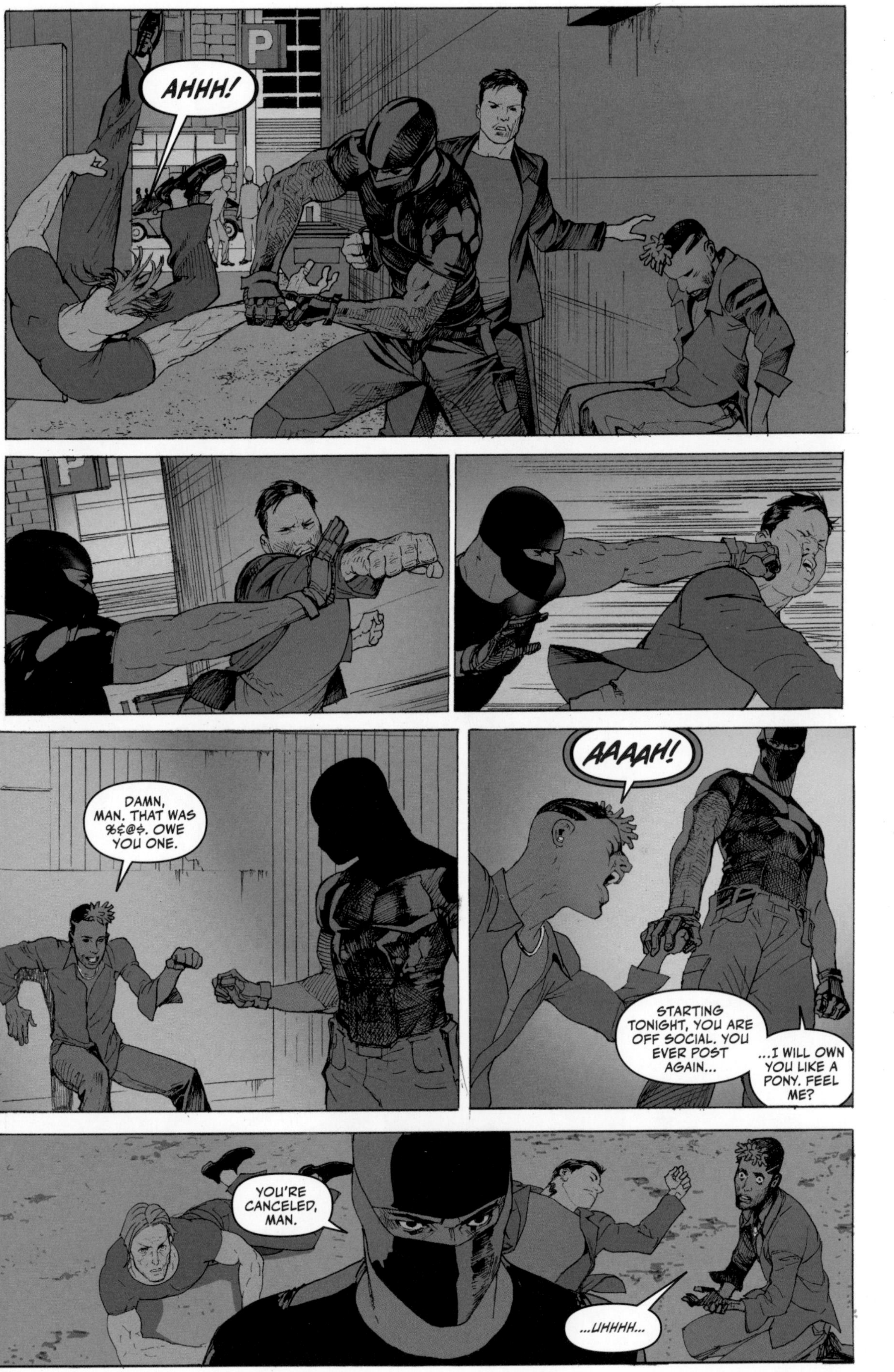
AHHH!
DAMN, MAN. THAT WAS %$@$. OWE YOU ONE.
AAAAH!
STARTING TONIGHT, YOU ARE OFF SOCIAL. YOU EVER POST AGAIN...
...I WILL OWN YOU LIKE A PONY. FEEL ME?
YOU'RE CANCELED, MAN.
...UHHHH...

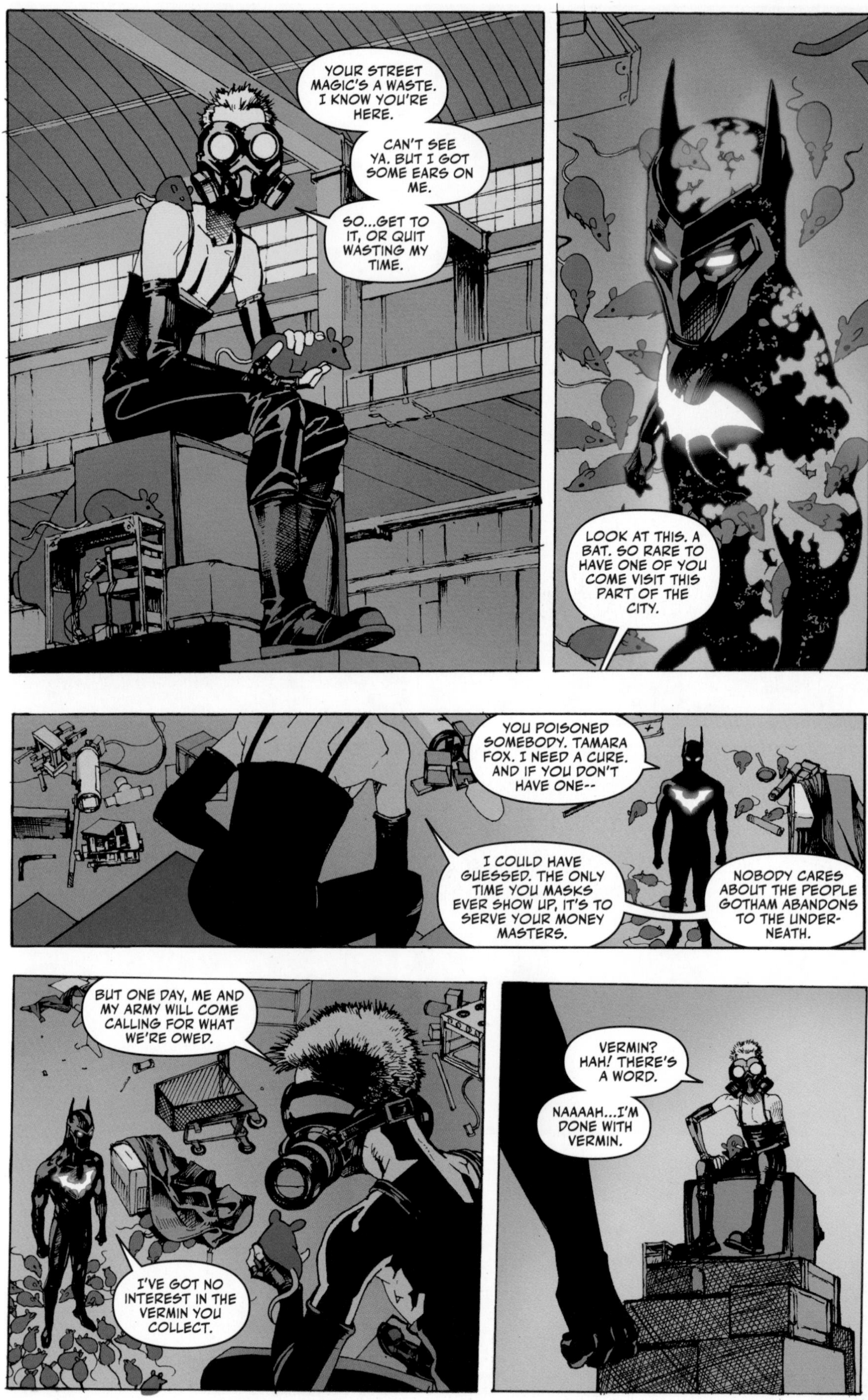
YOUR STREET MAGIC'S A WASTE. I KNOW YOU'RE HERE.
CAN'T SEE YA. BUT I GOT SOME EARS ON ME.
SO...GET TO IT, OR QUIT WASTING MY TIME.
LOOK AT THIS. A BAT. SO RARE TO HAVE ONE OF YOU COME VISIT THIS PART OF THE CITY.
YOU POISONED SOMEBODY. TAMARA FOX. I NEED A CURE. AND IF YOU DON'T HAVE ONE--
I COULD HAVE GUESSED. THE ONLY TIME YOU MASKS EVER SHOW UP, IT'S TO SERVE YOUR MONEY MASTERS.
NOBODY CARES ABOUT THE PEOPLE GOTHAM ABANDONS TO THE UNDER-NEATH.
BUT ONE DAY, ME AND MY ARMY WILL COME CALLING FOR WHAT WE'RE OWED.
I'VE GOT NO INTEREST IN THE VERMIN YOU COLLECT.
VERMIN? HAH! THERE'S A WORD.
NAAAAH...I'M DONE WITH VERMIN.

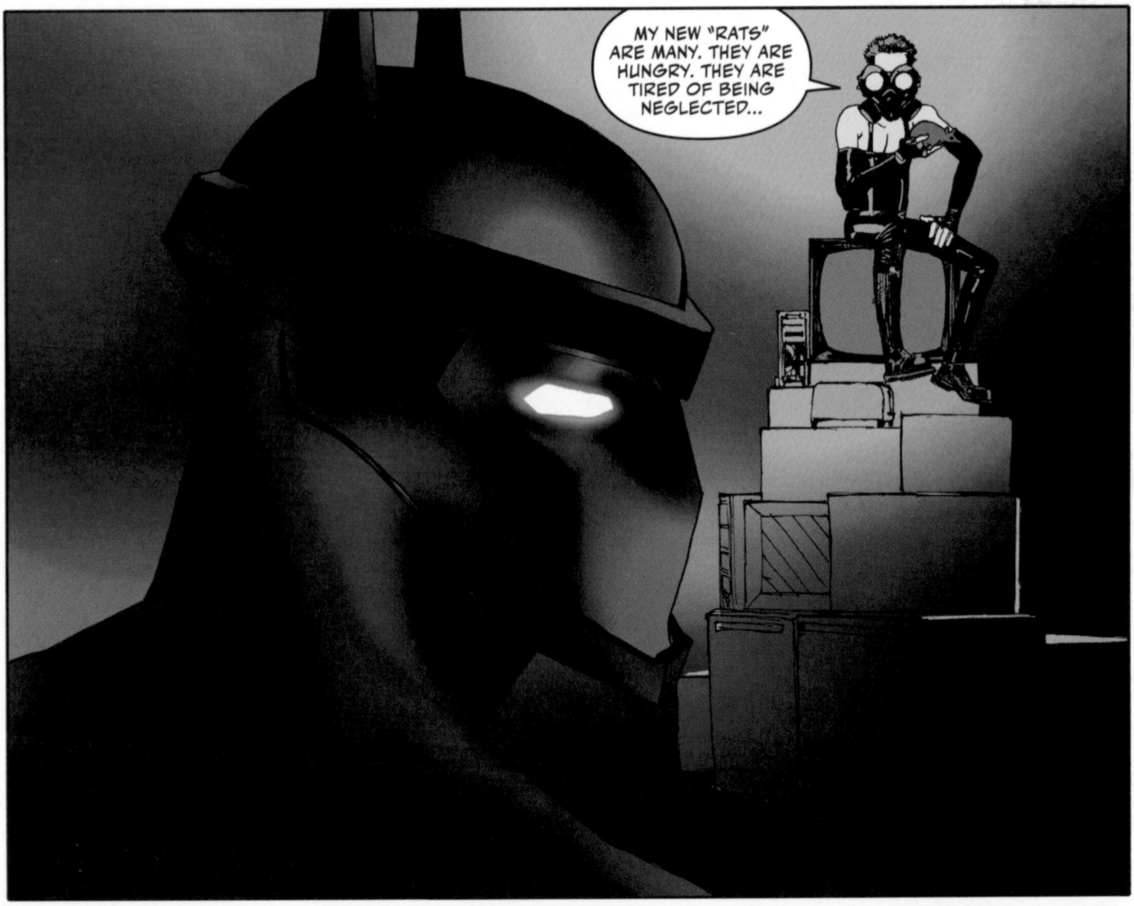
MY NEW "RATS" ARE MANY. THEY ARE HUNGRY. THEY ARE TIRED OF BEING NEGLECTED...

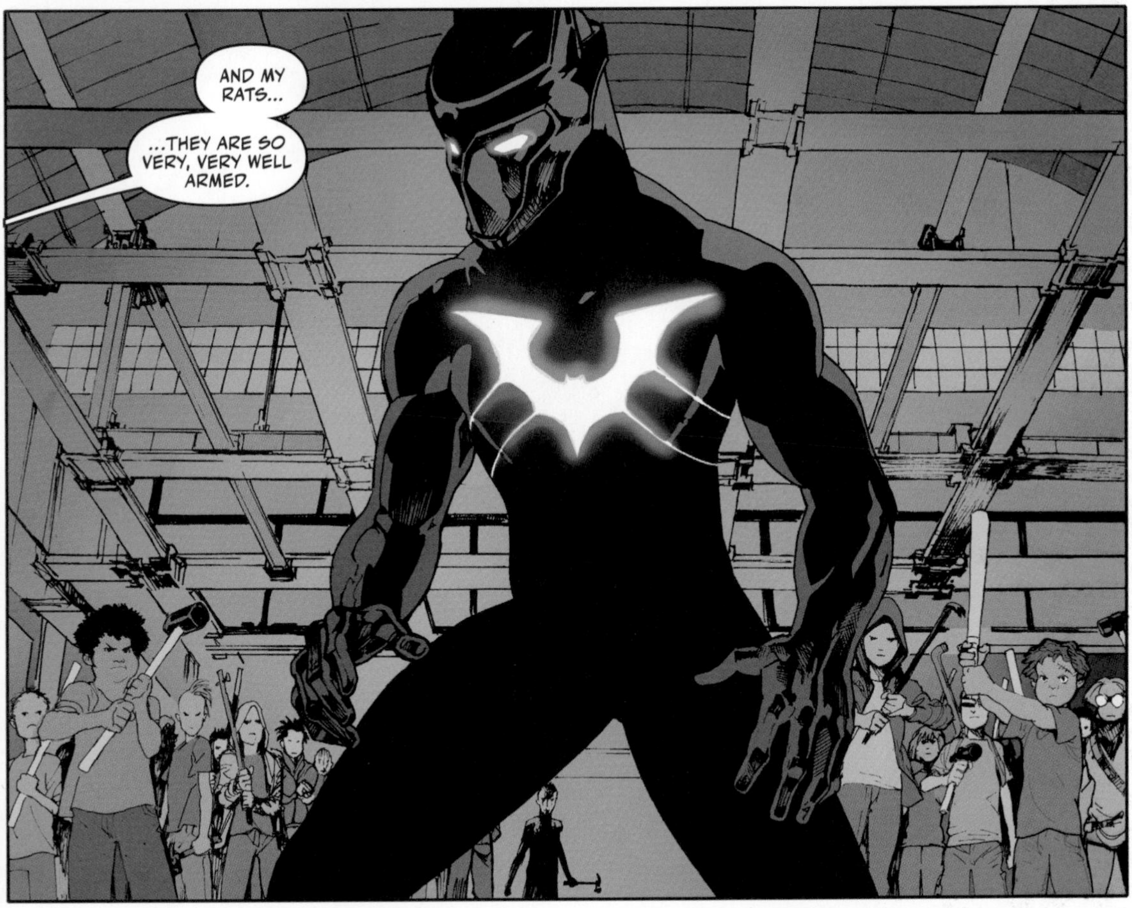
AND MY RATS...
...THEY ARE SO VERY, VERY WELL ARMED.

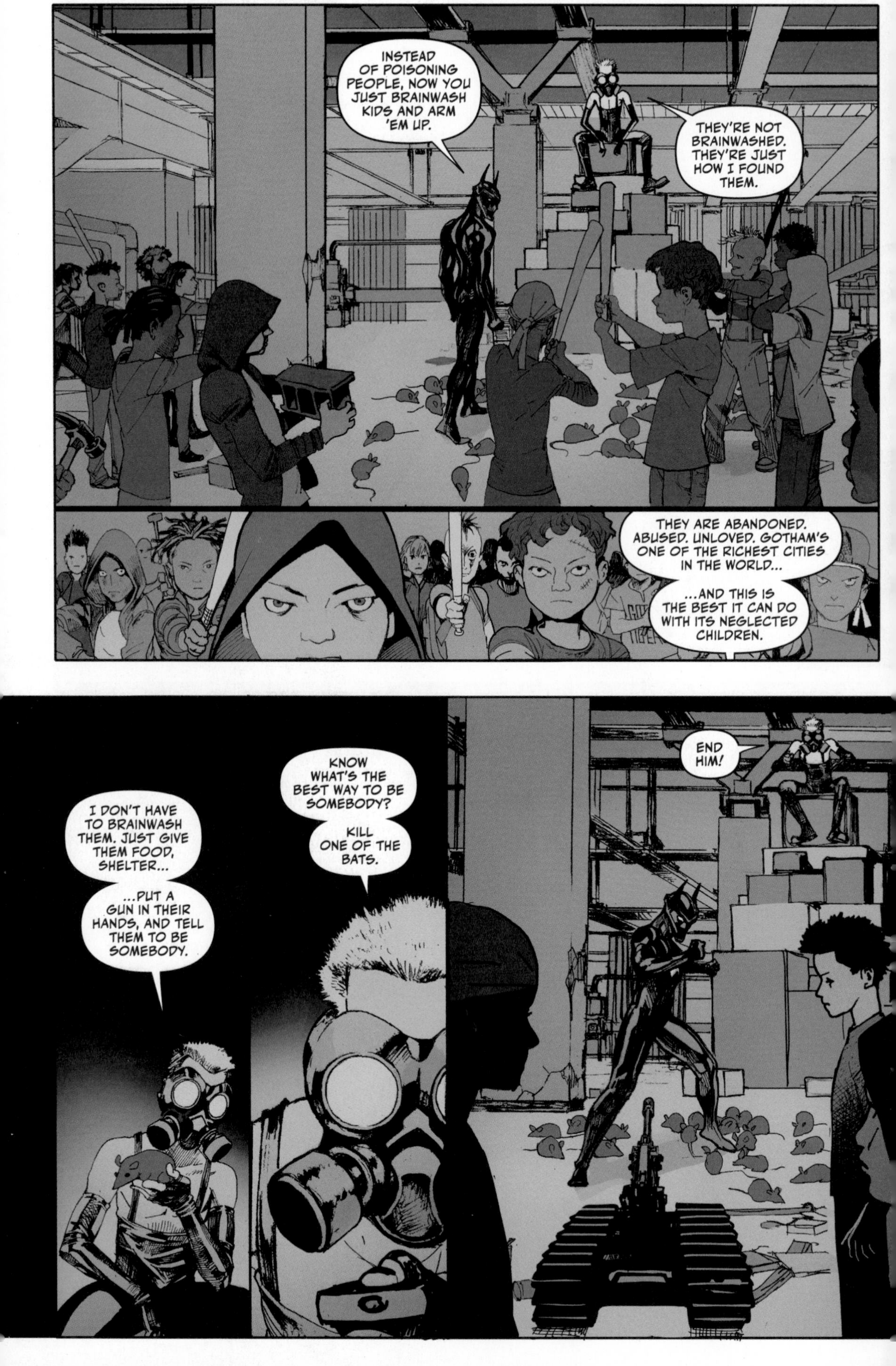
INSTEAD OF POISONING PEOPLE, NOW YOU JUST BRAINWASH KIDS AND ARM 'EM UP.
THEY'RE NOT BRAINWASHED. THEY'RE JUST HOW I FOUND THEM.
THEY ARE ABANDONED. ABUSED. UNLOVED. GOTHAM'S ONE OF THE RICHEST CITIES IN THE WORLD...
...AND THIS IS THE BEST IT CAN DO WITH ITS NEGLECTED CHILDREN.
I DON'T HAVE TO BRAINWASH THEM. JUST GIVE THEM FOOD, SHELTER...
...PUT A GUN IN THEIR HANDS, AND TELL THEM TO BE SOMEBODY.
KNOW WHAT'S THE BEST WAY TO BE SOMEBODY?
KILL ONE OF THE BATS.
END HIM!

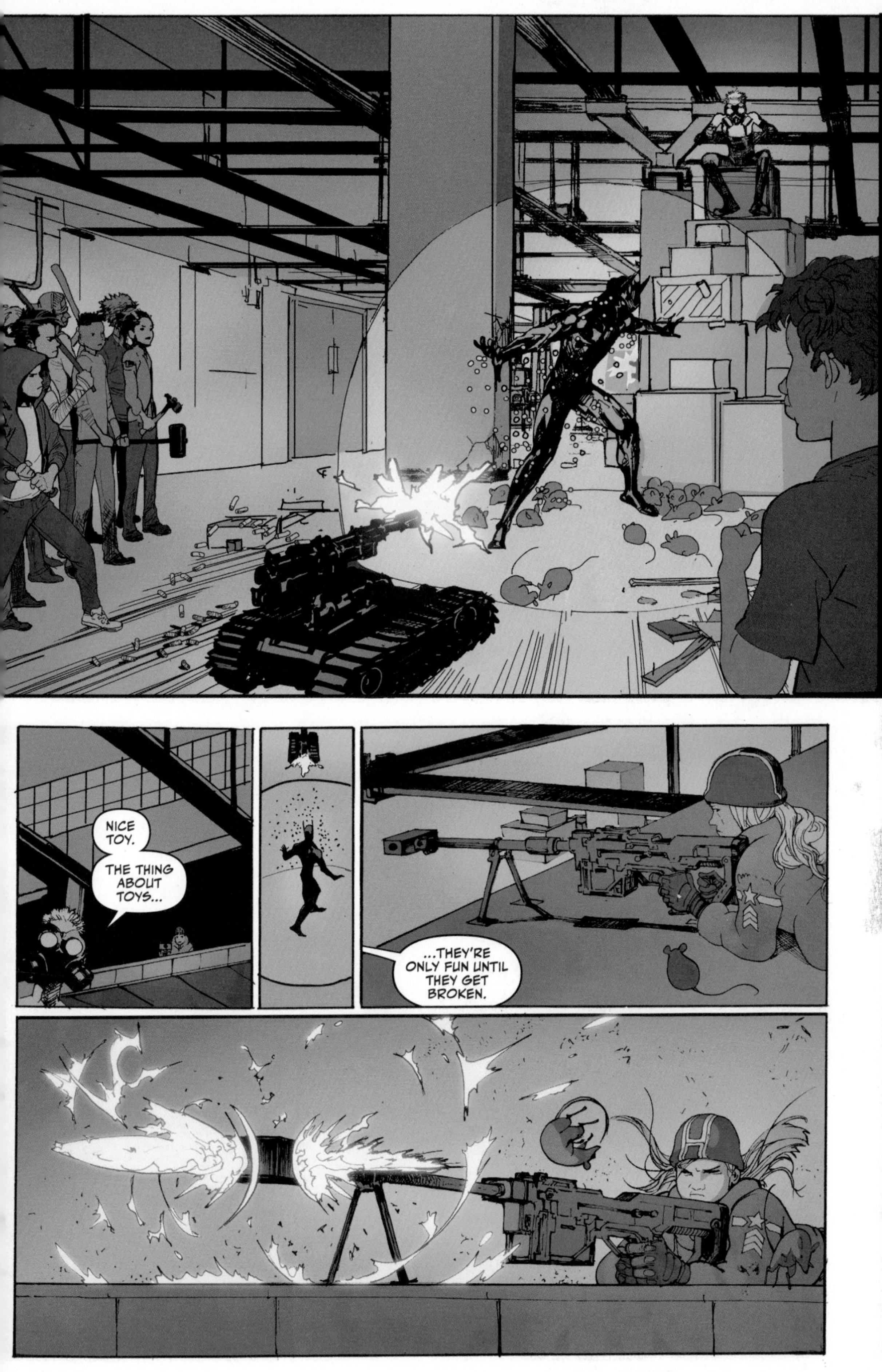
NICE TOY.
THE THING ABOUT TOYS...
...THEY'RE ONLY FUN UNTIL THEY GET BROKEN.

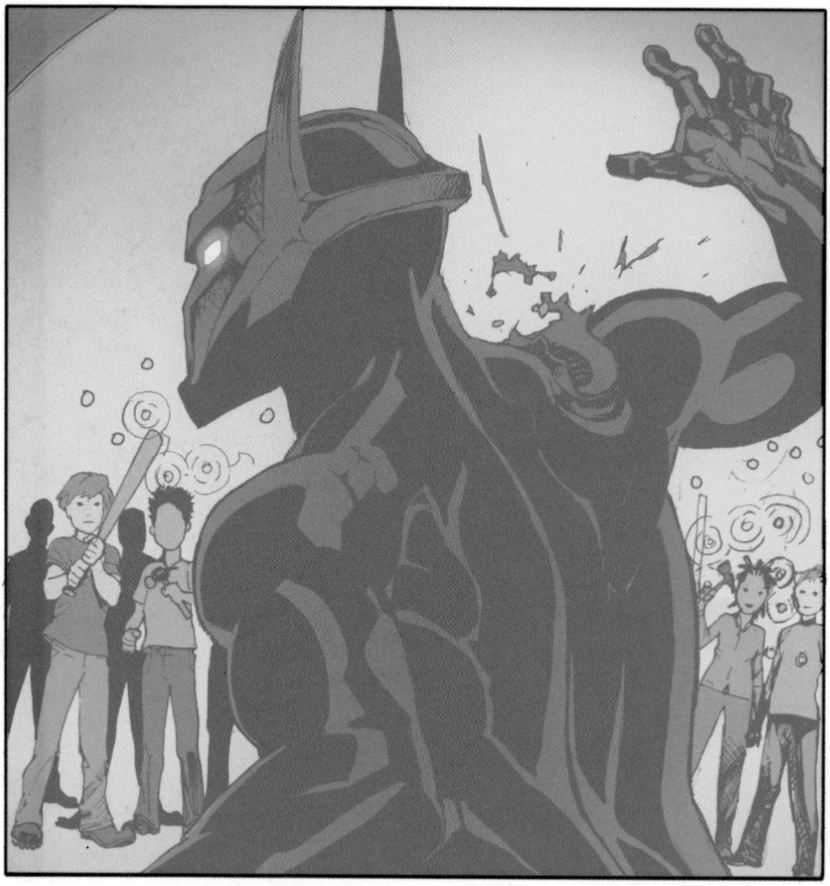

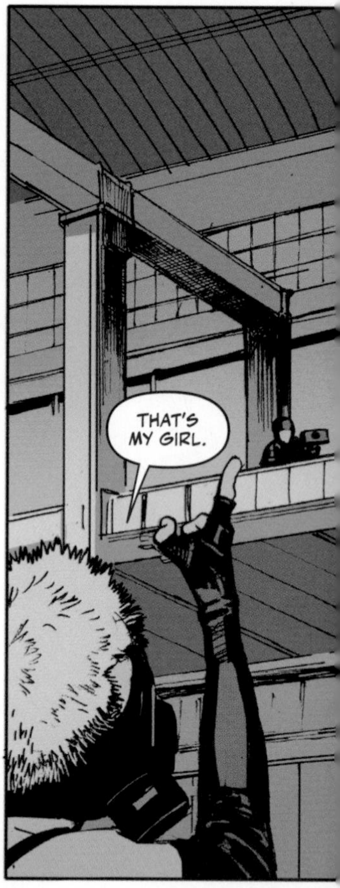
THAT'S MY GIRL.

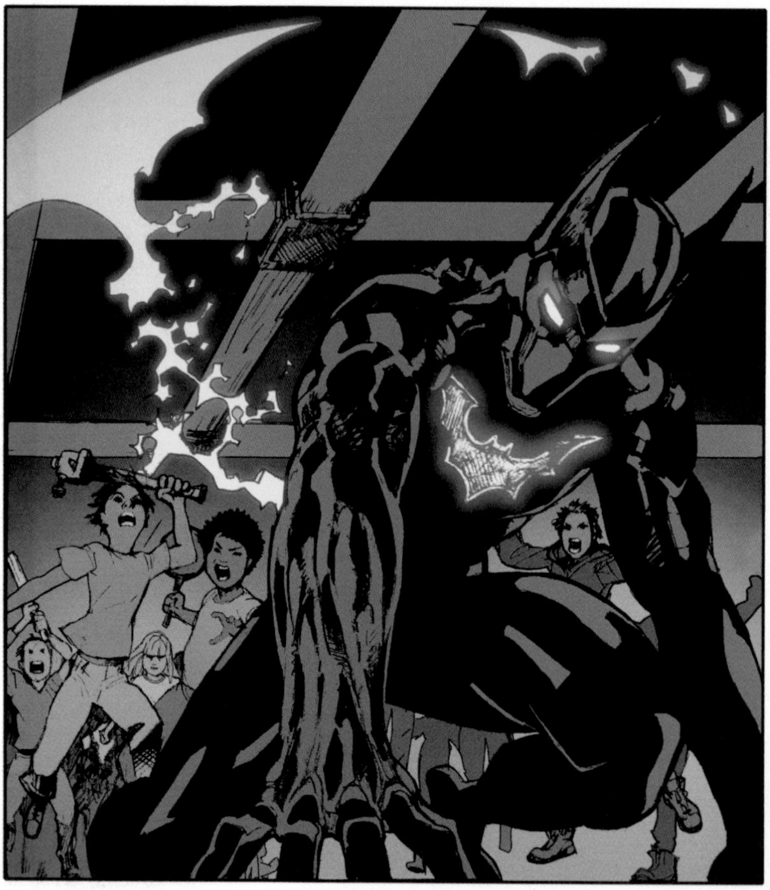

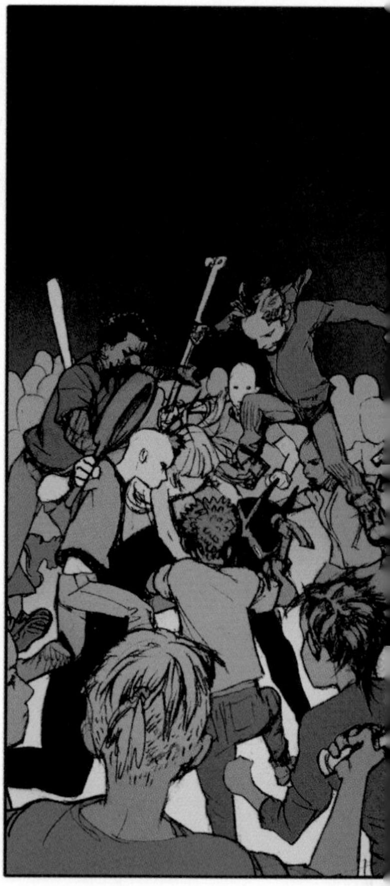

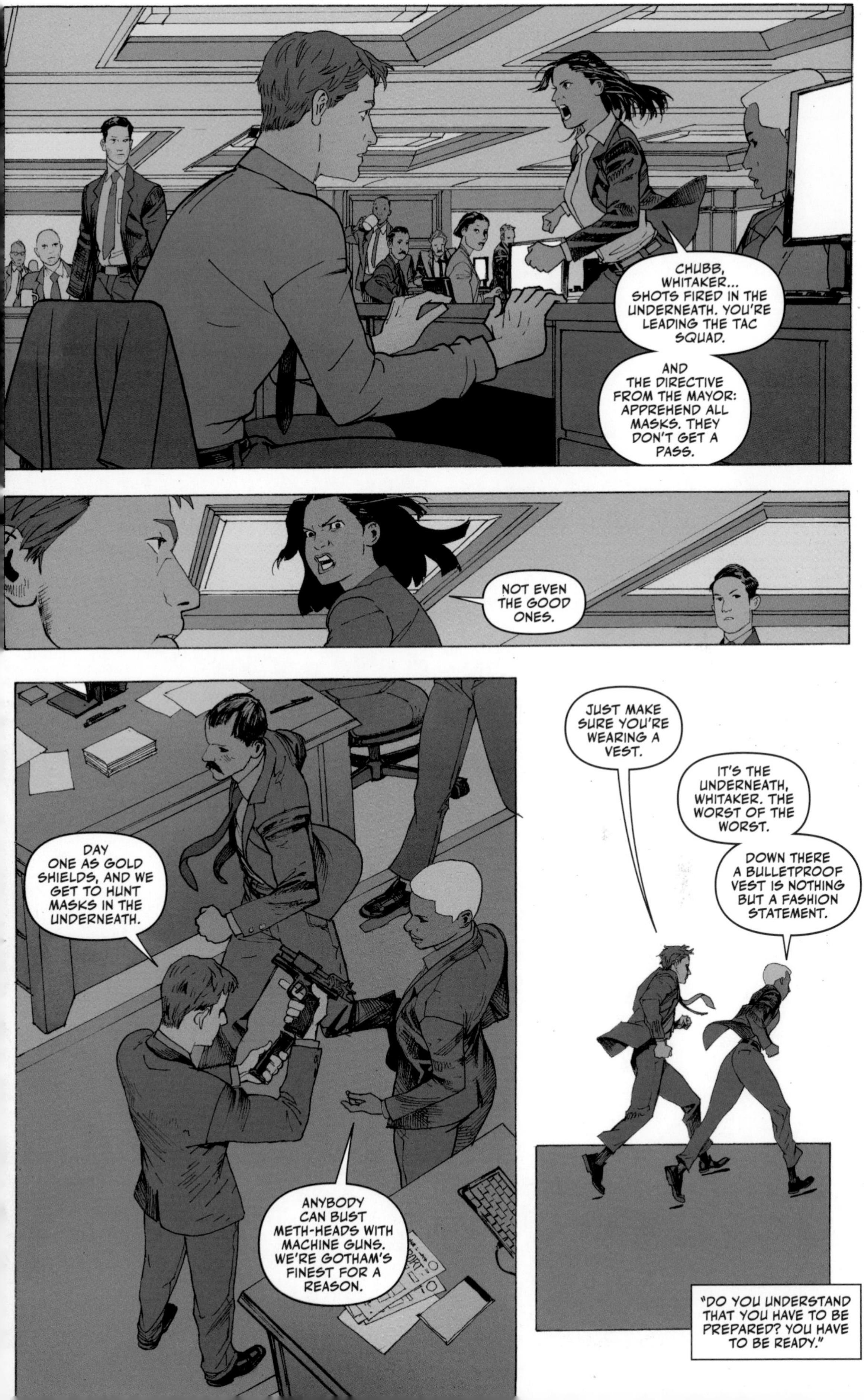
CHUBB, WHITAKER... SHOTS FIRED IN THE UNDERNEATH. YOU'RE LEADING THE TAC SQUAD.
AND THE DIRECTIVE FROM THE MAYOR: APPREHEND ALL MASKS. THEY DON'T GET A PASS.
NOT EVEN THE GOOD ONES.
DAY ONE AS GOLD SHIELDS, AND WE GET TO HUNT MASKS IN THE UNDERNEATH.
ANYBODY CAN BUST METH-HEADS WITH MACHINE GUNS. WE'RE GOTHAM'S FINEST FOR A REASON.
JUST MAKE SURE YOU'RE WEARING A VEST.
IT'S THE UNDERNEATH, WHITAKER. THE WORST OF THE WORST.
DOWN THERE A BULLETPROOF VEST IS NOTHING BUT A FASHION STATEMENT.
"DO YOU UNDERSTAND THAT YOU HAVE TO BE PREPARED? YOU HAVE TO BE READY."

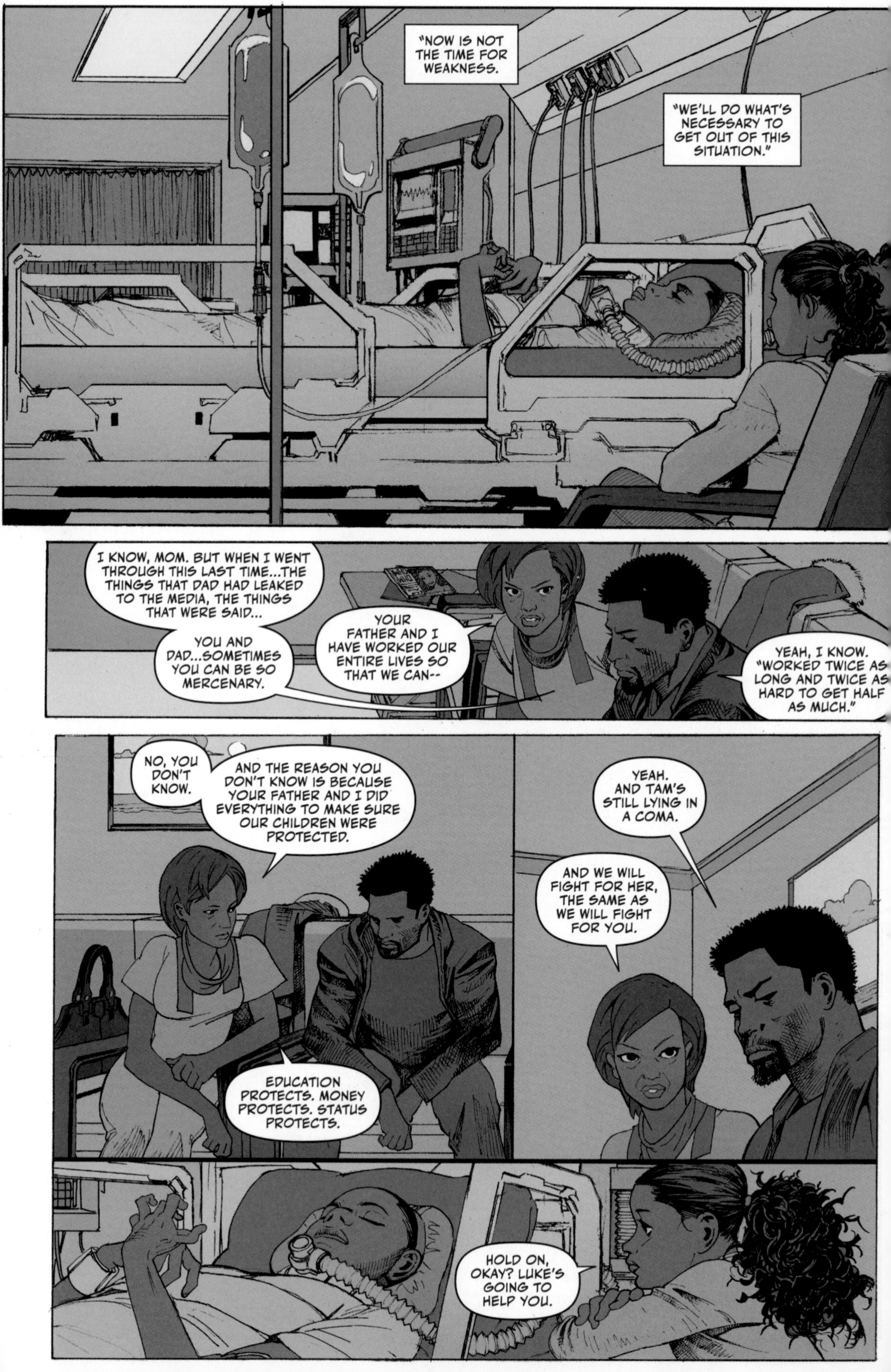
"NOW IS NOT THE TIME FOR WEAKNESS.
"WE'LL DO WHAT'S NECESSARY TO GET OUT OF THIS SITUATION."
I KNOW, MOM. BUT WHEN I WENT THROUGH THIS LAST TIME...THE THINGS THAT DAD HAD LEAKED TO THE MEDIA, THE THINGS THAT WERE SAID...
YOU AND DAD...SOMETIMES YOU CAN BE SO MERCENARY.
YOUR FATHER AND I HAVE WORKED OUR ENTIRE LIVES SO THAT WE CAN--
YEAH, I KNOW. "WORKED TWICE AS LONG AND TWICE AS HARD TO GET HALF AS MUCH."
NO, YOU DON'T KNOW.
AND THE REASON YOU DON'T KNOW IS BECAUSE YOUR FATHER AND I DID EVERYTHING TO MAKE SURE OUR CHILDREN WERE PROTECTED.
EDUCATION PROTECTS. MONEY PROTECTS. STATUS PROTECTS.
YEAH. AND TAM'S STILL LYING IN A COMA.
AND WE WILL FIGHT FOR HER, THE SAME AS WE WILL FIGHT FOR YOU.
HOLD ON, OKAY? LUKE'S GOING TO HELP YOU.

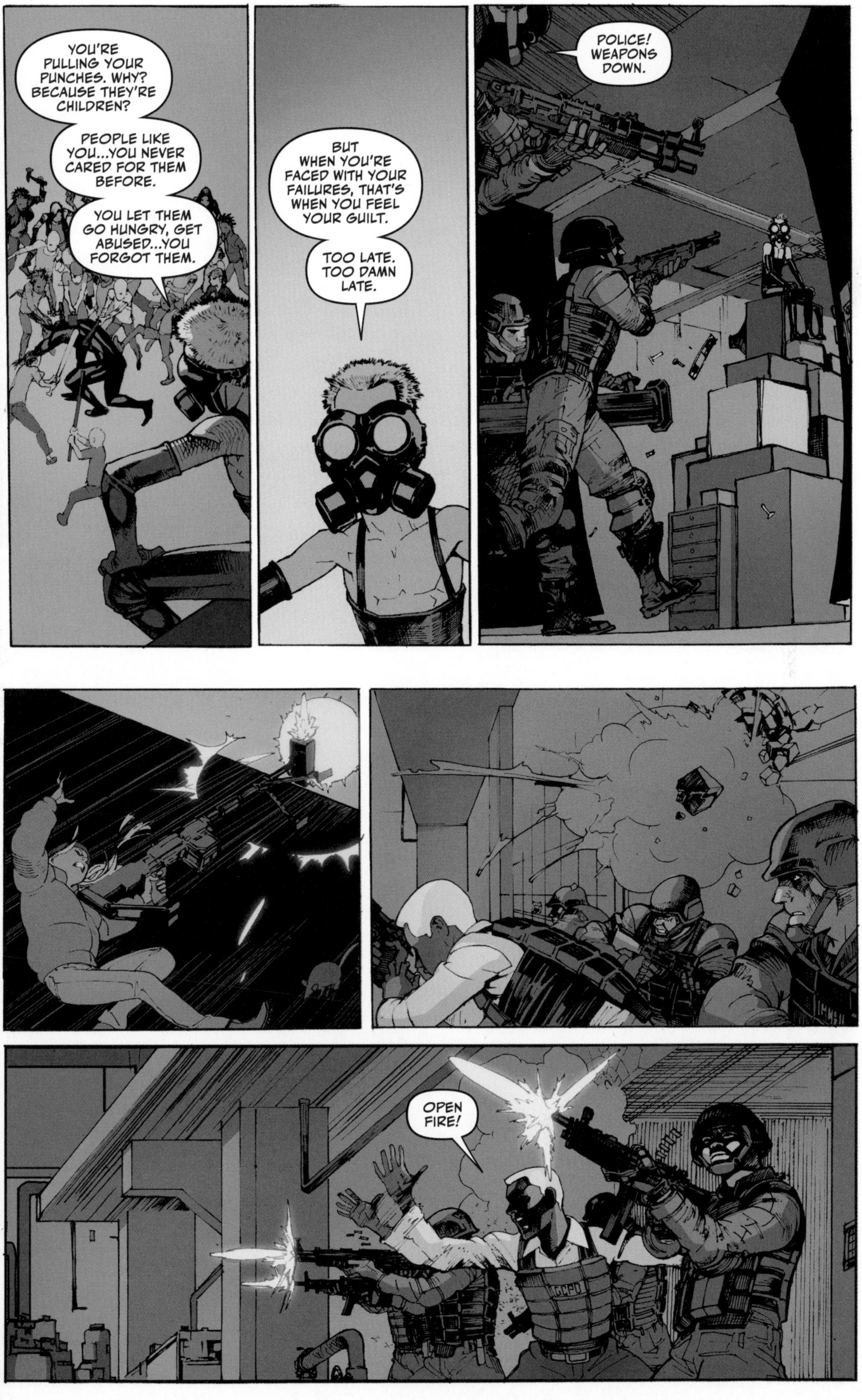
YOU'RE PULLING YOUR PUNCHES. WHY? BECAUSE THEY'RE CHILDREN?
PEOPLE LIKE YOU...YOU NEVER CARED FOR THEM BEFORE.
YOU LET THEM GO HUNGRY, GET ABUSED...YOU FORGOT THEM.
BUT WHEN YOU'RE FACED WITH YOUR FAILURES, THAT'S WHEN YOU FEEL YOUR GUILT.
TOO LATE. TOO DAMN LATE.
POLICE! WEAPONS DOWN.
OPEN FIRE!
GCPD

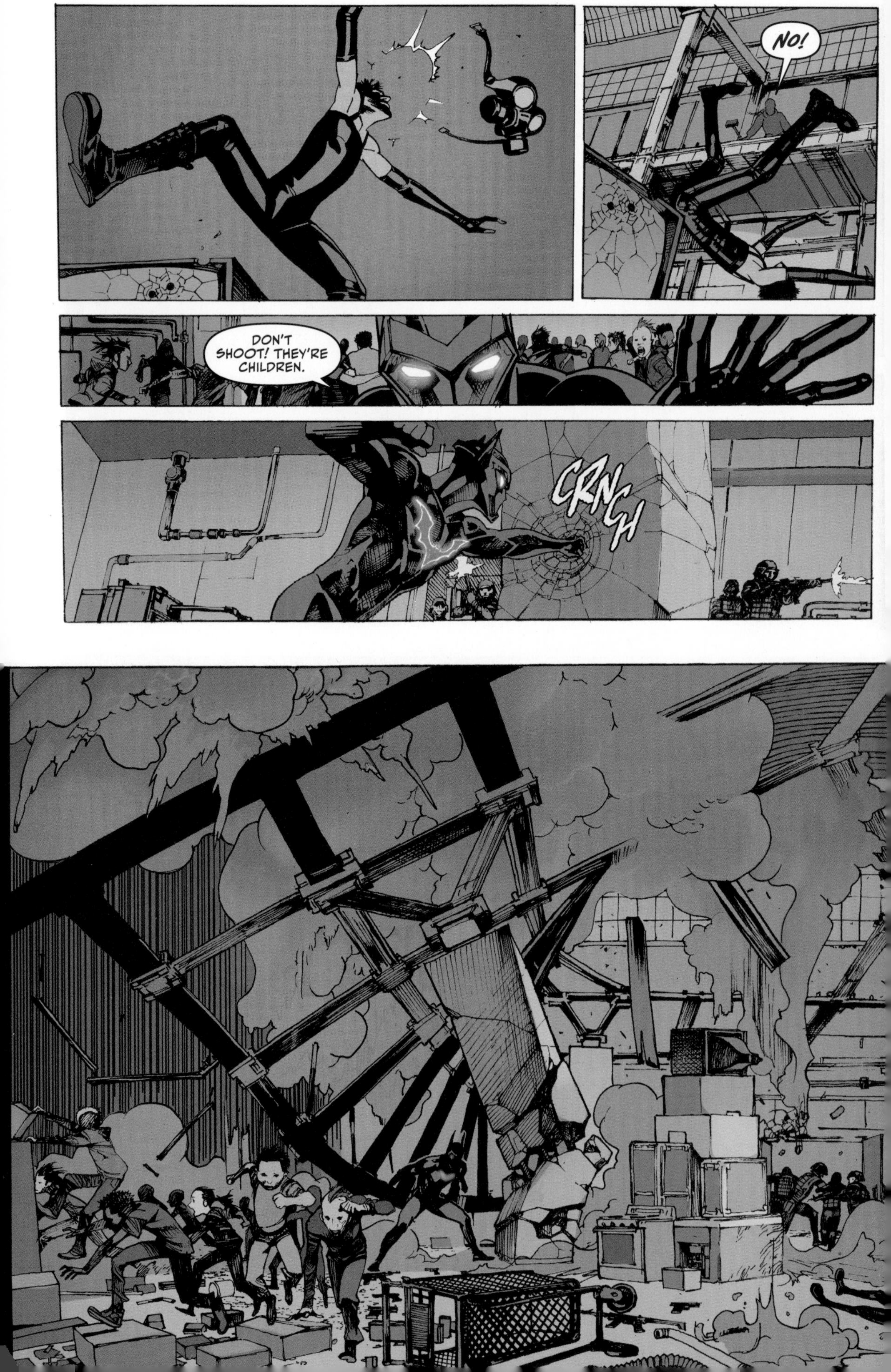
NO!
DON'T SHOOT! THEY'RE CHILDREN.
CRNCH

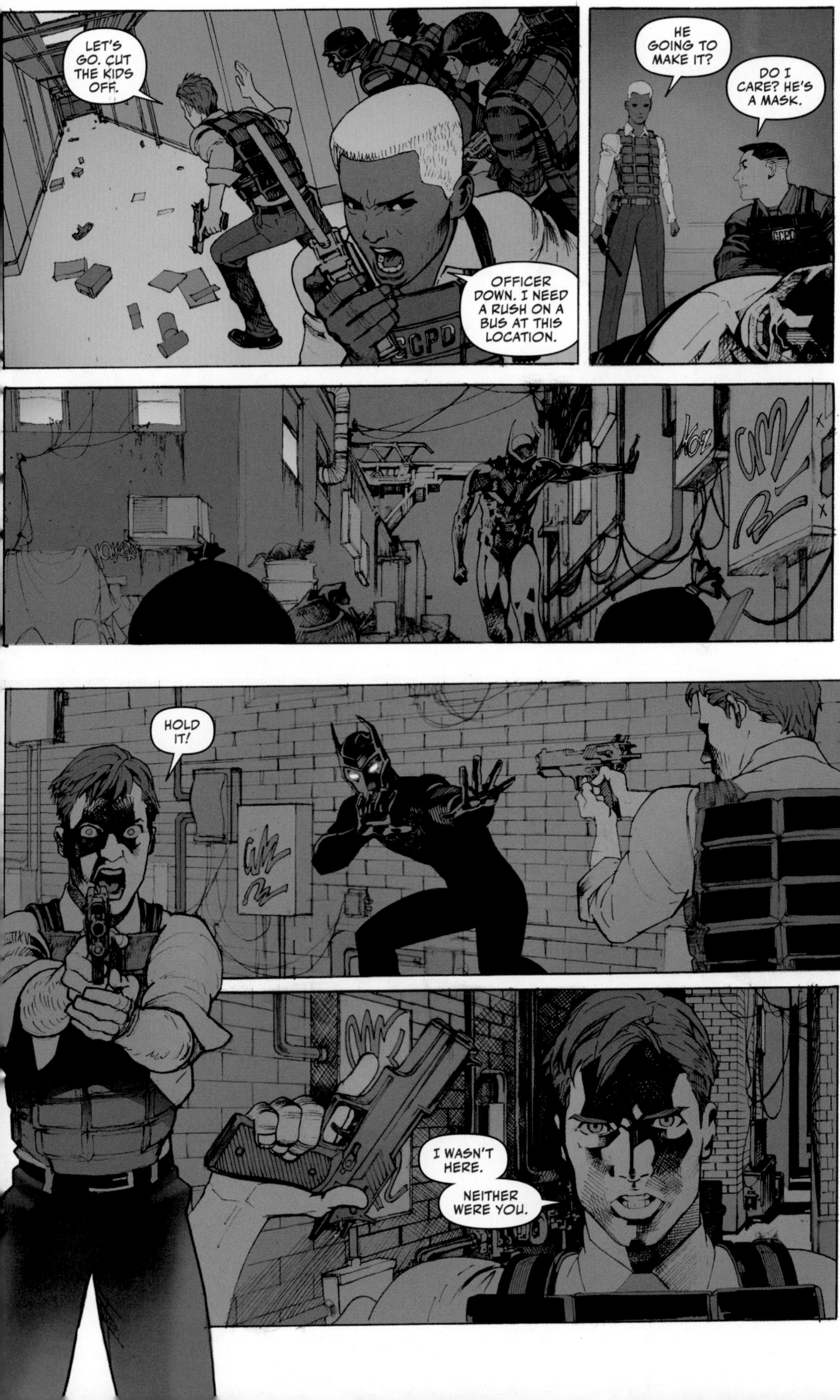
LET'S GO. CUT THE KIDS OFF.
OFFICER DOWN. I NEED A RUSH ON A BUS AT THIS LOCATION.
HE GOING TO MAKE IT?
DO I CARE? HE'S A MASK.
HOLD IT!
I WASN'T HERE.
NEITHER WERE YOU.

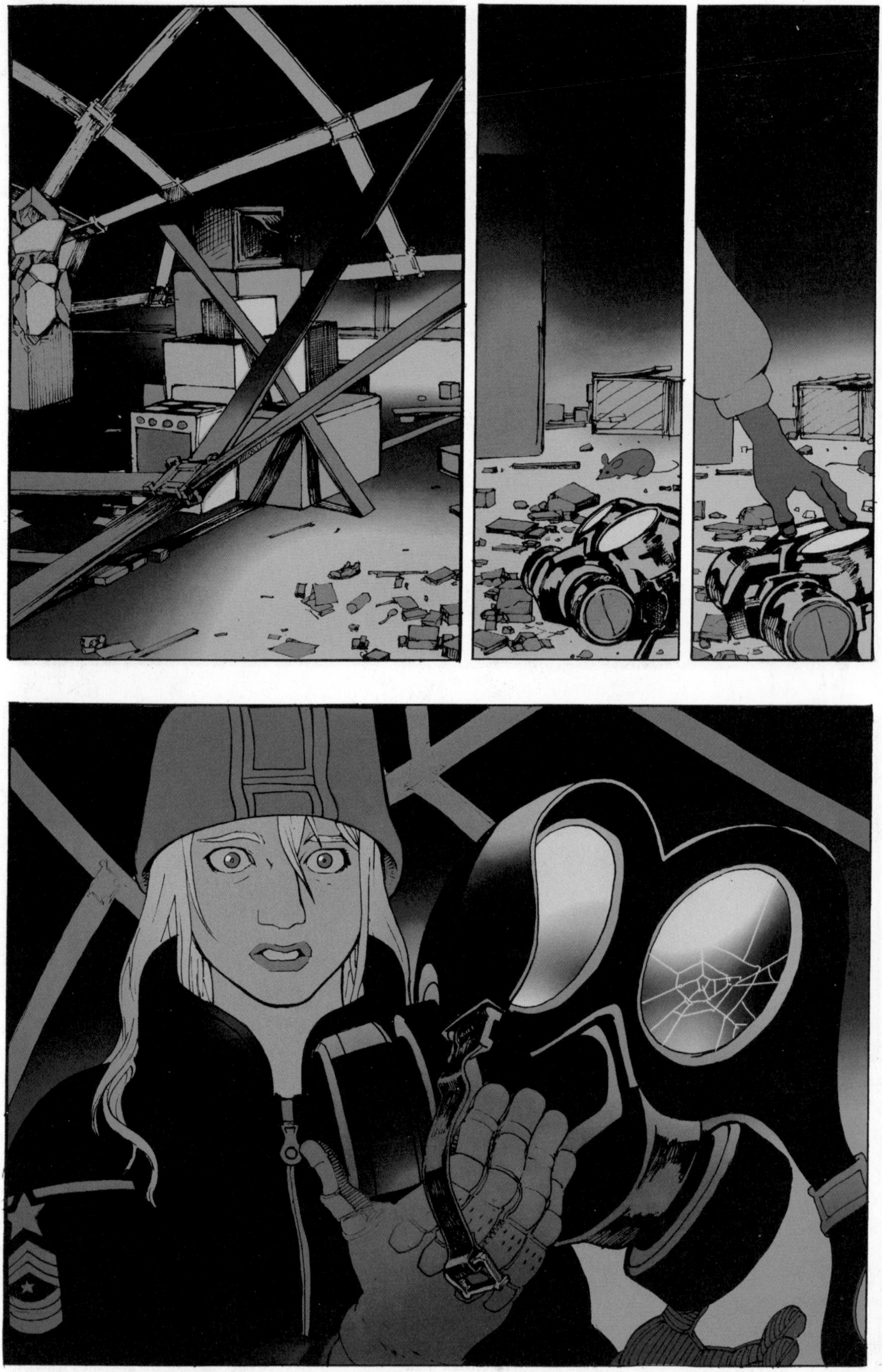

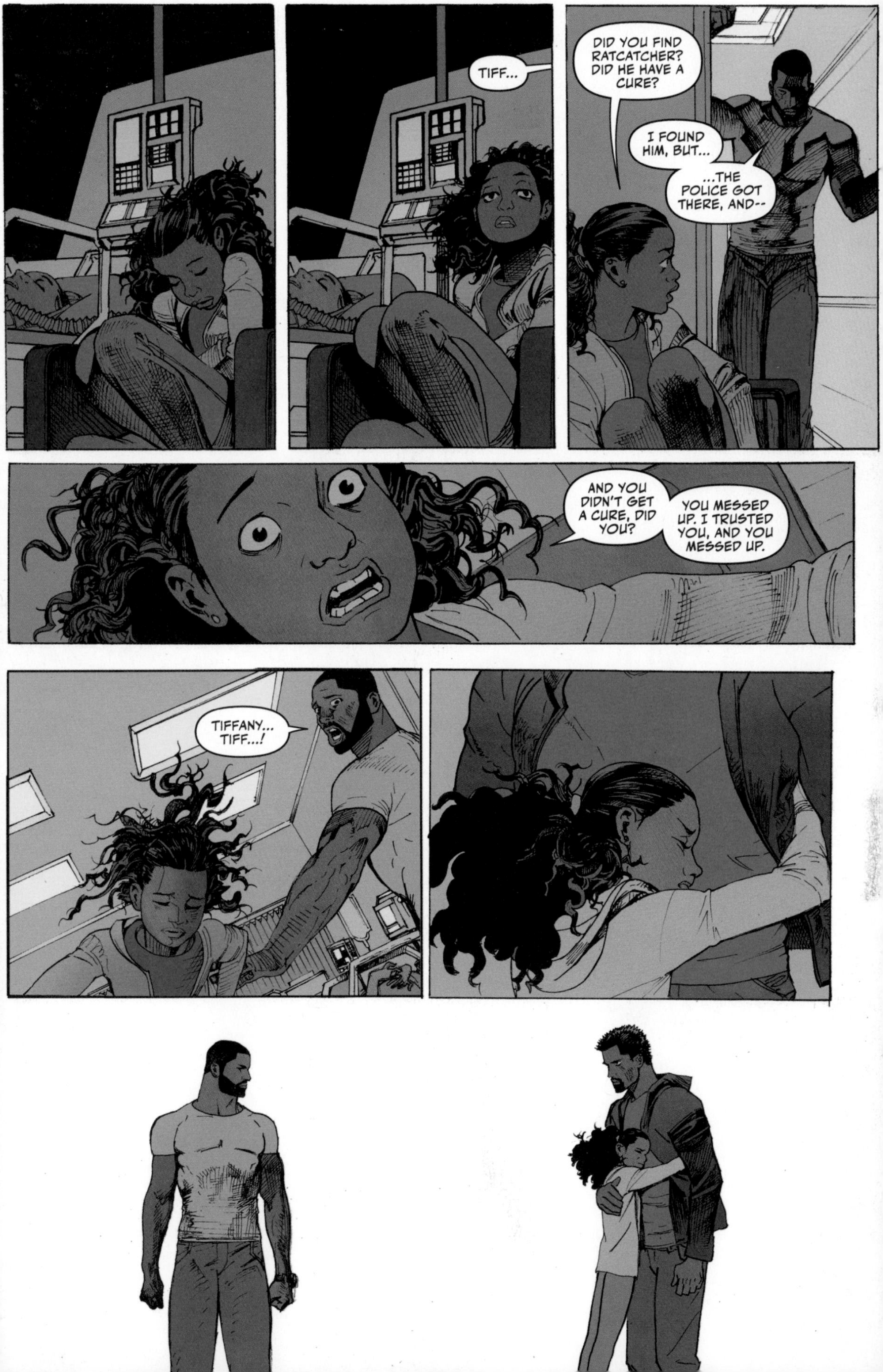
TIFF...
DID YOU FIND RATCATCHER? DID HE HAVE A CURE?
I FOUND HIM, BUT...
...THE POLICE GOT THERE, AND--
AND YOU DIDN'T GET A CURE, DID YOU?
YOU MESSED UP. I TRUSTED YOU, AND YOU MESSED UP.
TIFFANY... TIFF...!

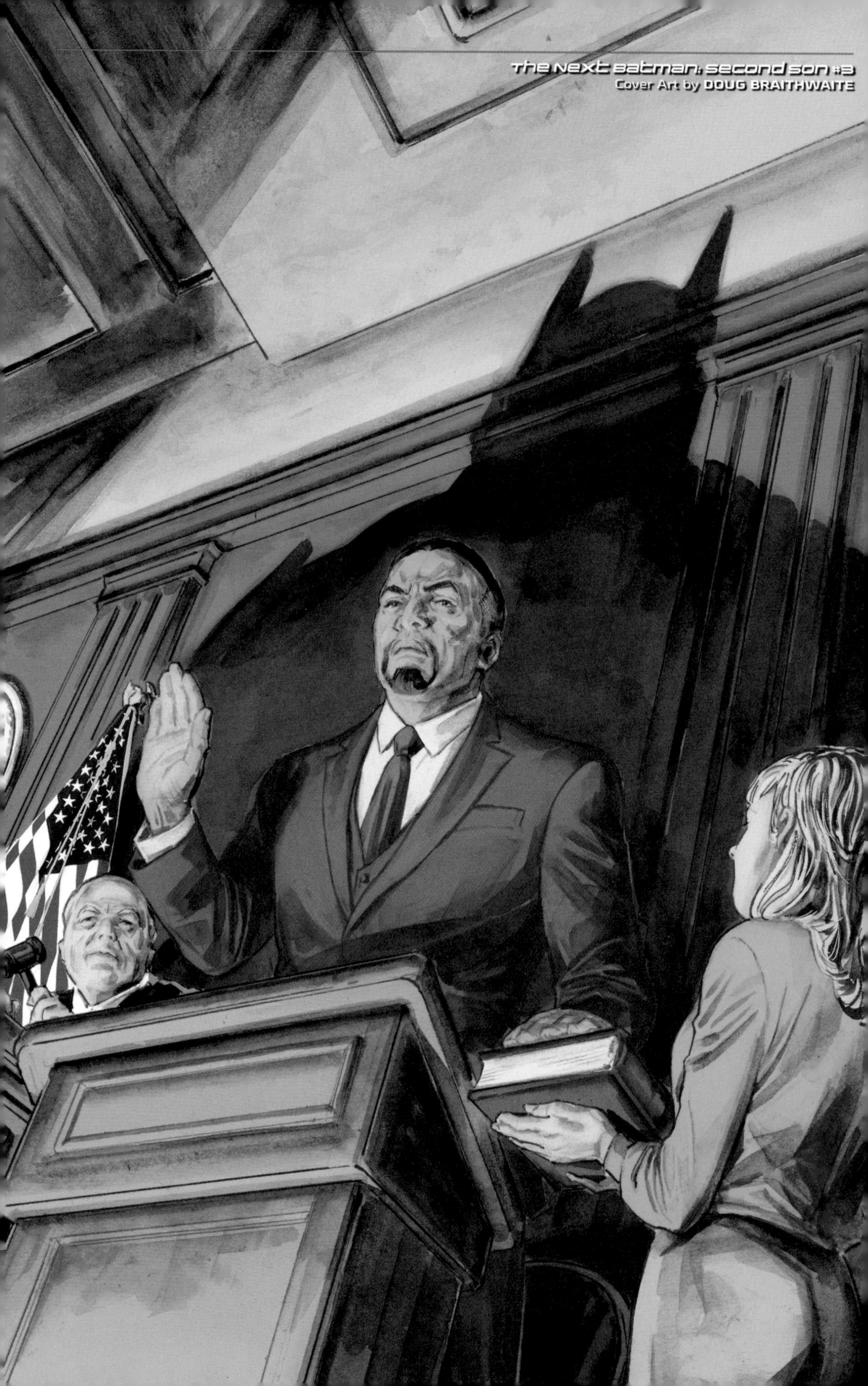

THE NEXT BATMAN: SECOND SON #3
Cover Art by DOUG BRAITHWAITE

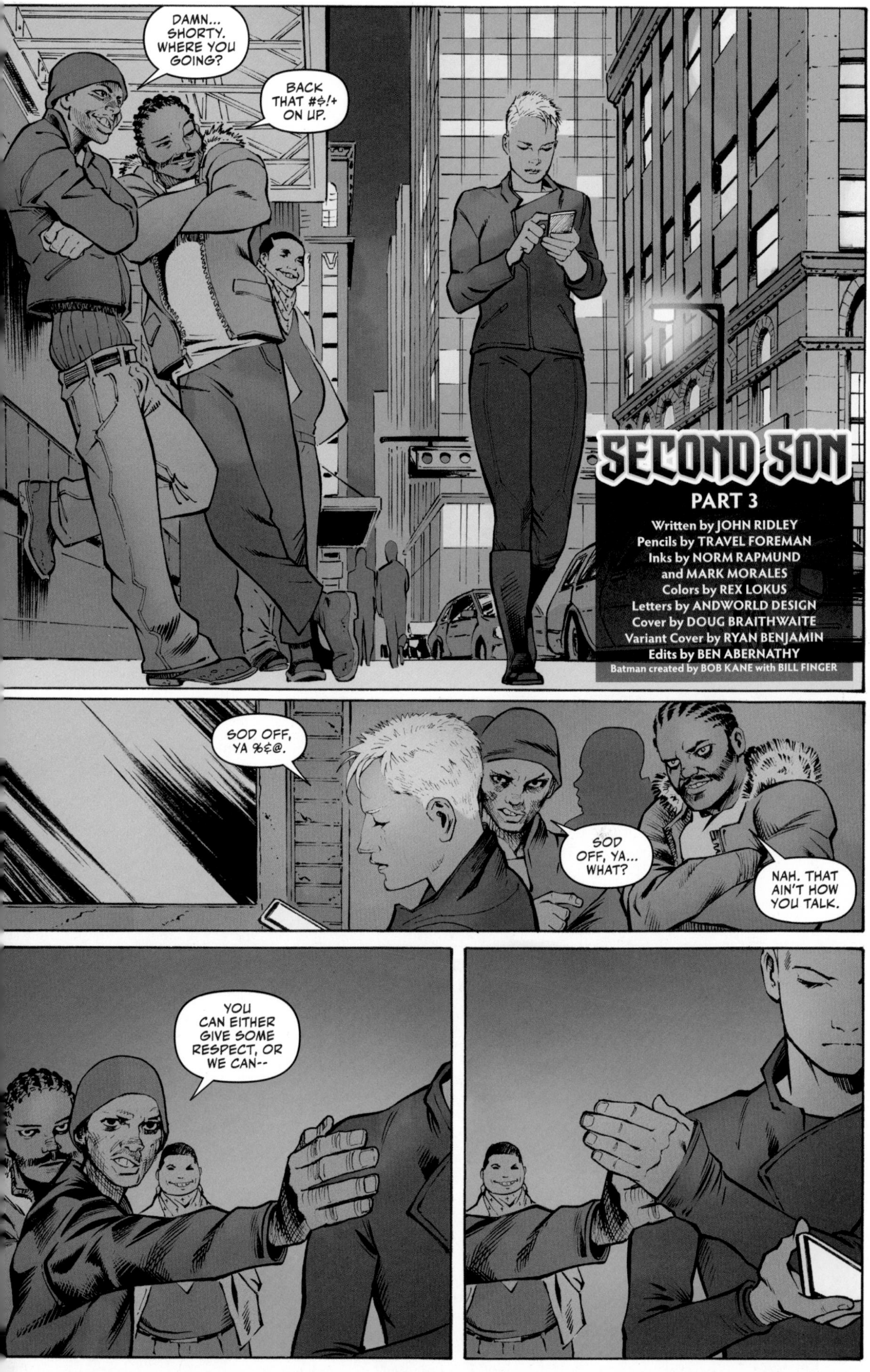
DAMN... SHORTY. WHERE YOU GOING?
BACK THAT #$!+ ON UP.
SECOND SON
PART 3
Written by JOHN RIDLEY
Pencils by TRAVEL FOREMAN
Inks by NORM RAPMUND and MARK MORALES
Colors by REX LOKUS
Letters by ANDWORLD DESIGN
Cover by DOUG BRAITHWAITE
Variant Cover by RYAN BENJAMIN
Edits by BEN ABERNATHY
Batman created by BOB KANE with BILL FINGER
SOD OFF, YA %$@.
SOD OFF, YA... WHAT?
NAH. THAT AIN'T HOW YOU TALK.
YOU CAN EITHER GIVE SOME RESPECT, OR WE CAN--

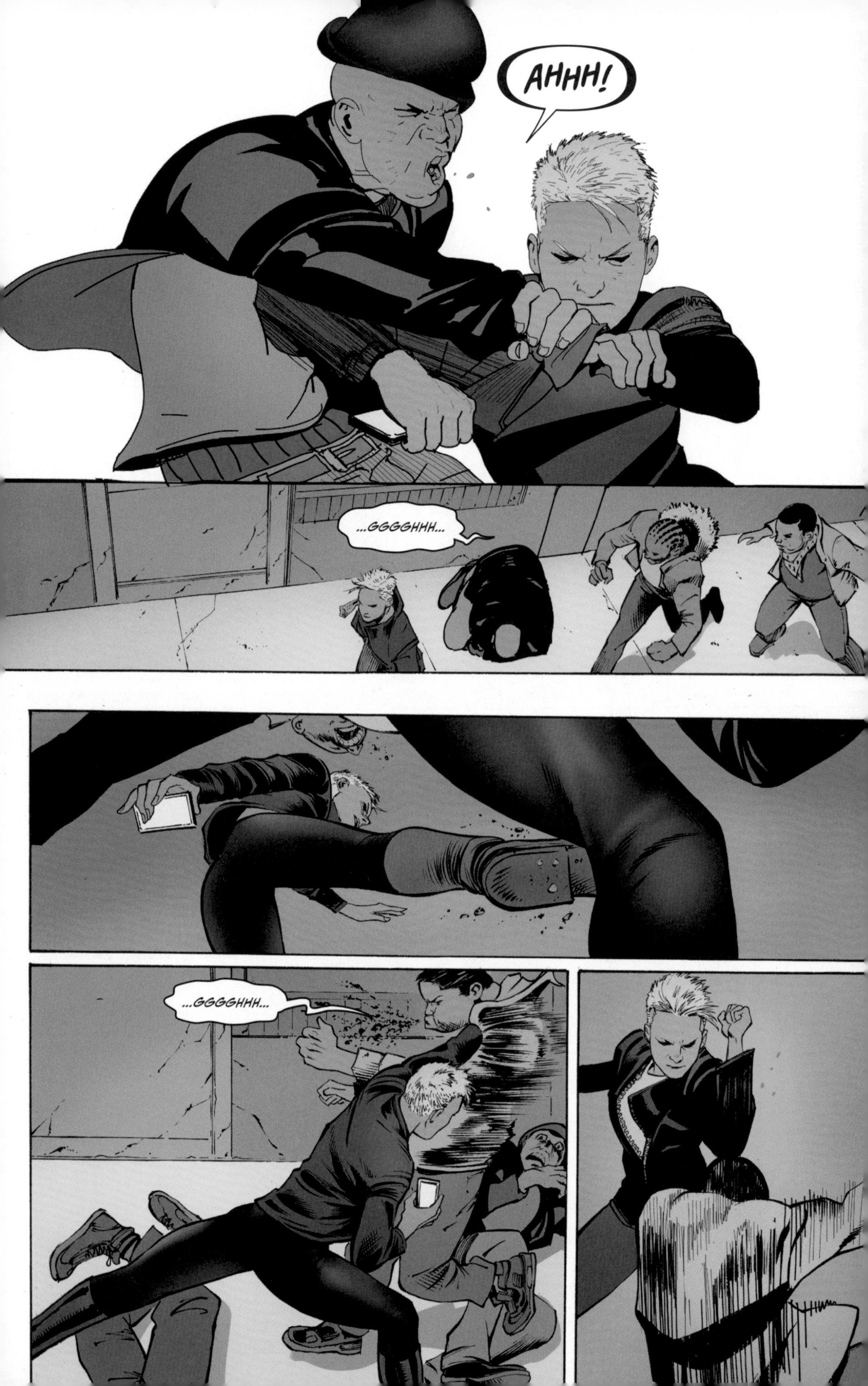
AHHH!
...GGGGHHH...
...GGGGHHH...

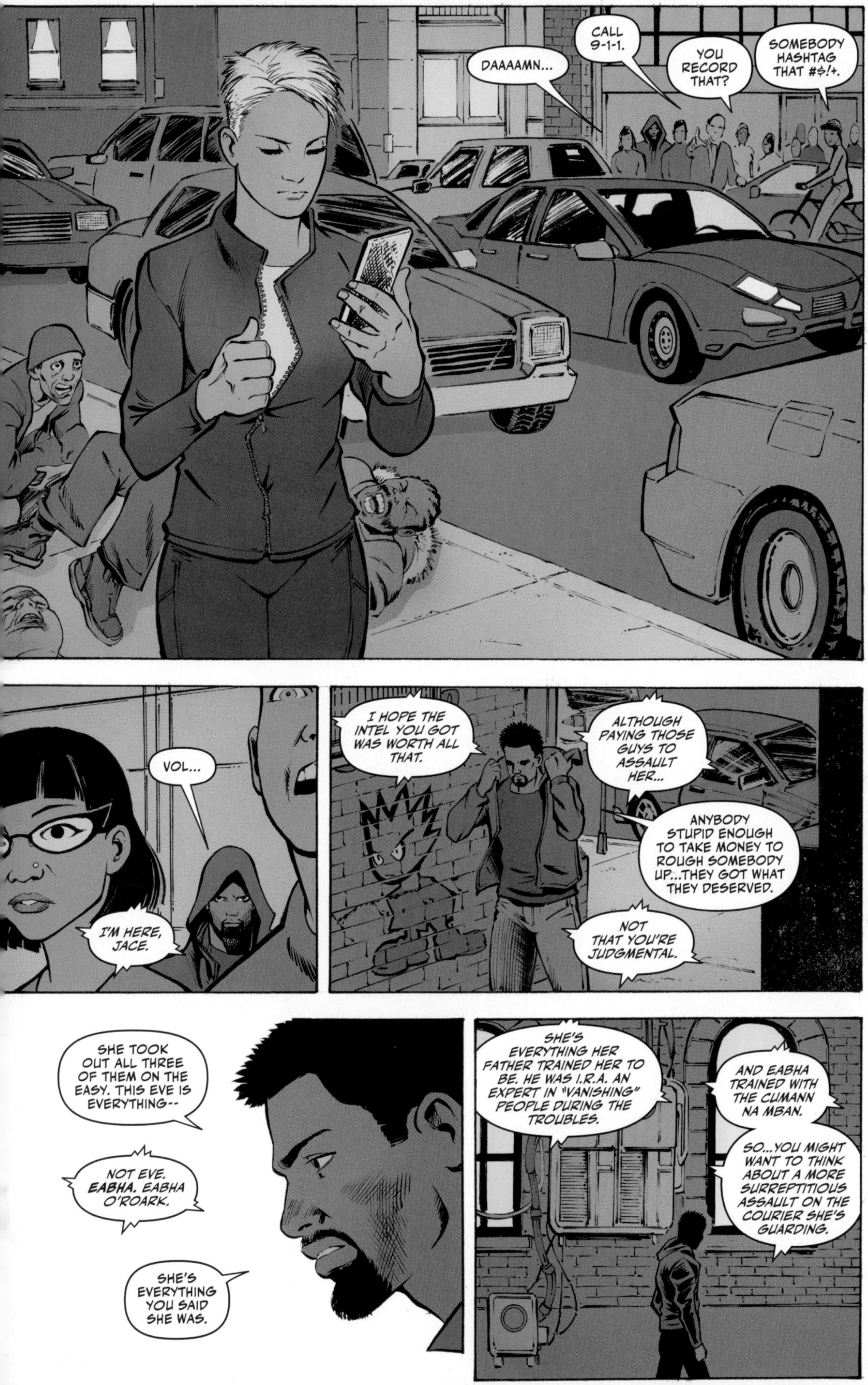
DAAAAMN...
CALL 9-1-1.
YOU RECORD THAT?
SOMEBODY HASHTAG THAT #$!+.
VOL...
I'M HERE, JACE.
I HOPE THE INTEL YOU GOT WAS WORTH ALL THAT.
ALTHOUGH PAYING THOSE GUYS TO ASSAULT HER...
ANYBODY STUPID ENOUGH TO TAKE MONEY TO ROUGH SOMEBODY UP...THEY GOT WHAT THEY DESERVED.
NOT THAT YOU'RE JUDGMENTAL.
SHE TOOK OUT ALL THREE OF THEM ON THE EASY. THIS EVE IS EVERYTHING--
NOT EVE. EABHA. EABHA O'ROARK.
SHE'S EVERYTHING YOU SAID SHE WAS.
SHE'S EVERYTHING HER FATHER TRAINED HER TO BE. HE WAS I.R.A. AN EXPERT IN "VANISHING" PEOPLE DURING THE TROUBLES.
AND EABHA TRAINED WITH THE CUMANN NA MBAN.
SO...YOU MIGHT WANT TO THINK ABOUT A MORE SURREPTITIOUS ASSAULT ON THE COURIER SHE'S GUARDING.

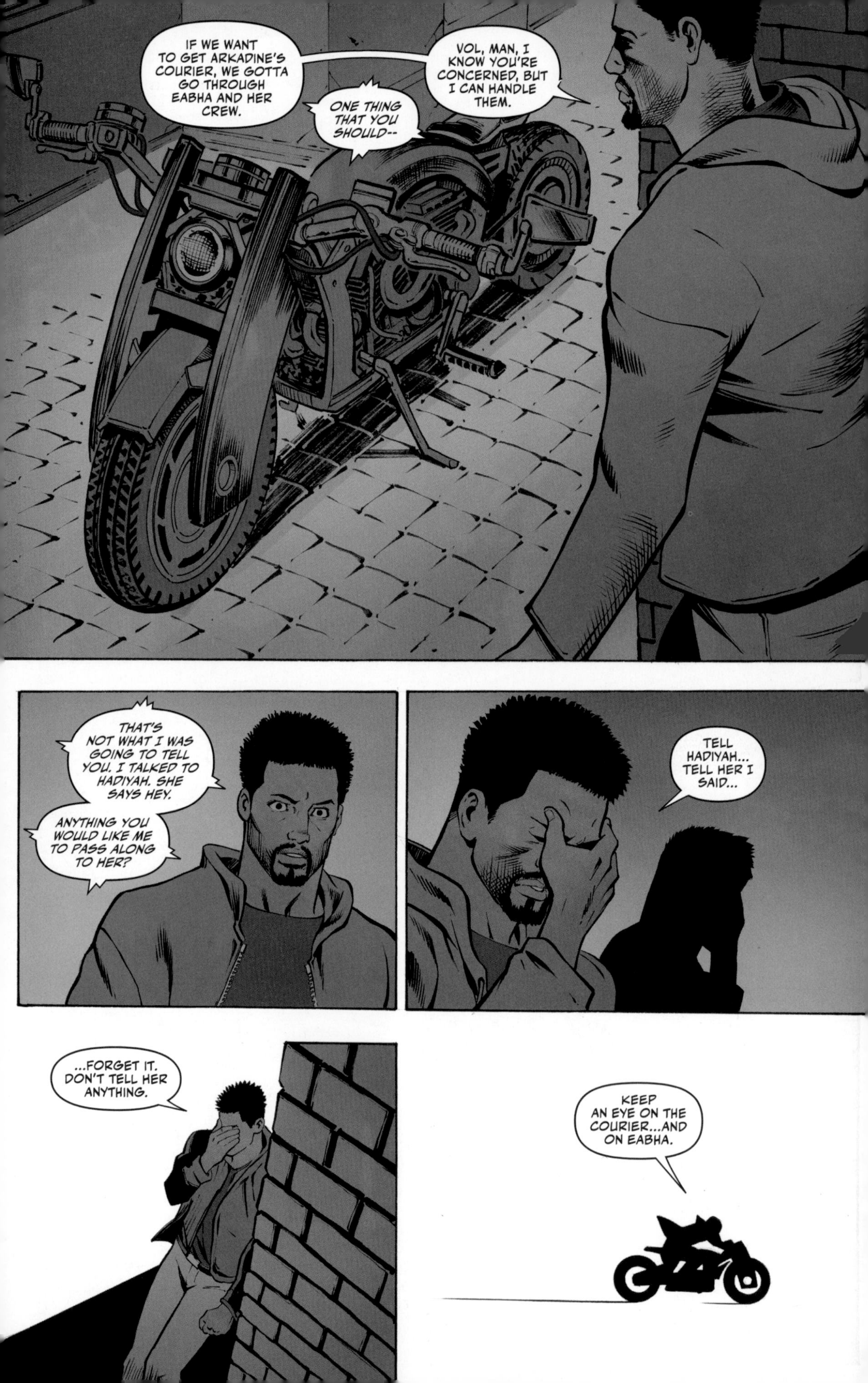
IF WE WANT TO GET ARKADINE'S COURIER, WE GOTTA GO THROUGH EABHA AND HER CREW.
VOL, MAN, I KNOW YOU'RE CONCERNED, BUT I CAN HANDLE THEM.
ONE THING THAT YOU SHOULD--
THAT'S NOT WHAT I WAS GOING TO TELL YOU. I TALKED TO HADIYAH. SHE SAYS HEY.
ANYTHING YOU WOULD LIKE ME TO PASS ALONG TO HER?
TELL HADIYAH... TELL HER I SAID...
...FORGET IT. DON'T TELL HER ANYTHING.
KEEP AN EYE ON THE COURIER...AND ON EABHA.

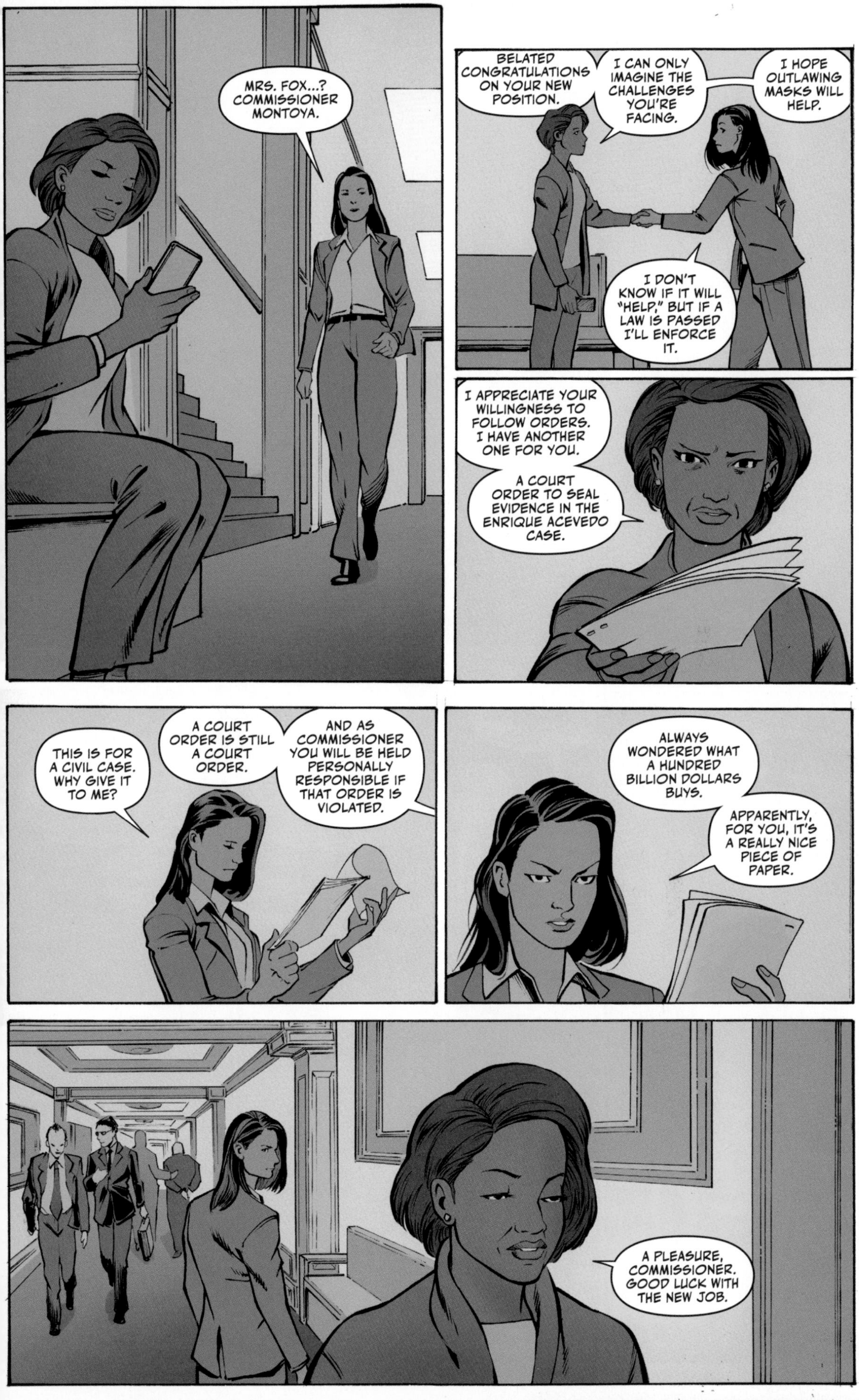
MRS. FOX...? COMMISSIONER MONTOYA.
BELATED CONGRATULATIONS ON YOUR NEW POSITION.
I CAN ONLY IMAGINE THE CHALLENGES YOU'RE FACING.
I HOPE OUTLAWING MASKS WILL HELP.
I DON'T KNOW IF IT WILL "HELP," BUT IF A LAW IS PASSED I'LL ENFORCE IT.
I APPRECIATE YOUR WILLINGNESS TO FOLLOW ORDERS. I HAVE ANOTHER ONE FOR YOU.
A COURT ORDER TO SEAL EVIDENCE IN THE ENRIQUE ACEVEDO CASE.
THIS IS FOR A CIVIL CASE. WHY GIVE IT TO ME?
A COURT ORDER IS STILL A COURT ORDER.
AND AS COMMISSIONER YOU WILL BE HELD PERSONALLY RESPONSIBLE IF THAT ORDER IS VIOLATED.
ALWAYS WONDERED WHAT A HUNDRED BILLION DOLLARS BUYS.
APPARENTLY, FOR YOU, IT'S A REALLY NICE PIECE OF PAPER.
A PLEASURE, COMMISSIONER. GOOD LUCK WITH THE NEW JOB.

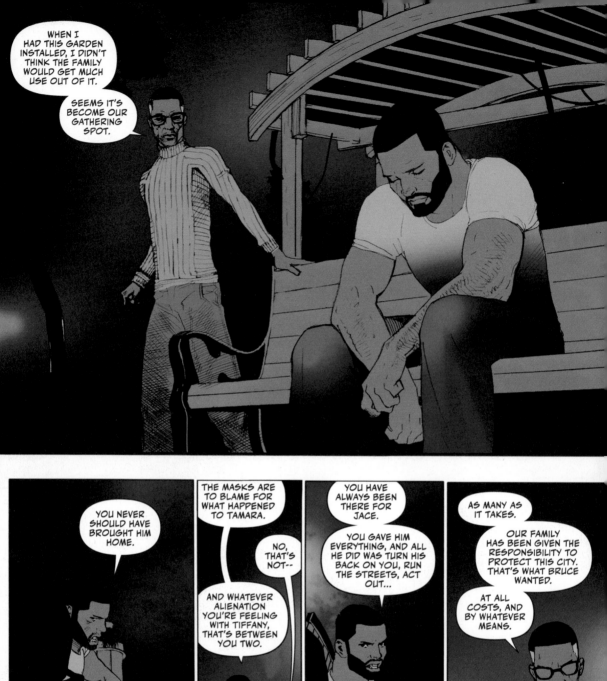

WHEN I HAD THIS GARDEN INSTALLED, I DIDN'T THINK THE FAMILY WOULD GET MUCH USE OUT OF IT.

SEEMS IT'S BECOME OUR GATHERING SPOT.

YOU NEVER SHOULD HAVE BROUGHT HIM HOME.

WHO, JACE? JACE IS PART OF OUR FAMILY. I COULDN'T HAVE DONE OTHERWISE.

SINCE HE GOT BACK, EVERYTHING'S GONE SOUTH. WITH TAM, WITH TIFF...

THE MASKS ARE TO BLAME FOR WHAT HAPPENED TO TAMARA.

NO, THAT'S NOT--

AND WHATEVER ALIENATION YOU'RE FEELING WITH TIFFANY, THAT'S BETWEEN YOU TWO.

YOU HAVE ALWAYS BEEN THERE FOR JACE.

YOU GAVE HIM EVERYTHING, AND ALL HE DID WAS TURN HIS BACK ON YOU, RUN THE STREETS, ACT OUT...

HOW MANY CHANCES ARE YOU GOING TO GIVE HIM?

AS MANY AS IT TAKES.

OUR FAMILY HAS BEEN GIVEN THE RESPONSIBILITY TO PROTECT THIS CITY. THAT'S WHAT BRUCE WANTED.

AT ALL COSTS, AND BY WHATEVER MEANS.

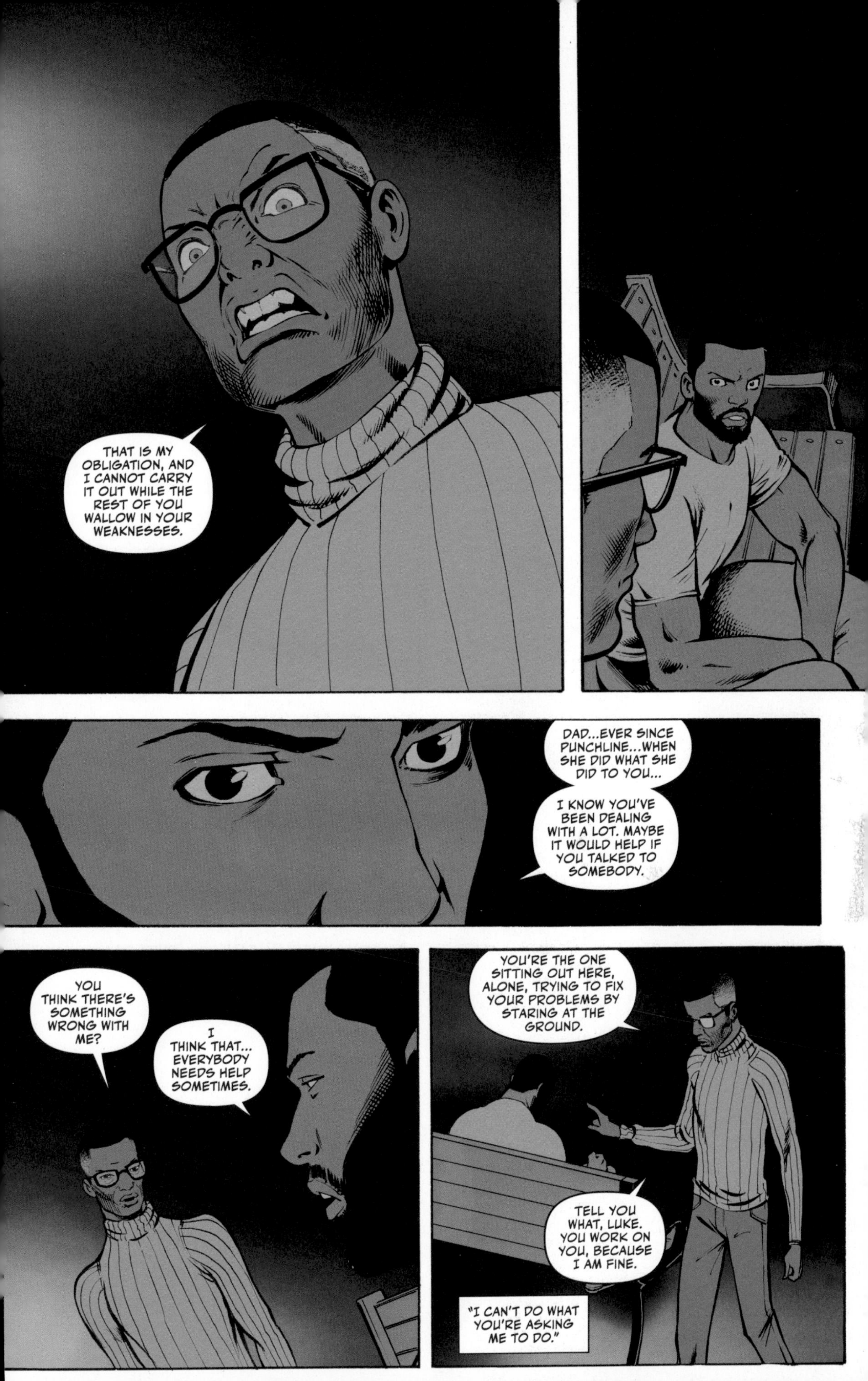
THAT IS MY OBLIGATION, AND I CANNOT CARRY IT OUT WHILE THE REST OF YOU WALLOW IN YOUR WEAKNESSES.
DAD...EVER SINCE PUNCHLINE...WHEN SHE DID WHAT SHE DID TO YOU...
I KNOW YOU'VE BEEN DEALING WITH A LOT. MAYBE IT WOULD HELP IF YOU TALKED TO SOMEBODY.
YOU THINK THERE'S SOMETHING WRONG WITH ME?
I THINK THAT... EVERYBODY NEEDS HELP SOMETIMES.
YOU'RE THE ONE SITTING OUT HERE, ALONE, TRYING TO FIX YOUR PROBLEMS BY STARING AT THE GROUND.
TELL YOU WHAT, LUKE. YOU WORK ON YOU, BECAUSE I AM FINE.
"I CAN'T DO WHAT YOU'RE ASKING ME TO DO."

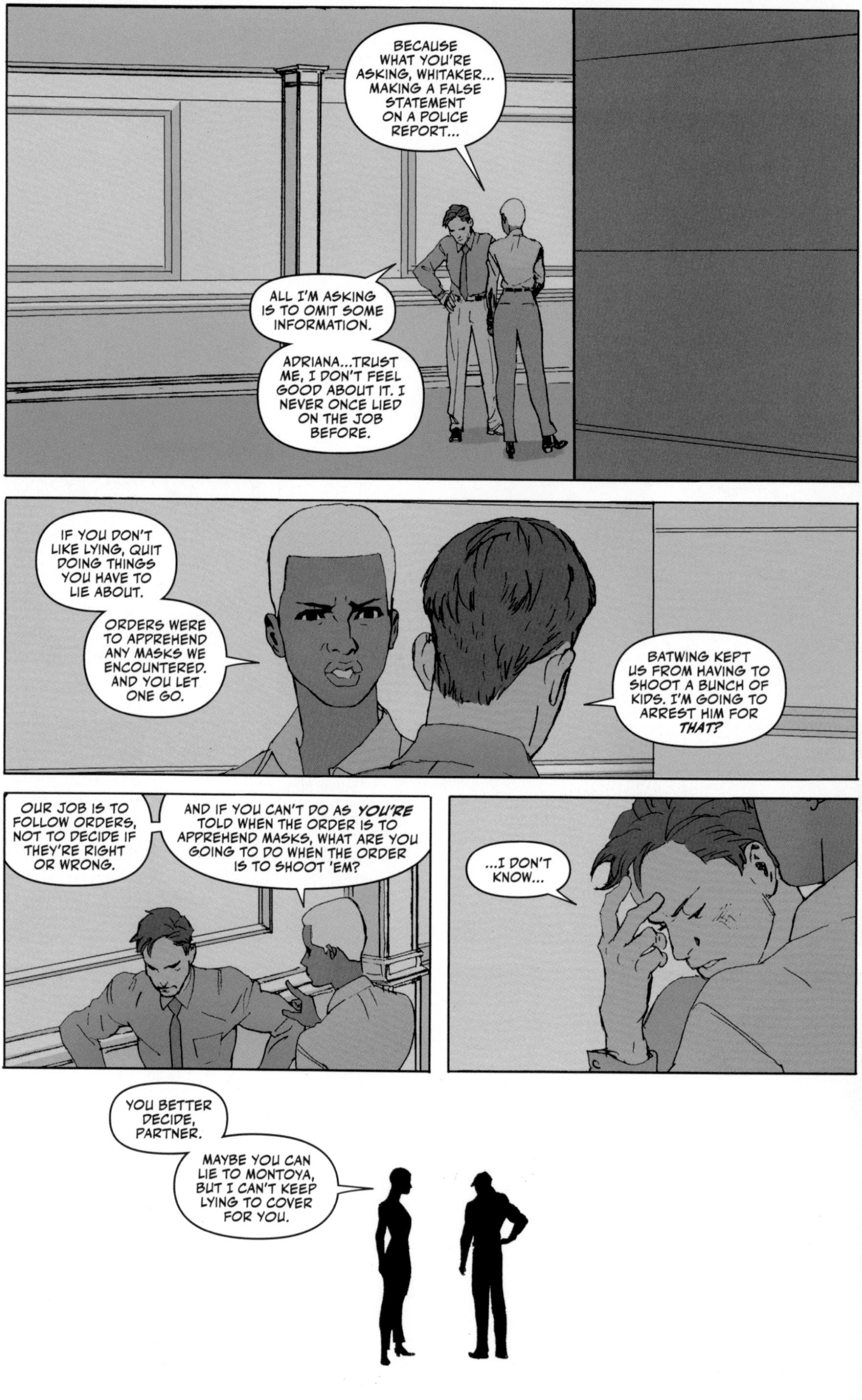
BECAUSE WHAT YOU'RE ASKING, WHITAKER... MAKING A FALSE STATEMENT ON A POLICE REPORT...
ALL I'M ASKING IS TO OMIT SOME INFORMATION.
ADRIANA...TRUST ME, I DON'T FEEL GOOD ABOUT IT. I NEVER ONCE LIED ON THE JOB BEFORE.
IF YOU DON'T LIKE LYING, QUIT DOING THINGS YOU HAVE TO LIE ABOUT.
ORDERS WERE TO APPREHEND ANY MASKS WE ENCOUNTERED. AND YOU LET ONE GO.
BATWING KEPT US FROM HAVING TO SHOOT A BUNCH OF KIDS. I'M GOING TO ARREST HIM FOR *THAT?*
OUR JOB IS TO FOLLOW ORDERS, NOT TO DECIDE IF THEY'RE RIGHT OR WRONG.
AND IF YOU CAN'T DO AS *YOU'RE* TOLD WHEN THE ORDER IS TO APPREHEND MASKS, WHAT ARE YOU GOING TO DO WHEN THE ORDER IS TO SHOOT 'EM?
...I DON'T KNOW...
YOU BETTER DECIDE, PARTNER.
MAYBE YOU CAN LIE TO MONTOYA, BUT I CAN'T KEEP LYING TO COVER FOR YOU.

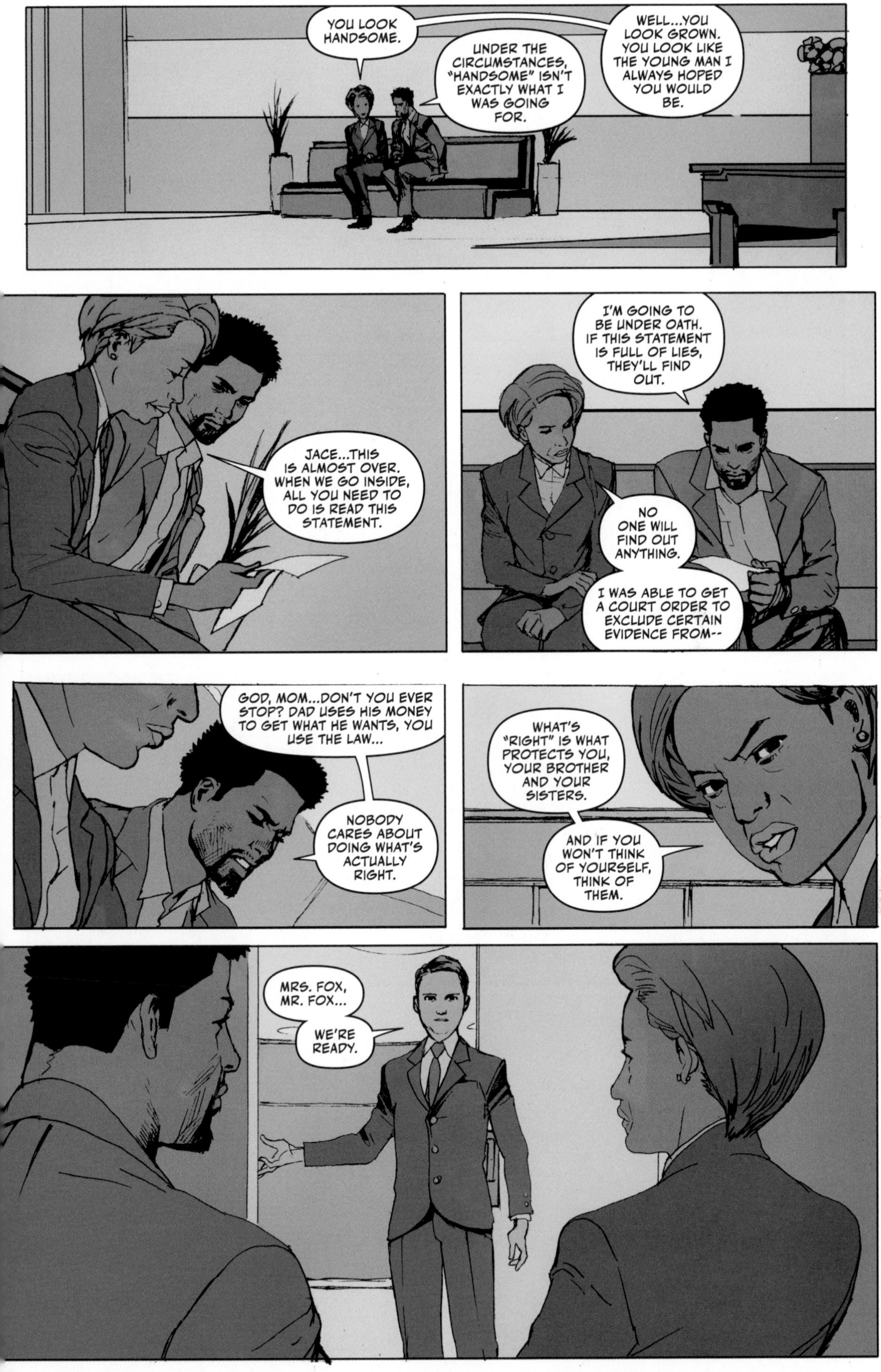
YOU LOOK HANDSOME.
UNDER THE CIRCUMSTANCES, "HANDSOME" ISN'T EXACTLY WHAT I WAS GOING FOR.
WELL...YOU LOOK GROWN. YOU LOOK LIKE THE YOUNG MAN I ALWAYS HOPED YOU WOULD BE.
JACE...THIS IS ALMOST OVER. WHEN WE GO INSIDE, ALL YOU NEED TO DO IS READ THIS STATEMENT.
I'M GOING TO BE UNDER OATH. IF THIS STATEMENT IS FULL OF LIES, THEY'LL FIND OUT.
NO ONE WILL FIND OUT ANYTHING.
I WAS ABLE TO GET A COURT ORDER TO EXCLUDE CERTAIN EVIDENCE FROM--
GOD, MOM...DON'T YOU EVER STOP? DAD USES HIS MONEY TO GET WHAT HE WANTS, YOU USE THE LAW...
NOBODY CARES ABOUT DOING WHAT'S ACTUALLY RIGHT.
WHAT'S "RIGHT" IS WHAT PROTECTS YOU, YOUR BROTHER AND YOUR SISTERS.
AND IF YOU WON'T THINK OF YOURSELF, THINK OF THEM.
MRS. FOX, MR. FOX...
WE'RE READY.

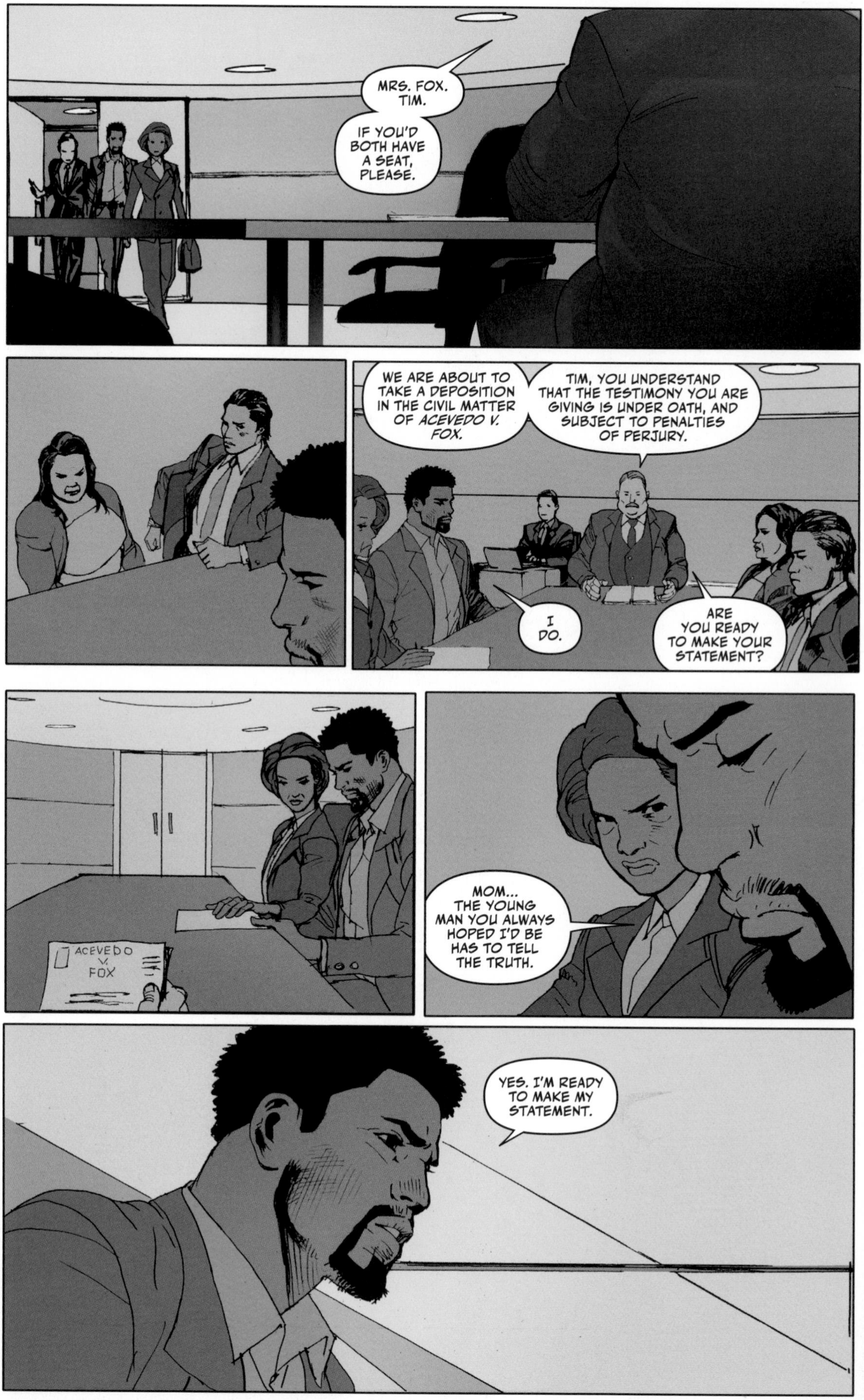
MRS. FOX. TIM.
IF YOU'D BOTH HAVE A SEAT, PLEASE.
WE ARE ABOUT TO TAKE A DEPOSITION IN THE CIVIL MATTER OF *ACEVEDO V. FOX.*
TIM, YOU UNDERSTAND THAT THE TESTIMONY YOU ARE GIVING IS UNDER OATH, AND SUBJECT TO PENALTIES OF PERJURY.
I DO.
ARE YOU READY TO MAKE YOUR STATEMENT?
ACEVEDO V. FOX
MOM... THE YOUNG MAN YOU ALWAYS HOPED I'D BE HAS TO TELL THE TRUTH.
YES. I'M READY TO MAKE MY STATEMENT.

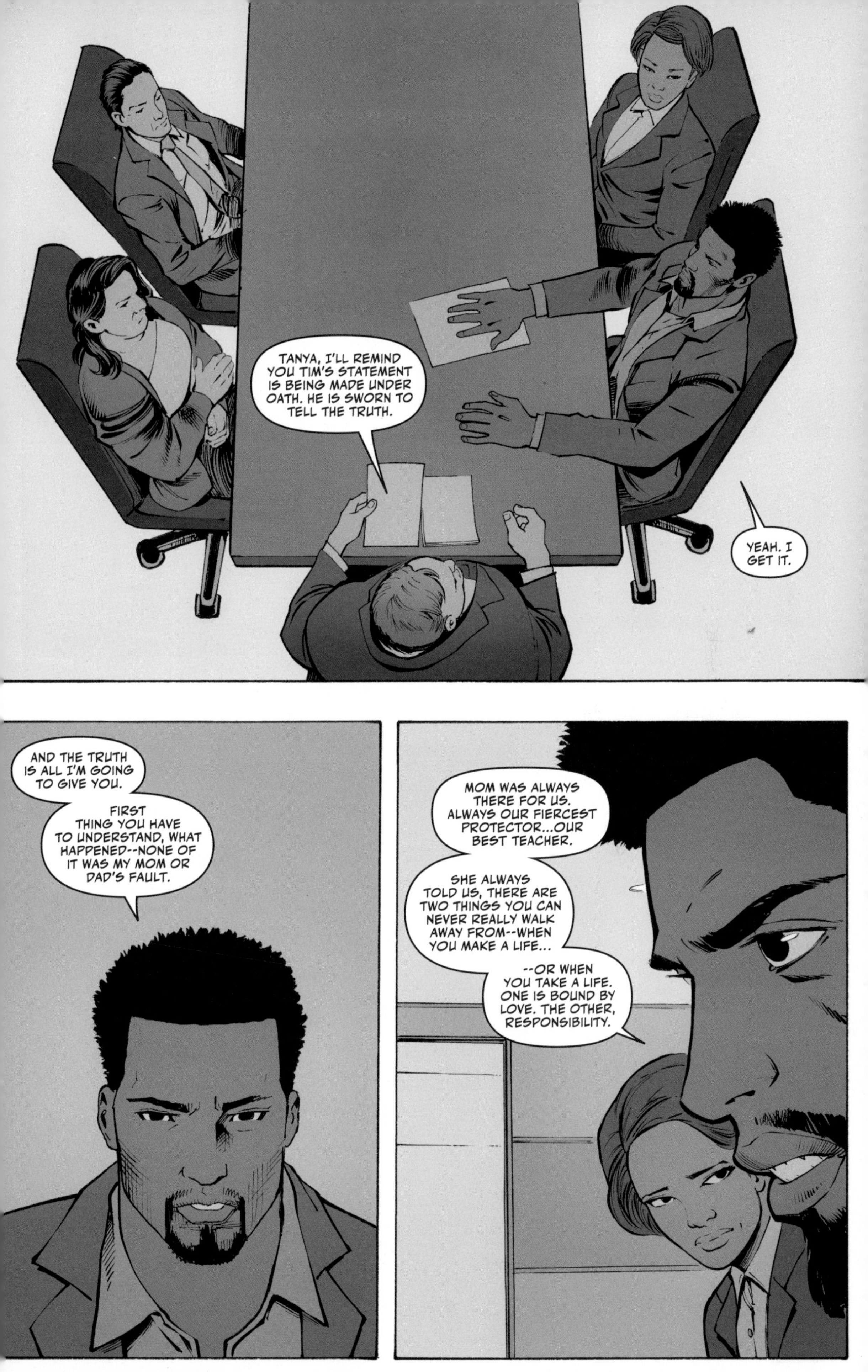
TANYA, I'LL REMIND YOU TIM'S STATEMENT IS BEING MADE UNDER OATH. HE IS SWORN TO TELL THE TRUTH.
YEAH. I GET IT.
AND THE TRUTH IS ALL I'M GOING TO GIVE YOU.
FIRST THING YOU HAVE TO UNDERSTAND, WHAT HAPPENED--NONE OF IT WAS MY MOM OR DAD'S FAULT.
MOM WAS ALWAYS THERE FOR US. ALWAYS OUR FIERCEST PROTECTOR...OUR BEST TEACHER.
SHE ALWAYS TOLD US, THERE ARE TWO THINGS YOU CAN NEVER REALLY WALK AWAY FROM--WHEN YOU MAKE A LIFE...
--OR WHEN YOU TAKE A LIFE. ONE IS BOUND BY LOVE. THE OTHER, RESPONSIBILITY.

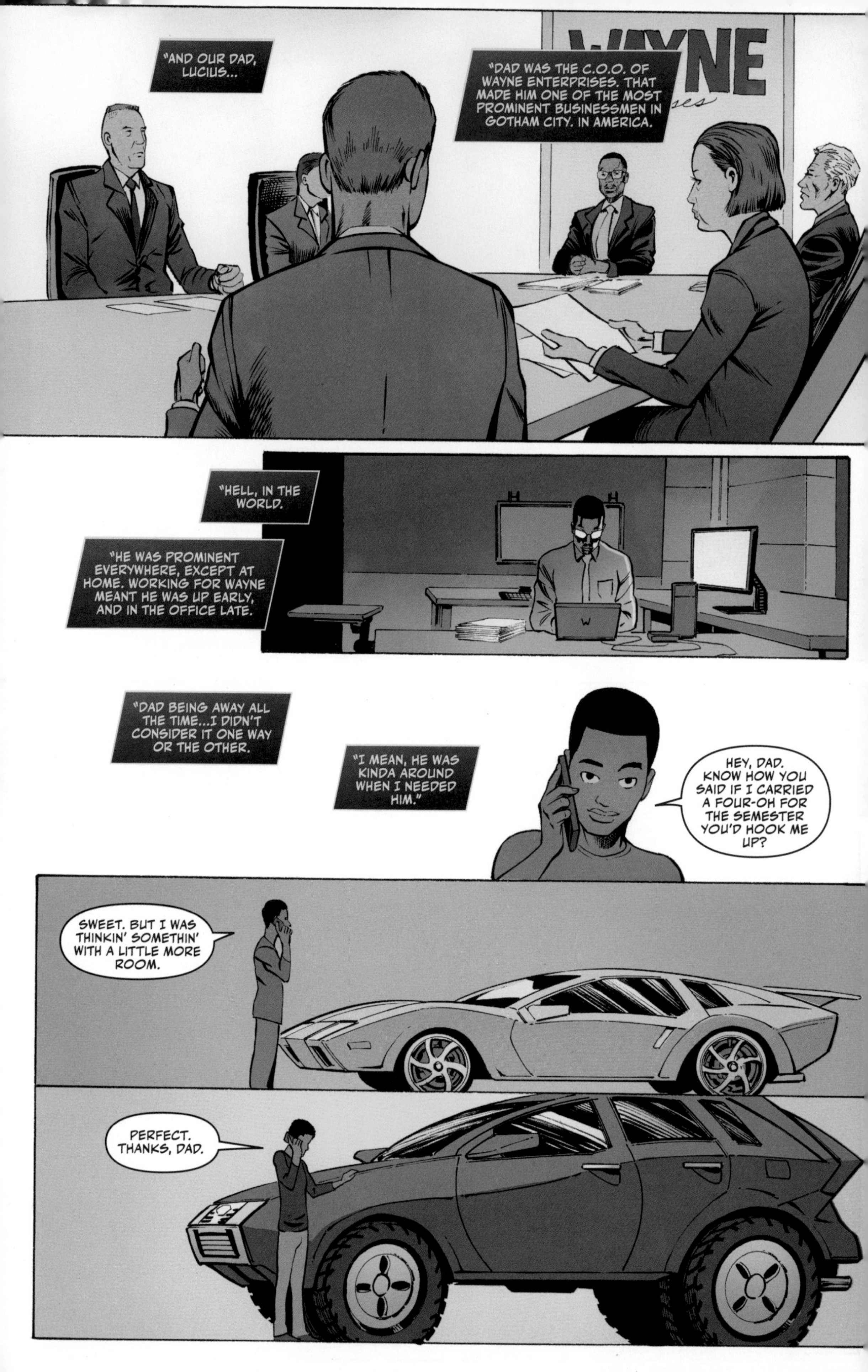
"AND OUR DAD, LUCIUS...
"DAD WAS THE C.O.O. OF WAYNE ENTERPRISES. THAT MADE HIM ONE OF THE MOST PROMINENT BUSINESSMEN IN GOTHAM CITY. IN AMERICA.
WAYNE
"HELL, IN THE WORLD.
"HE WAS PROMINENT EVERYWHERE, EXCEPT AT HOME. WORKING FOR WAYNE MEANT HE WAS UP EARLY, AND IN THE OFFICE LATE.
"DAD BEING AWAY ALL THE TIME...I DIDN'T CONSIDER IT ONE WAY OR THE OTHER.
"I MEAN, HE WAS KINDA AROUND WHEN I NEEDED HIM."
HEY, DAD. KNOW HOW YOU SAID IF I CARRIED A FOUR-OH FOR THE SEMESTER YOU'D HOOK ME UP?
SWEET. BUT I WAS THINKIN' SOMETHIN' WITH A LITTLE MORE ROOM.
PERFECT. THANKS, DAD.

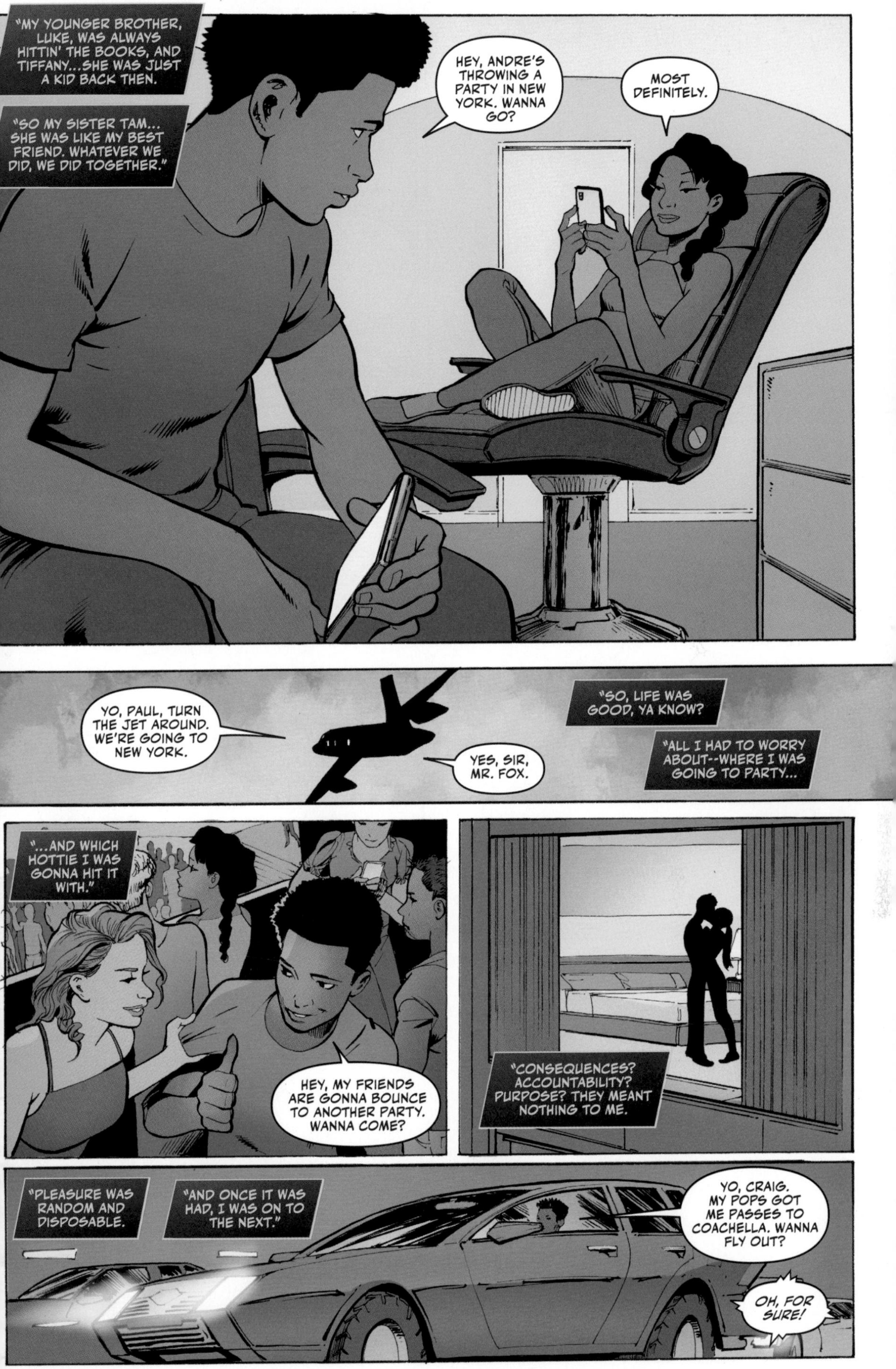
"MY YOUNGER BROTHER, LUKE, WAS ALWAYS HITTIN' THE BOOKS, AND TIFFANY...SHE WAS JUST A KID BACK THEN.
"SO MY SISTER TAM... SHE WAS LIKE MY BEST FRIEND. WHATEVER WE DID, WE DID TOGETHER."
HEY, ANDRE'S THROWING A PARTY IN NEW YORK. WANNA GO?
MOST DEFINITELY.
YO, PAUL, TURN THE JET AROUND. WE'RE GOING TO NEW YORK.
YES, SIR, MR. FOX.
"SO, LIFE WAS GOOD, YA KNOW?
"ALL I HAD TO WORRY ABOUT--WHERE I WAS GOING TO PARTY...
"...AND WHICH HOTTIE I WAS GONNA HIT IT WITH."
HEY, MY FRIENDS ARE GONNA BOUNCE TO ANOTHER PARTY. WANNA COME?
"CONSEQUENCES? ACCOUNTABILITY? PURPOSE? THEY MEANT NOTHING TO ME.
"PLEASURE WAS RANDOM AND DISPOSABLE.
"AND ONCE IT WAS HAD, I WAS ON TO THE NEXT."
YO, CRAIG. MY POPS GOT ME PASSES TO COACHELLA. WANNA FLY OUT?
OH, FOR SURE!

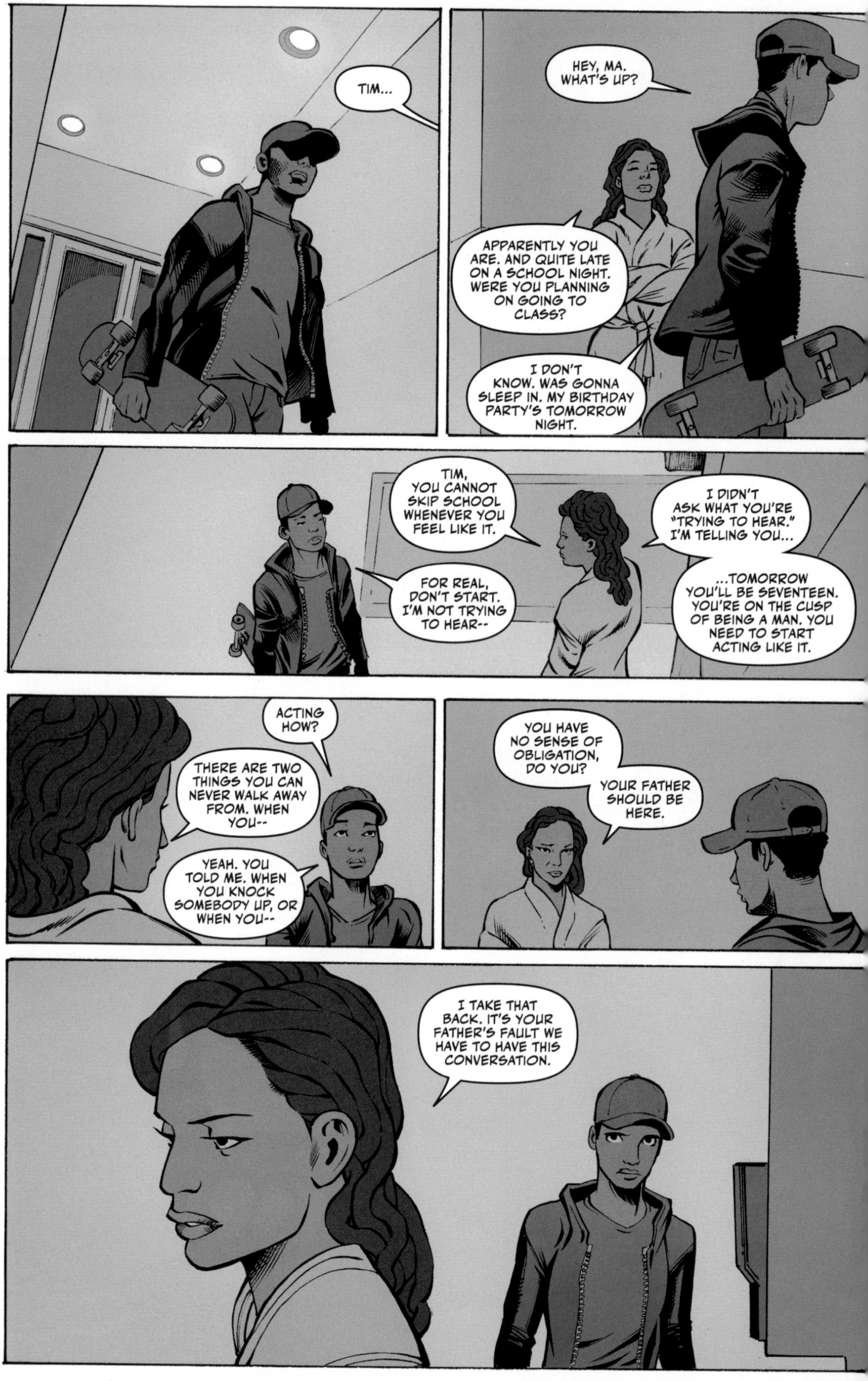
TIM...
HEY, MA. WHAT'S UP?
APPARENTLY YOU ARE. AND QUITE LATE ON A SCHOOL NIGHT. WERE YOU PLANNING ON GOING TO CLASS?
I DON'T KNOW. WAS GONNA SLEEP IN. MY BIRTHDAY PARTY'S TOMORROW NIGHT.
TIM, YOU CANNOT SKIP SCHOOL WHENEVER YOU FEEL LIKE IT.
FOR REAL, DON'T START. I'M NOT TRYING TO HEAR--
I DIDN'T ASK WHAT YOU'RE "TRYING TO HEAR." I'M TELLING YOU...
...TOMORROW YOU'LL BE SEVENTEEN. YOU'RE ON THE CUSP OF BEING A MAN. YOU NEED TO START ACTING LIKE IT.
ACTING HOW?
THERE ARE TWO THINGS YOU CAN NEVER WALK AWAY FROM. WHEN YOU--
YEAH. YOU TOLD ME. WHEN YOU KNOCK SOMEBODY UP, OR WHEN YOU--
YOU HAVE NO SENSE OF OBLIGATION, DO YOU?
YOUR FATHER SHOULD BE HERE.
I TAKE THAT BACK. IT'S YOUR FATHER'S FAULT WE HAVE TO HAVE THIS CONVERSATION.

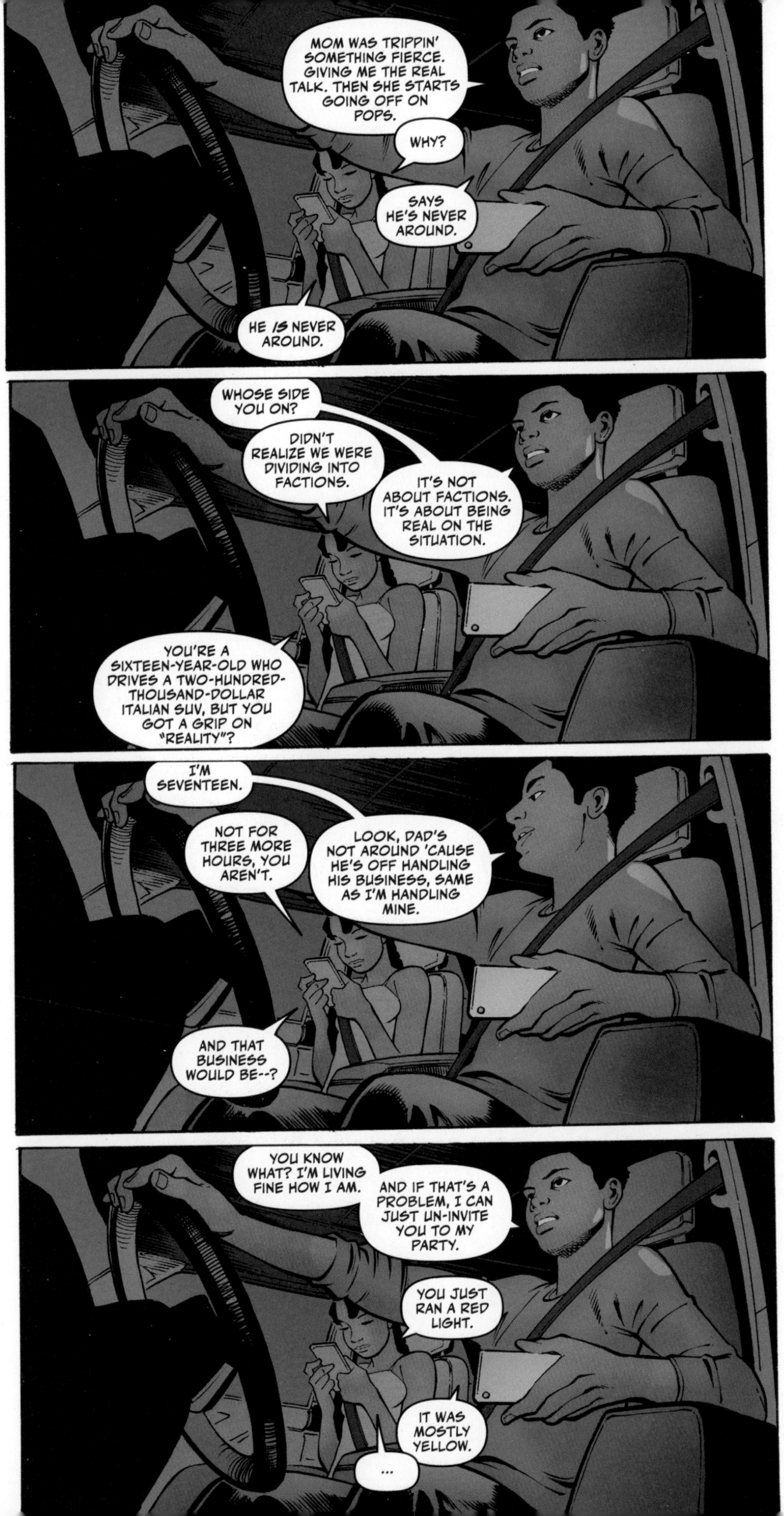
MOM WAS TRIPPIN' SOMETHING FIERCE. GIVING ME THE REAL TALK. THEN SHE STARTS GOING OFF ON POPS.
WHY?
SAYS HE'S NEVER AROUND.
HE *IS* NEVER AROUND.
WHOSE SIDE YOU ON?
DIDN'T REALIZE WE WERE DIVIDING INTO FACTIONS.
IT'S NOT ABOUT FACTIONS. IT'S ABOUT BEING REAL ON THE SITUATION.
YOU'RE A SIXTEEN-YEAR-OLD WHO DRIVES A TWO-HUNDRED-THOUSAND-DOLLAR ITALIAN SUV, BUT YOU GOT A GRIP ON "REALITY"?
I'M SEVENTEEN.
NOT FOR THREE MORE HOURS, YOU AREN'T.
LOOK, DAD'S NOT AROUND 'CAUSE HE'S OFF HANDLING HIS BUSINESS, SAME AS I'M HANDLING MINE.
AND THAT BUSINESS WOULD BE--?
YOU KNOW WHAT? I'M LIVING FINE HOW I AM.
AND IF THAT'S A PROBLEM, I CAN JUST UN-INVITE YOU TO MY PARTY.
YOU JUST RAN A RED LIGHT.
IT WAS MOSTLY YELLOW.
...

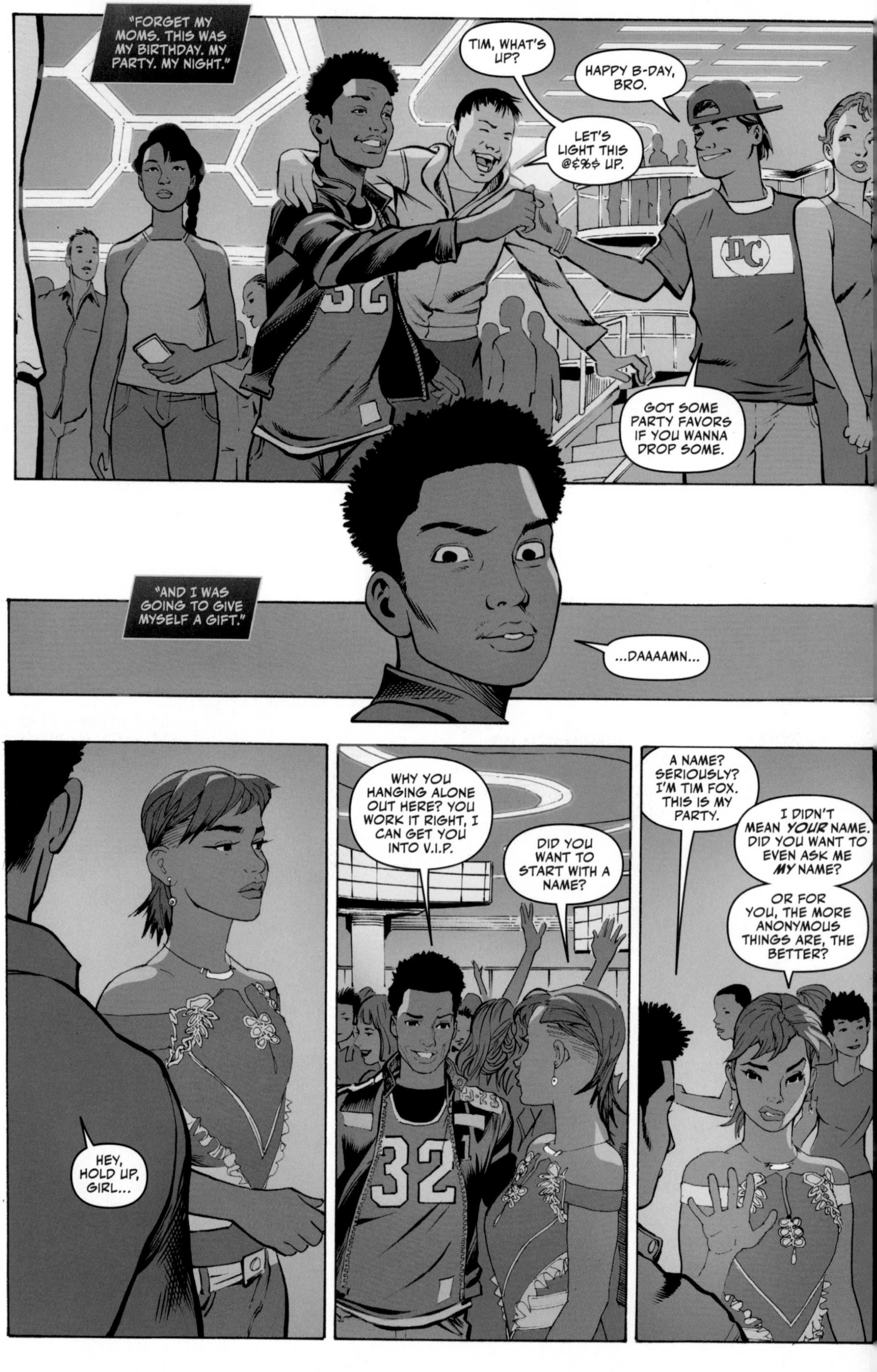
"FORGET MY MOMS. THIS WAS MY BIRTHDAY. MY PARTY. MY NIGHT."
TIM, WHAT'S UP?
HAPPY B-DAY, BRO.
LET'S LIGHT THIS @$%$ UP.
GOT SOME PARTY FAVORS IF YOU WANNA DROP SOME.
"AND I WAS GOING TO GIVE MYSELF A GIFT."
...DAAAAMN...
HEY, HOLD UP, GIRL...
WHY YOU HANGING ALONE OUT HERE? YOU WORK IT RIGHT, I CAN GET YOU INTO V.I.P.
DID YOU WANT TO START WITH A NAME?
A NAME? SERIOUSLY? I'M TIM FOX. THIS IS MY PARTY.
I DIDN'T MEAN YOUR NAME. DID YOU WANT TO EVEN ASK ME MY NAME?
OR FOR YOU, THE MORE ANONYMOUS THINGS ARE, THE BETTER?

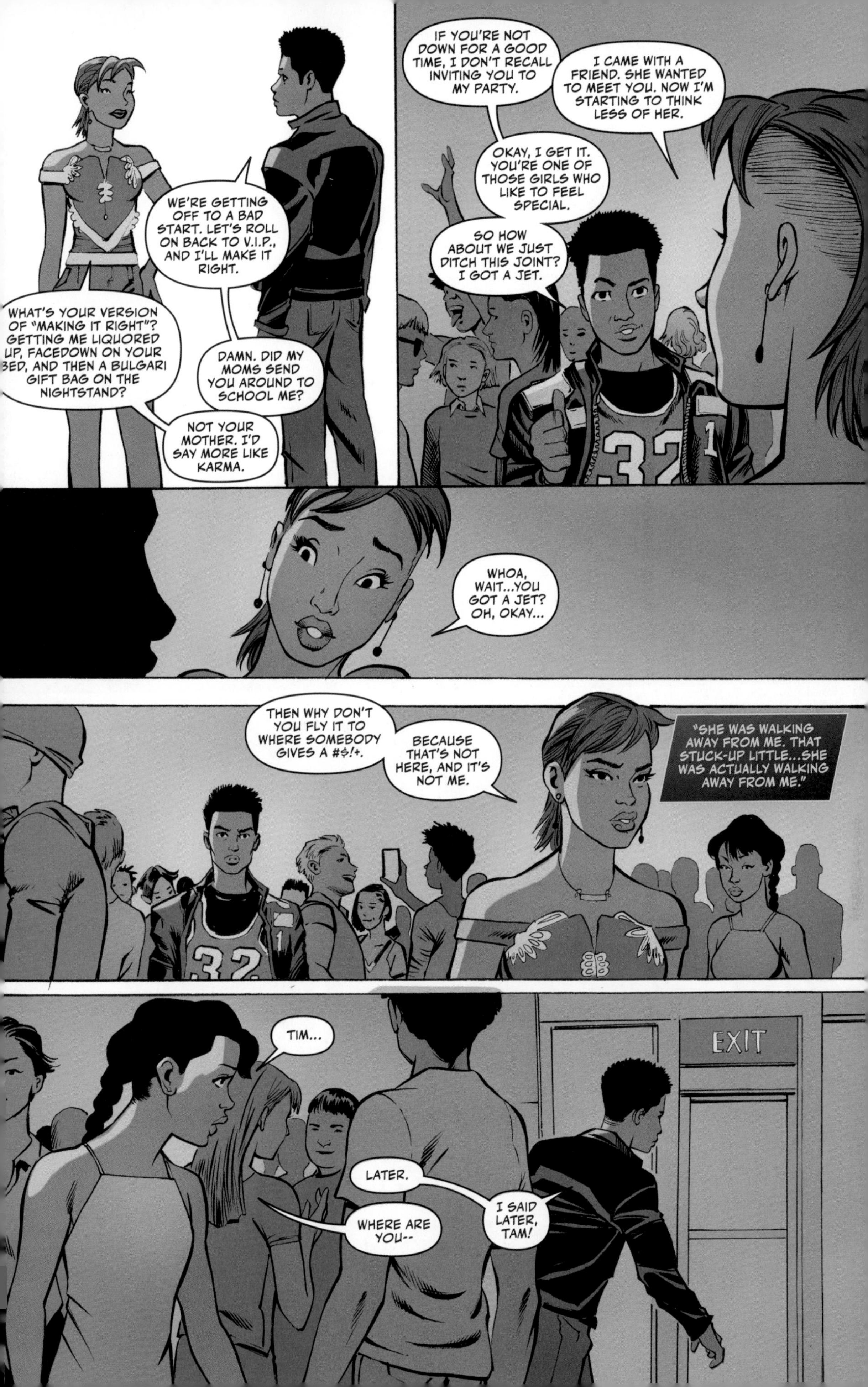
WE'RE GETTING OFF TO A BAD START. LET'S ROLL ON BACK TO V.I.P., AND I'LL MAKE IT RIGHT.
WHAT'S YOUR VERSION OF "MAKING IT RIGHT"? GETTING ME LIQUORED UP, FACEDOWN ON YOUR BED, AND THEN A BULGARI GIFT BAG ON THE NIGHTSTAND?
DAMN. DID MY MOMS SEND YOU AROUND TO SCHOOL ME?
NOT YOUR MOTHER. I'D SAY MORE LIKE KARMA.
IF YOU'RE NOT DOWN FOR A GOOD TIME, I DON'T RECALL INVITING YOU TO MY PARTY.
I CAME WITH A FRIEND. SHE WANTED TO MEET YOU. NOW I'M STARTING TO THINK LESS OF HER.
OKAY, I GET IT. YOU'RE ONE OF THOSE GIRLS WHO LIKE TO FEEL SPECIAL.
SO HOW ABOUT WE JUST DITCH THIS JOINT? I GOT A JET.
WHOA, WAIT...YOU GOT A JET? OH, OKAY...
THEN WHY DON'T YOU FLY IT TO WHERE SOMEBODY GIVES A #$!+.
BECAUSE THAT'S NOT HERE, AND IT'S NOT ME.
"SHE WAS WALKING AWAY FROM ME. THAT STUCK-UP LITTLE...SHE WAS ACTUALLY WALKING AWAY FROM ME."
TIM...
EXIT
LATER.
WHERE ARE YOU--
I SAID LATER, TAM!

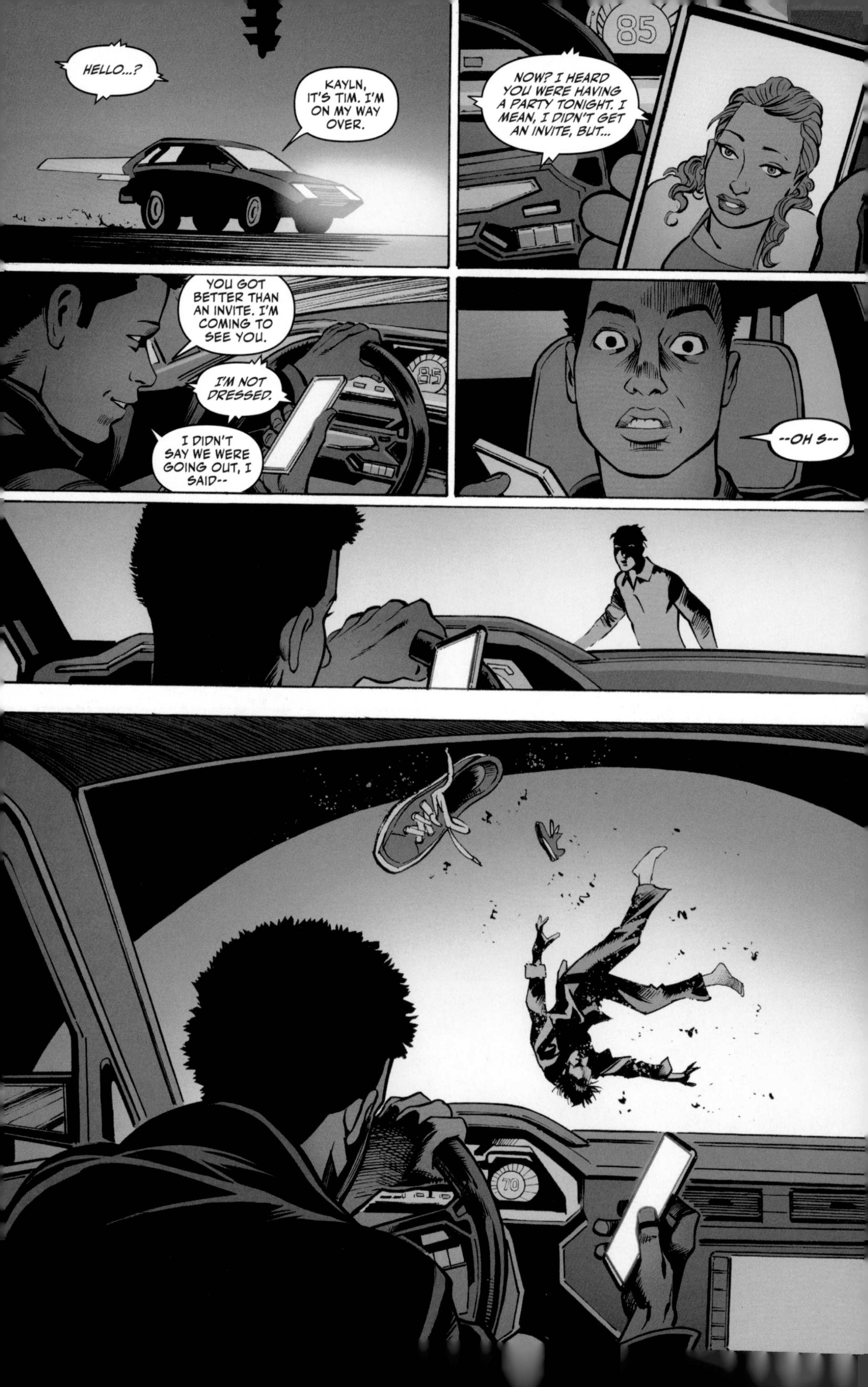
HELLO...?
KAYLN, IT'S TIM. I'M ON MY WAY OVER.
NOW? I HEARD YOU WERE HAVING A PARTY TONIGHT. I MEAN, I DIDN'T GET AN INVITE, BUT...
YOU GOT BETTER THAN AN INVITE. I'M COMING TO SEE YOU.
I'M NOT DRESSED.
I DIDN'T SAY WE WERE GOING OUT, I SAID--
--OH S--

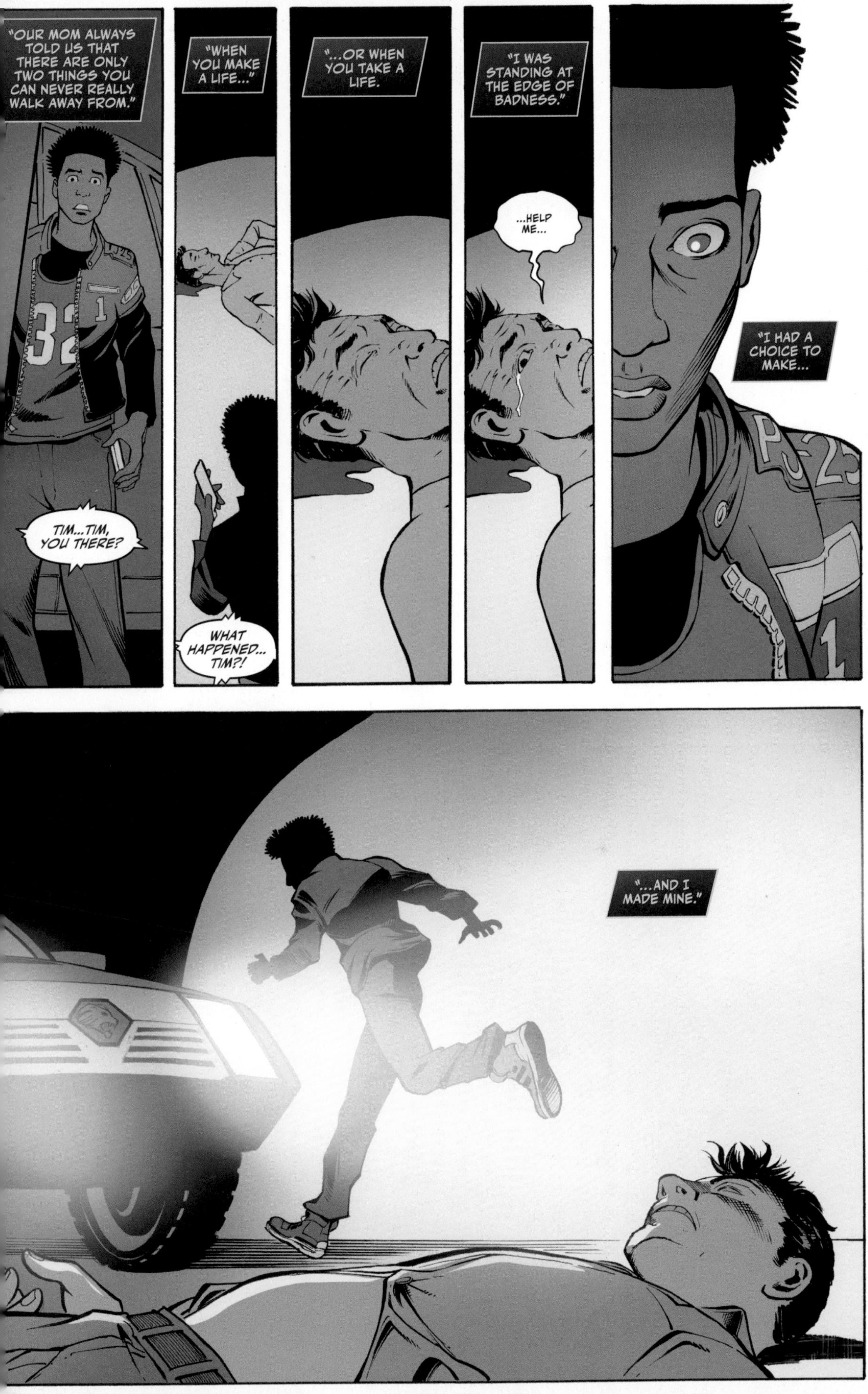

"OUR MOM ALWAYS TOLD US THAT THERE ARE ONLY TWO THINGS YOU CAN NEVER REALLY WALK AWAY FROM."
TIM...TIM, YOU THERE?
"WHEN YOU MAKE A LIFE..."
WHAT HAPPENED... TIM?!
"...OR WHEN YOU TAKE A LIFE.
"I WAS STANDING AT THE EDGE OF BADNESS."
...HELP ME...
"I HAD A CHOICE TO MAKE...
"...AND I MADE MINE."

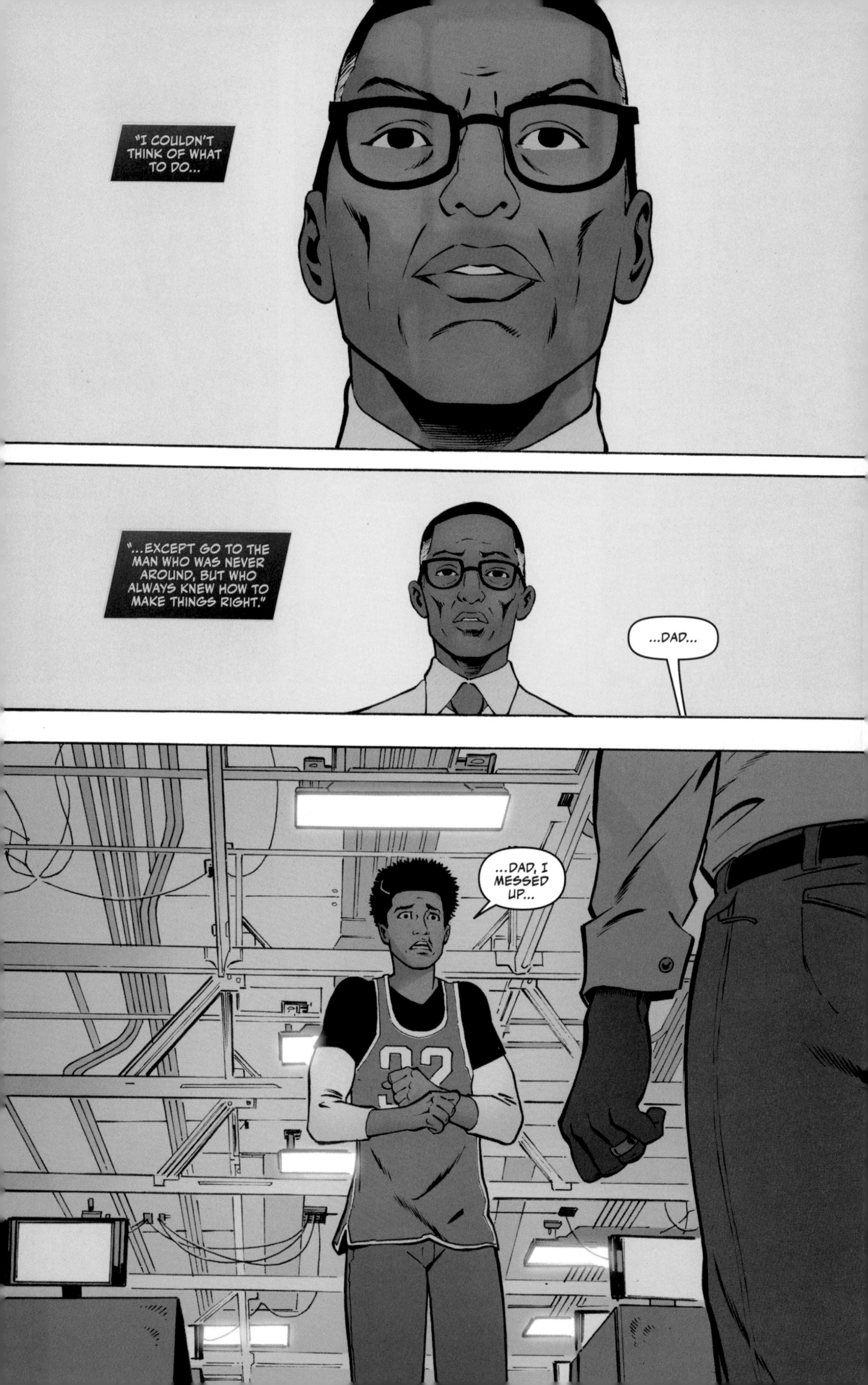
"I COULDN'T THINK OF WHAT TO DO...
"...EXCEPT GO TO THE MAN WHO WAS NEVER AROUND, BUT WHO ALWAYS KNEW HOW TO MAKE THINGS RIGHT."
...DAD...
...DAD, I MESSED UP...

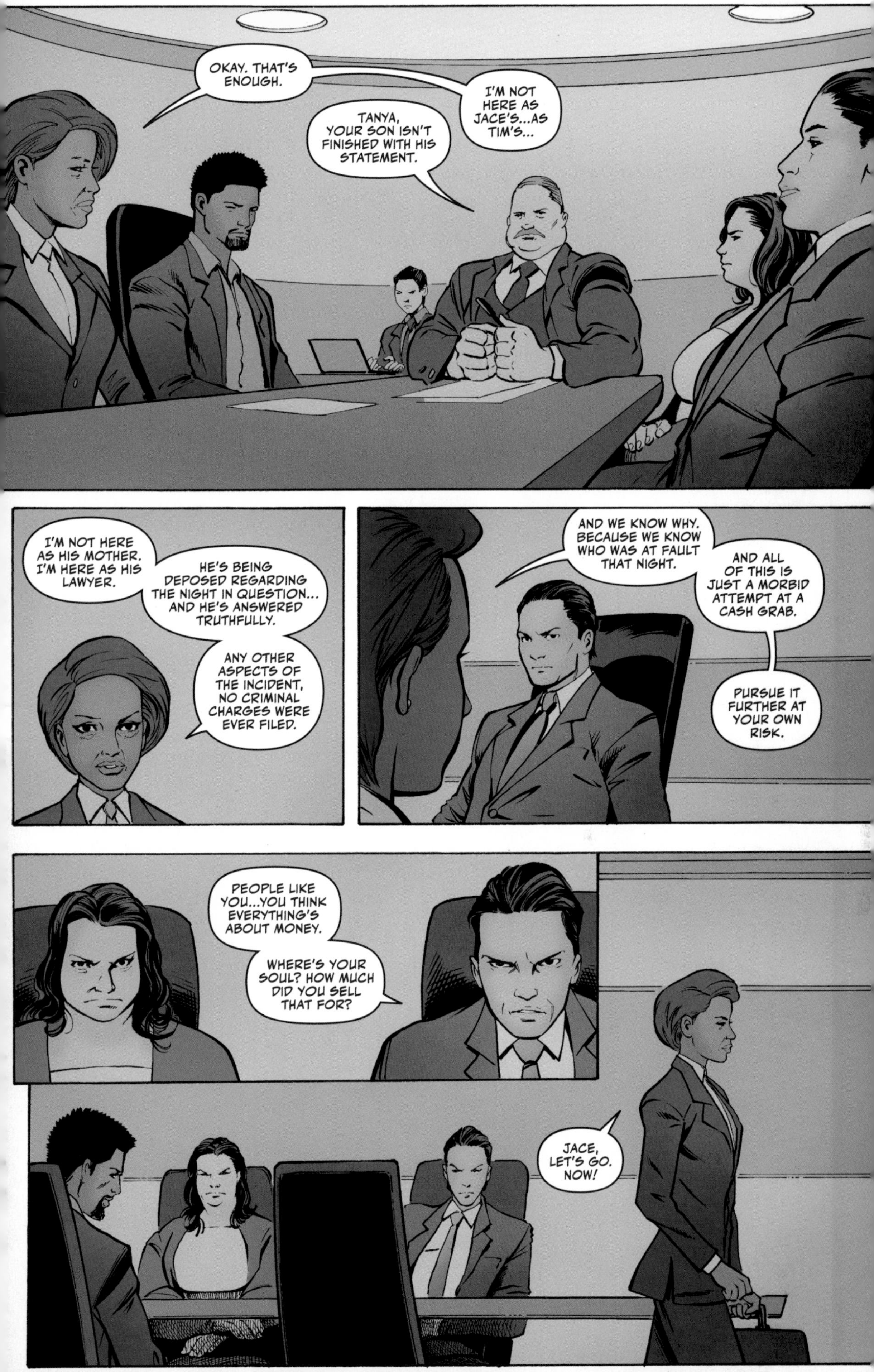
OKAY. THAT'S ENOUGH.
TANYA, YOUR SON ISN'T FINISHED WITH HIS STATEMENT.
I'M NOT HERE AS JACE'S...AS TIM'S...
I'M NOT HERE AS HIS MOTHER. I'M HERE AS HIS LAWYER.
HE'S BEING DEPOSED REGARDING THE NIGHT IN QUESTION... AND HE'S ANSWERED TRUTHFULLY.
ANY OTHER ASPECTS OF THE INCIDENT, NO CRIMINAL CHARGES WERE EVER FILED.
AND WE KNOW WHY. BECAUSE WE KNOW WHO WAS AT FAULT THAT NIGHT.
AND ALL OF THIS IS JUST A MORBID ATTEMPT AT A CASH GRAB.
PURSUE IT FURTHER AT YOUR OWN RISK.
PEOPLE LIKE YOU...YOU THINK EVERYTHING'S ABOUT MONEY.
WHERE'S YOUR SOUL? HOW MUCH DID YOU SELL THAT FOR?
JACE, LET'S GO. NOW!

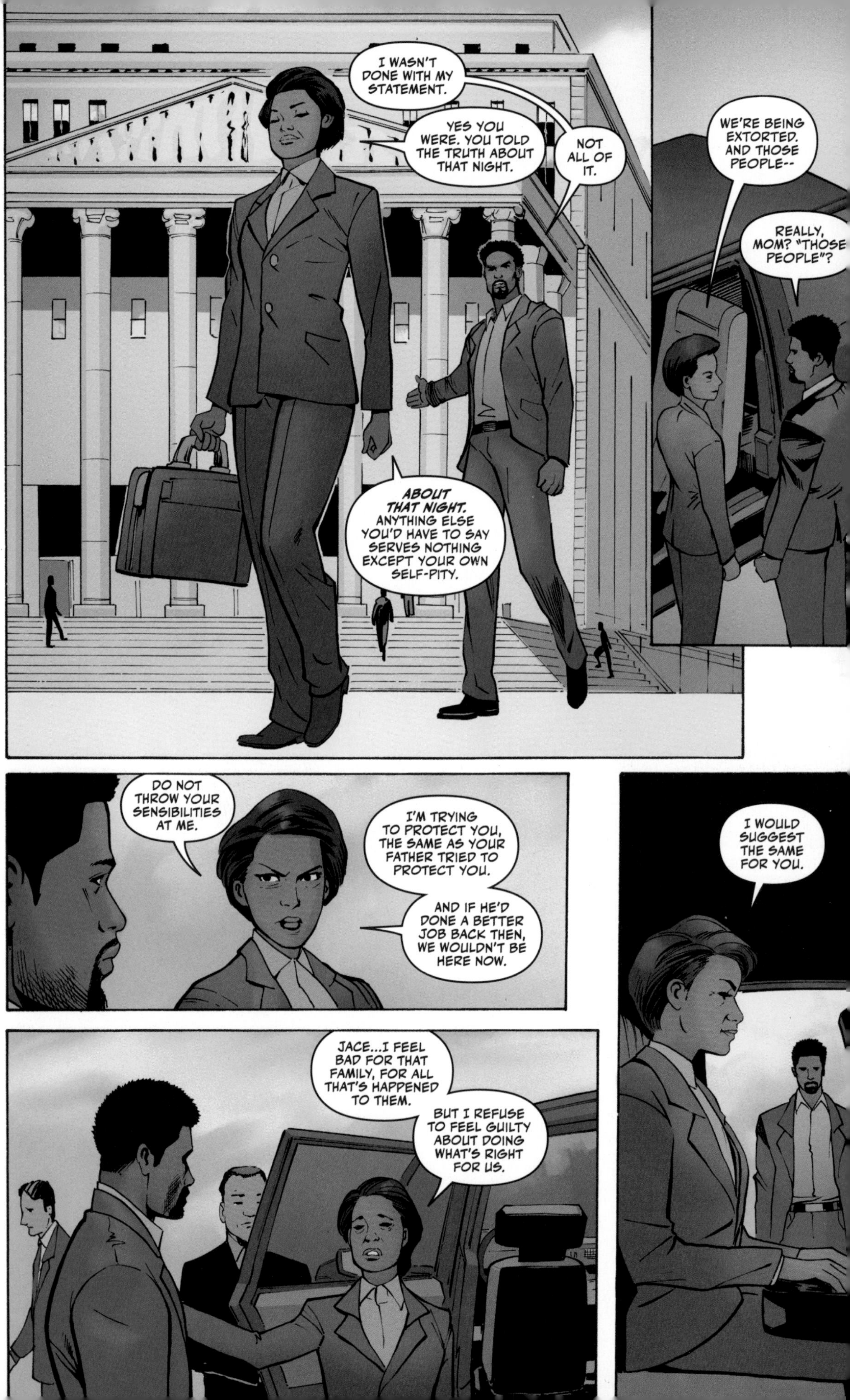
I WASN'T DONE WITH MY STATEMENT.
YES YOU WERE. YOU TOLD THE TRUTH ABOUT THAT NIGHT.
NOT ALL OF IT.
ABOUT THAT NIGHT. ANYTHING ELSE YOU'D HAVE TO SAY SERVES NOTHING EXCEPT YOUR OWN SELF-PITY.
WE'RE BEING EXTORTED. AND THOSE PEOPLE--
REALLY, MOM? "THOSE PEOPLE"?
DO NOT THROW YOUR SENSIBILITIES AT ME.
I'M TRYING TO PROTECT YOU, THE SAME AS YOUR FATHER TRIED TO PROTECT YOU.
AND IF HE'D DONE A BETTER JOB BACK THEN, WE WOULDN'T BE HERE NOW.
I WOULD SUGGEST THE SAME FOR YOU.
JACE...I FEEL BAD FOR THAT FAMILY, FOR ALL THAT'S HAPPENED TO THEM.
BUT I REFUSE TO FEEL GUILTY ABOUT DOING WHAT'S RIGHT FOR US.

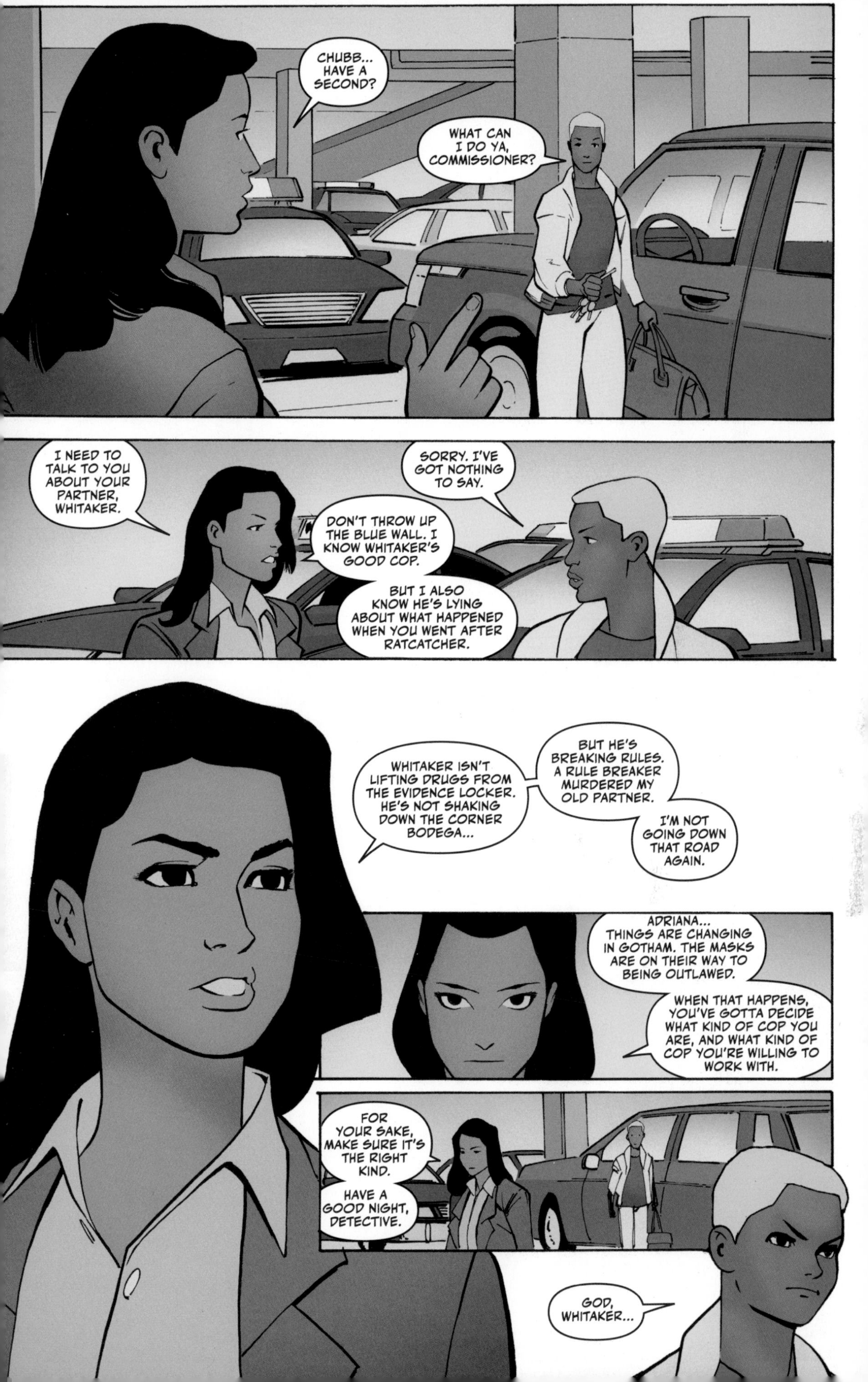
CHUBB... HAVE A SECOND?
WHAT CAN I DO YA, COMMISSIONER?
I NEED TO TALK TO YOU ABOUT YOUR PARTNER, WHITAKER.
SORRY. I'VE GOT NOTHING TO SAY.
DON'T THROW UP THE BLUE WALL. I KNOW WHITAKER'S GOOD COP.
BUT I ALSO KNOW HE'S LYING ABOUT WHAT HAPPENED WHEN YOU WENT AFTER RATCATCHER.
WHITAKER ISN'T LIFTING DRUGS FROM THE EVIDENCE LOCKER. HE'S NOT SHAKING DOWN THE CORNER BODEGA...
BUT HE'S BREAKING RULES. A RULE BREAKER MURDERED MY OLD PARTNER.
I'M NOT GOING DOWN THAT ROAD AGAIN.
ADRIANA... THINGS ARE CHANGING IN GOTHAM. THE MASKS ARE ON THEIR WAY TO BEING OUTLAWED.
WHEN THAT HAPPENS, YOU'VE GOTTA DECIDE WHAT KIND OF COP YOU ARE, AND WHAT KIND OF COP YOU'RE WILLING TO WORK WITH.
FOR YOUR SAKE, MAKE SURE IT'S THE RIGHT KIND.
HAVE A GOOD NIGHT, DETECTIVE.
GOD, WHITAKER...

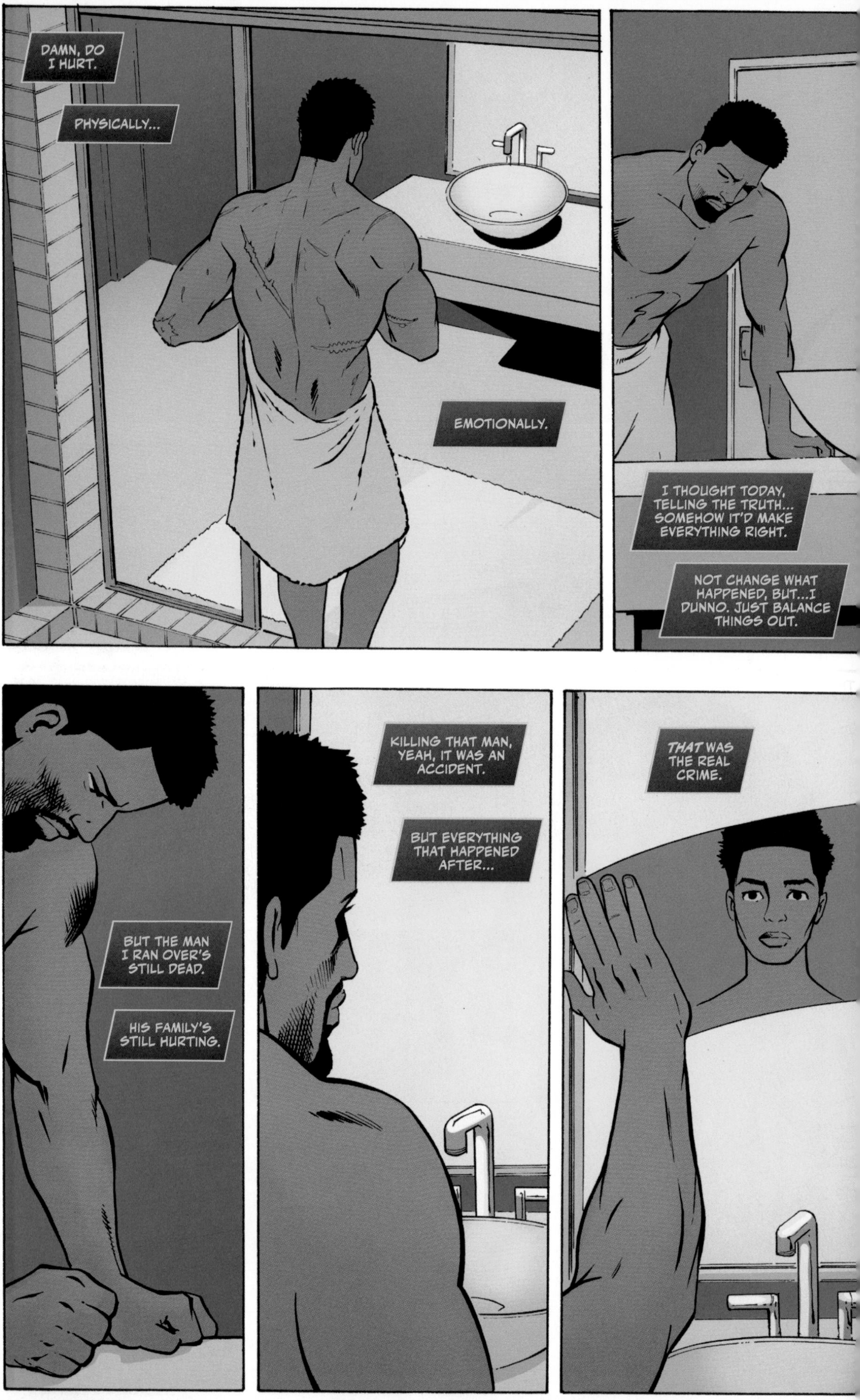
DAMN, DO I HURT.
PHYSICALLY...
EMOTIONALLY.
I THOUGHT TODAY, TELLING THE TRUTH... SOMEHOW IT'D MAKE EVERYTHING RIGHT.
NOT CHANGE WHAT HAPPENED, BUT...I DUNNO. JUST BALANCE THINGS OUT.
BUT THE MAN I RAN OVER'S STILL DEAD.
HIS FAMILY'S STILL HURTING.
KILLING THAT MAN, YEAH, IT WAS AN ACCIDENT.
BUT EVERYTHING THAT HAPPENED AFTER...
THAT WAS THE REAL CRIME.

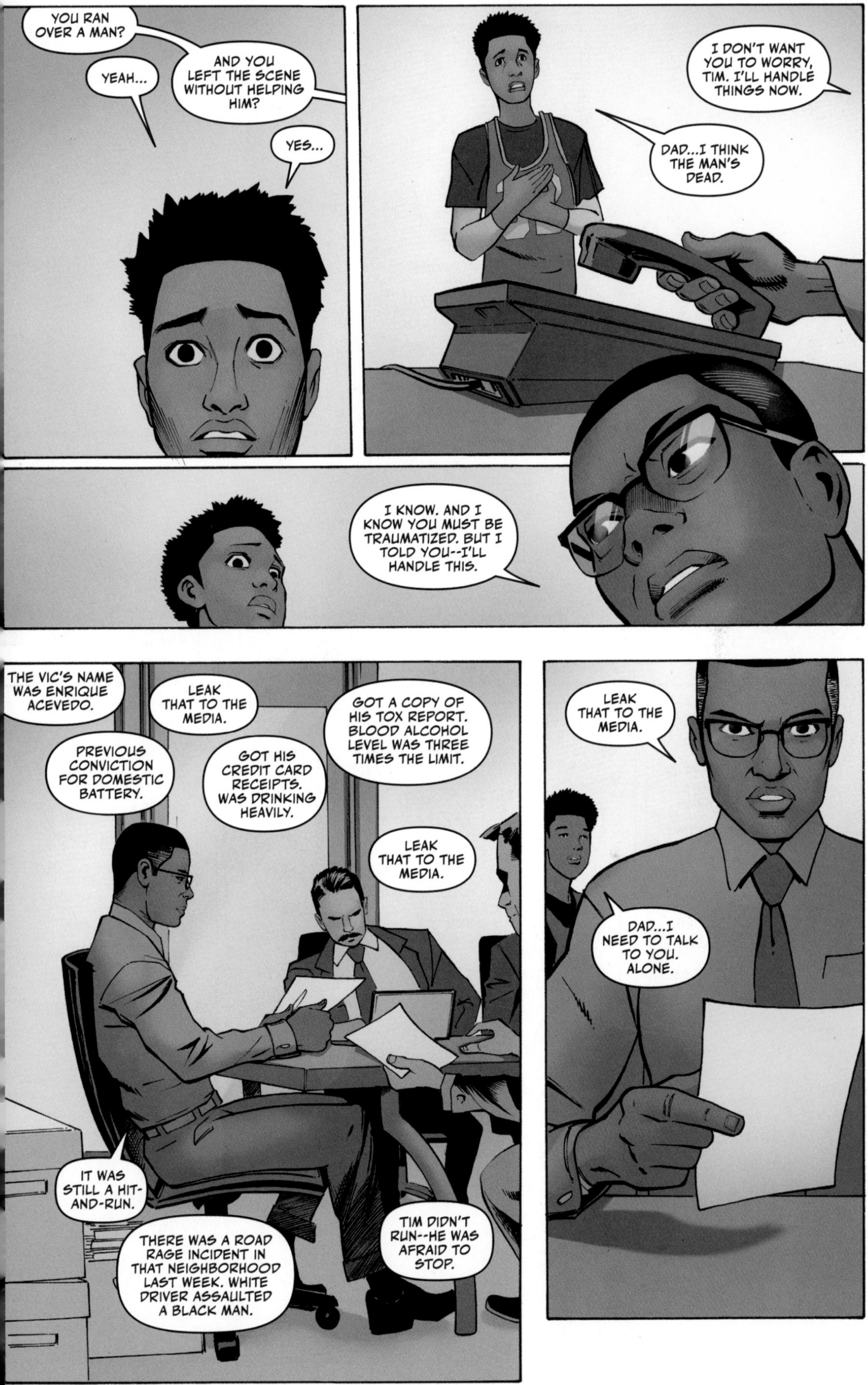
YOU RAN OVER A MAN?
YEAH...
AND YOU LEFT THE SCENE WITHOUT HELPING HIM?
YES...
I DON'T WANT YOU TO WORRY, TIM. I'LL HANDLE THINGS NOW.
DAD...I THINK THE MAN'S DEAD.
I KNOW. AND I KNOW YOU MUST BE TRAUMATIZED. BUT I TOLD YOU--I'LL HANDLE THIS.
THE VIC'S NAME WAS ENRIQUE ACEVEDO.
LEAK THAT TO THE MEDIA.
PREVIOUS CONVICTION FOR DOMESTIC BATTERY.
GOT HIS CREDIT CARD RECEIPTS. WAS DRINKING HEAVILY.
GOT A COPY OF HIS TOX REPORT. BLOOD ALCOHOL LEVEL WAS THREE TIMES THE LIMIT.
LEAK THAT TO THE MEDIA.
IT WAS STILL A HIT-AND-RUN.
TIM DIDN'T RUN--HE WAS AFRAID TO STOP.
THERE WAS A ROAD RAGE INCIDENT IN THAT NEIGHBORHOOD LAST WEEK. WHITE DRIVER ASSAULTED A BLACK MAN.
LEAK THAT TO THE MEDIA.
DAD...I NEED TO TALK TO YOU. ALONE.

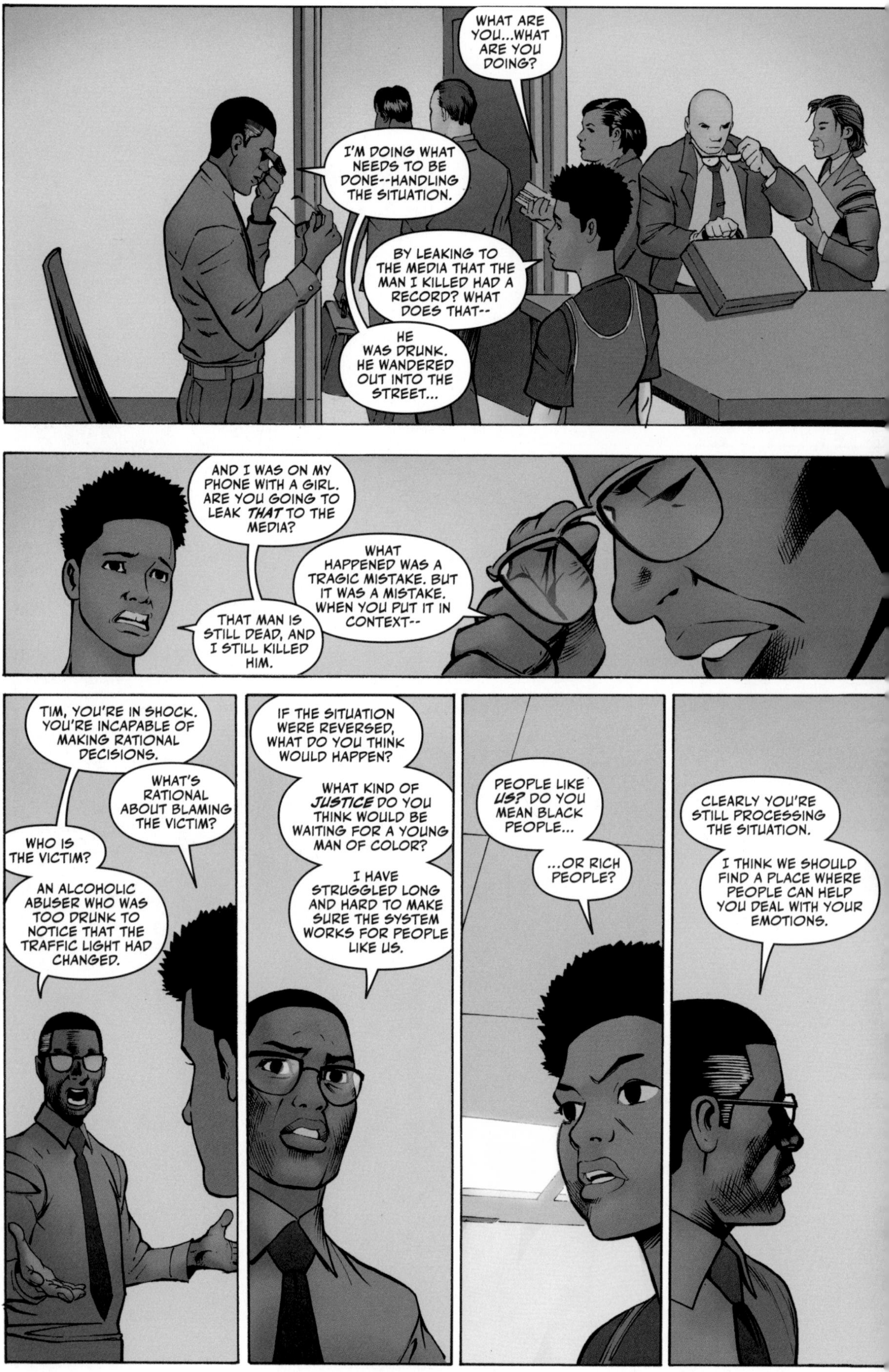
WHAT ARE YOU...WHAT ARE YOU DOING?
I'M DOING WHAT NEEDS TO BE DONE--HANDLING THE SITUATION.
BY LEAKING TO THE MEDIA THAT THE MAN I KILLED HAD A RECORD? WHAT DOES THAT--
HE WAS DRUNK. HE WANDERED OUT INTO THE STREET...
AND I WAS ON MY PHONE WITH A GIRL. ARE YOU GOING TO LEAK *THAT* TO THE MEDIA?
WHAT HAPPENED WAS A TRAGIC MISTAKE. BUT IT WAS A MISTAKE. WHEN YOU PUT IT IN CONTEXT--
THAT MAN IS STILL DEAD, AND I STILL KILLED HIM.
TIM, YOU'RE IN SHOCK. YOU'RE INCAPABLE OF MAKING RATIONAL DECISIONS.
WHAT'S RATIONAL ABOUT BLAMING THE VICTIM?
WHO IS THE VICTIM?
AN ALCOHOLIC ABUSER WHO WAS TOO DRUNK TO NOTICE THAT THE TRAFFIC LIGHT HAD CHANGED.
IF THE SITUATION WERE REVERSED, WHAT DO YOU THINK WOULD HAPPEN?
WHAT KIND OF *JUSTICE* DO YOU THINK WOULD BE WAITING FOR A YOUNG MAN OF COLOR?
I HAVE STRUGGLED LONG AND HARD TO MAKE SURE THE SYSTEM WORKS FOR PEOPLE LIKE US.
PEOPLE LIKE *US?* DO YOU MEAN BLACK PEOPLE...
...OR RICH PEOPLE?
CLEARLY YOU'RE STILL PROCESSING THE SITUATION.
I THINK WE SHOULD FIND A PLACE WHERE PEOPLE CAN HELP YOU DEAL WITH YOUR EMOTIONS.

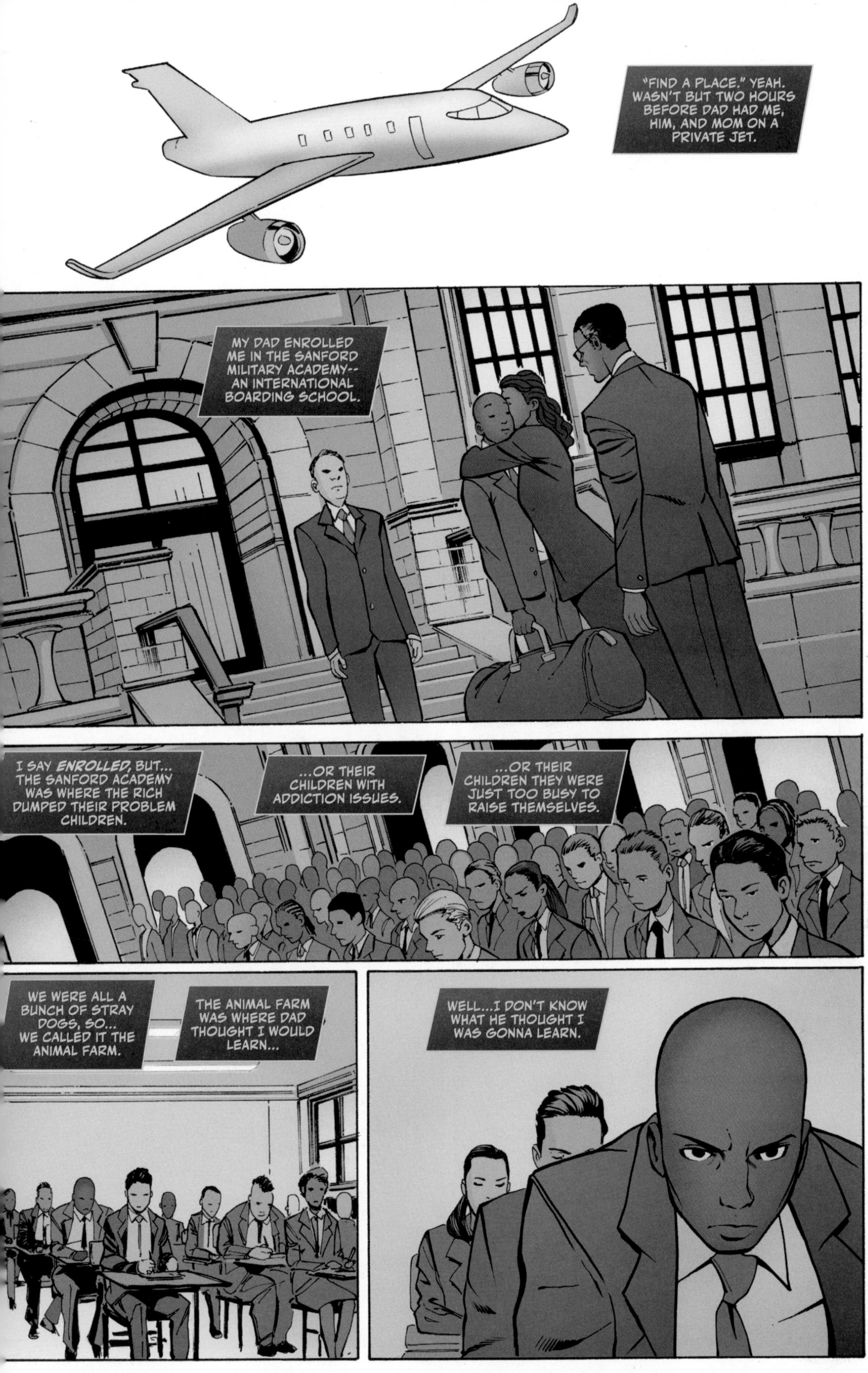
"FIND A PLACE." YEAH. WASN'T BUT TWO HOURS BEFORE DAD HAD ME, HIM, AND MOM ON A PRIVATE JET.
MY DAD ENROLLED ME IN THE SANFORD MILITARY ACADEMY-- AN INTERNATIONAL BOARDING SCHOOL.
I SAY *ENROLLED*, BUT... THE SANFORD ACADEMY WAS WHERE THE RICH DUMPED THEIR PROBLEM CHILDREN.
...OR THEIR CHILDREN WITH ADDICTION ISSUES.
...OR THEIR CHILDREN THEY WERE JUST TOO BUSY TO RAISE THEMSELVES.
WE WERE ALL A BUNCH OF STRAY DOGS, SO... WE CALLED IT THE ANIMAL FARM.
THE ANIMAL FARM WAS WHERE DAD THOUGHT I WOULD LEARN...
WELL...I DON'T KNOW WHAT HE THOUGHT I WAS GONNA LEARN.

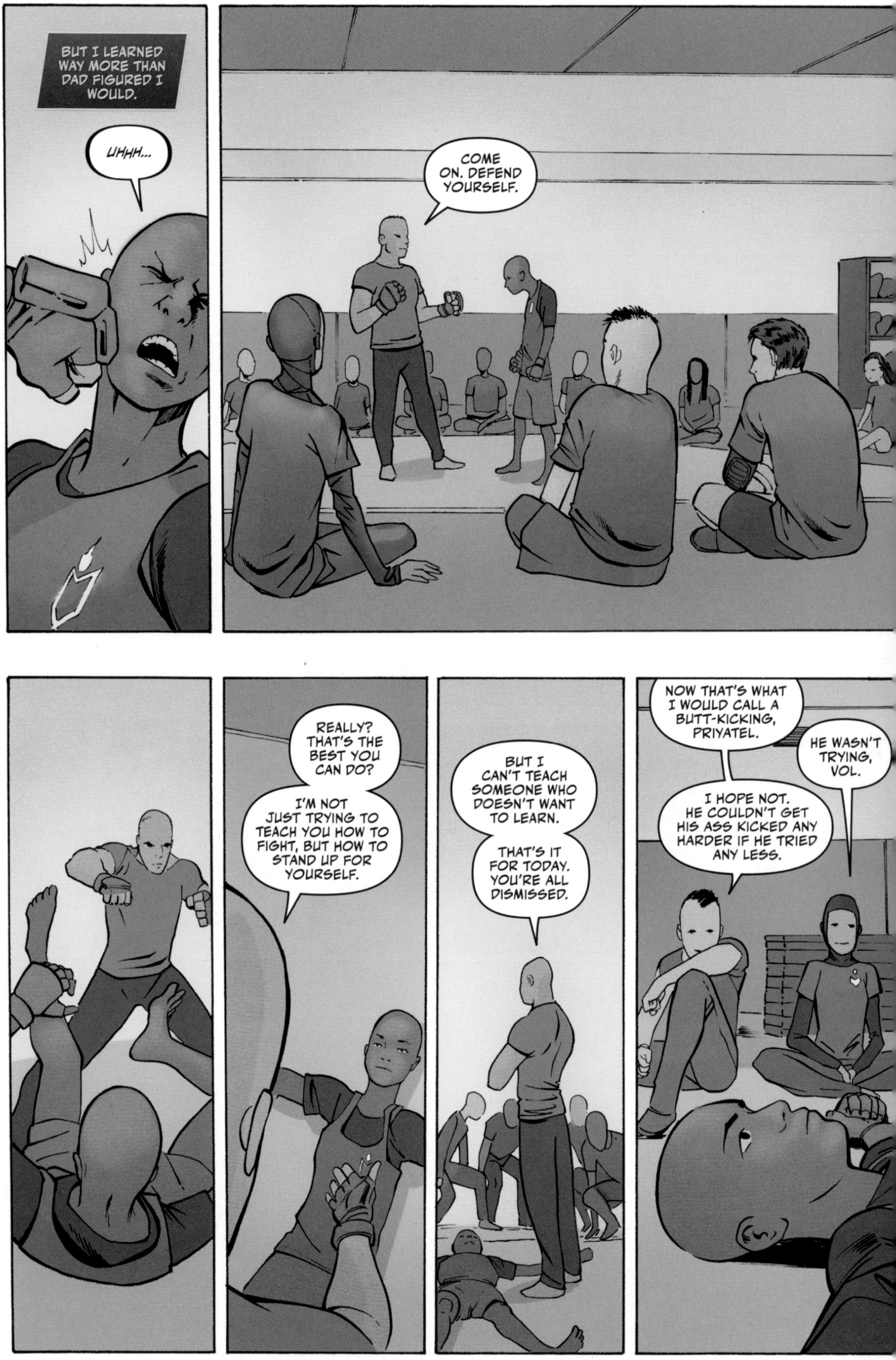
BUT I LEARNED WAY MORE THAN DAD FIGURED I WOULD.
UHHH...
COME ON. DEFEND YOURSELF.
REALLY? THAT'S THE BEST YOU CAN DO?
I'M NOT JUST TRYING TO TEACH YOU HOW TO FIGHT, BUT HOW TO STAND UP FOR YOURSELF.
BUT I CAN'T TEACH SOMEONE WHO DOESN'T WANT TO LEARN.
THAT'S IT FOR TODAY. YOU'RE ALL DISMISSED.
NOW THAT'S WHAT I WOULD CALL A BUTT-KICKING, PRIYATEL.
HE WASN'T TRYING, VOL.
I HOPE NOT. HE COULDN'T GET HIS ASS KICKED ANY HARDER IF HE TRIED ANY LESS.

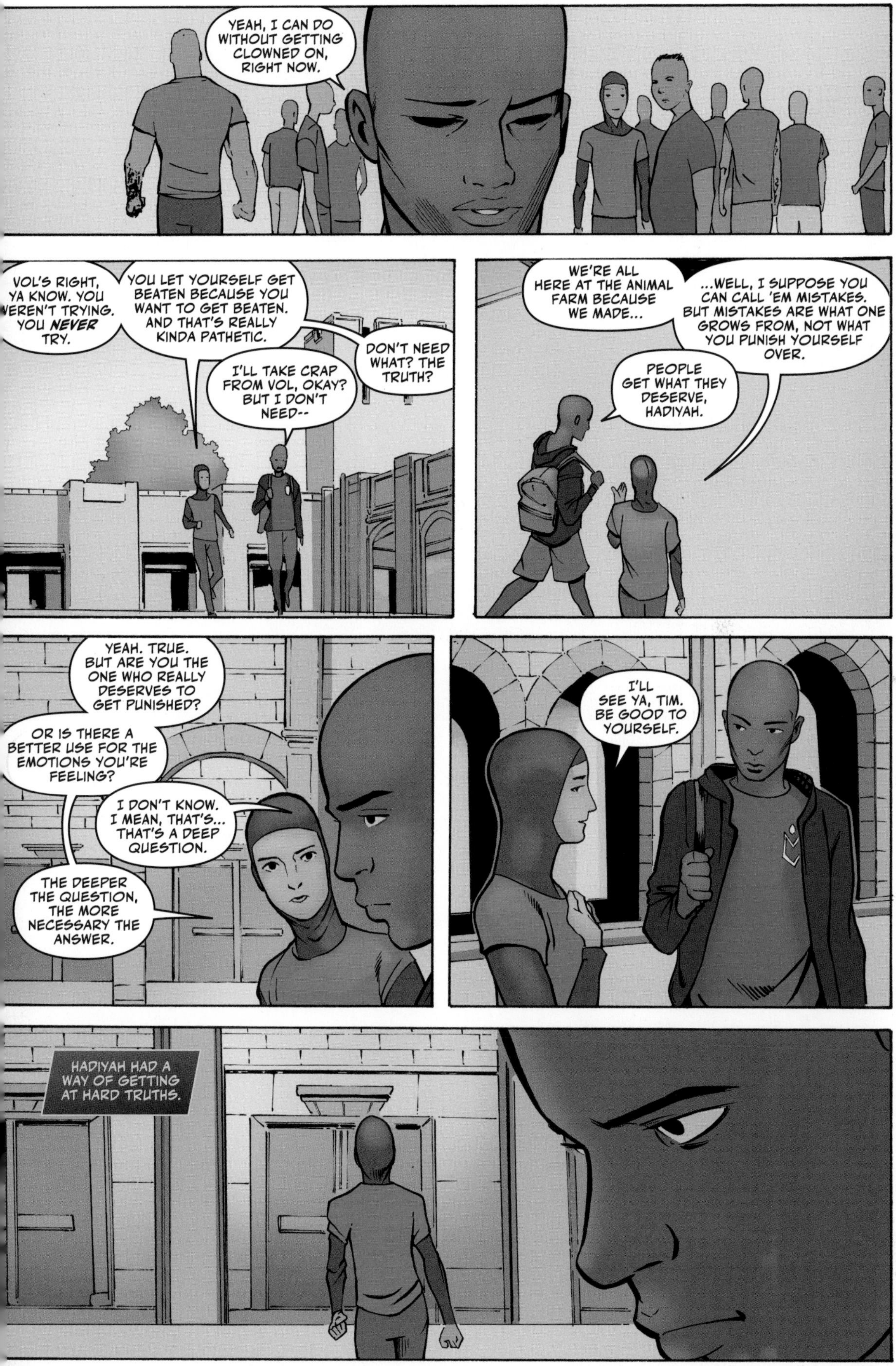
YEAH, I CAN DO WITHOUT GETTING CLOWNED ON, RIGHT NOW.
VOL'S RIGHT, YA KNOW. YOU WEREN'T TRYING. YOU NEVER TRY.
YOU LET YOURSELF GET BEATEN BECAUSE YOU WANT TO GET BEATEN. AND THAT'S REALLY KINDA PATHETIC.
I'LL TAKE CRAP FROM VOL, OKAY? BUT I DON'T NEED--
DON'T NEED WHAT? THE TRUTH?
WE'RE ALL HERE AT THE ANIMAL FARM BECAUSE WE MADE...
...WELL, I SUPPOSE YOU CAN CALL 'EM MISTAKES. BUT MISTAKES ARE WHAT ONE GROWS FROM, NOT WHAT YOU PUNISH YOURSELF OVER.
PEOPLE GET WHAT THEY DESERVE, HADIYAH.
YEAH. TRUE. BUT ARE YOU THE ONE WHO REALLY DESERVES TO GET PUNISHED?
OR IS THERE A BETTER USE FOR THE EMOTIONS YOU'RE FEELING?
I DON'T KNOW. I MEAN, THAT'S... THAT'S A DEEP QUESTION.
THE DEEPER THE QUESTION, THE MORE NECESSARY THE ANSWER.
I'LL SEE YA, TIM. BE GOOD TO YOURSELF.
HADIYAH HAD A WAY OF GETTING AT HARD TRUTHS.

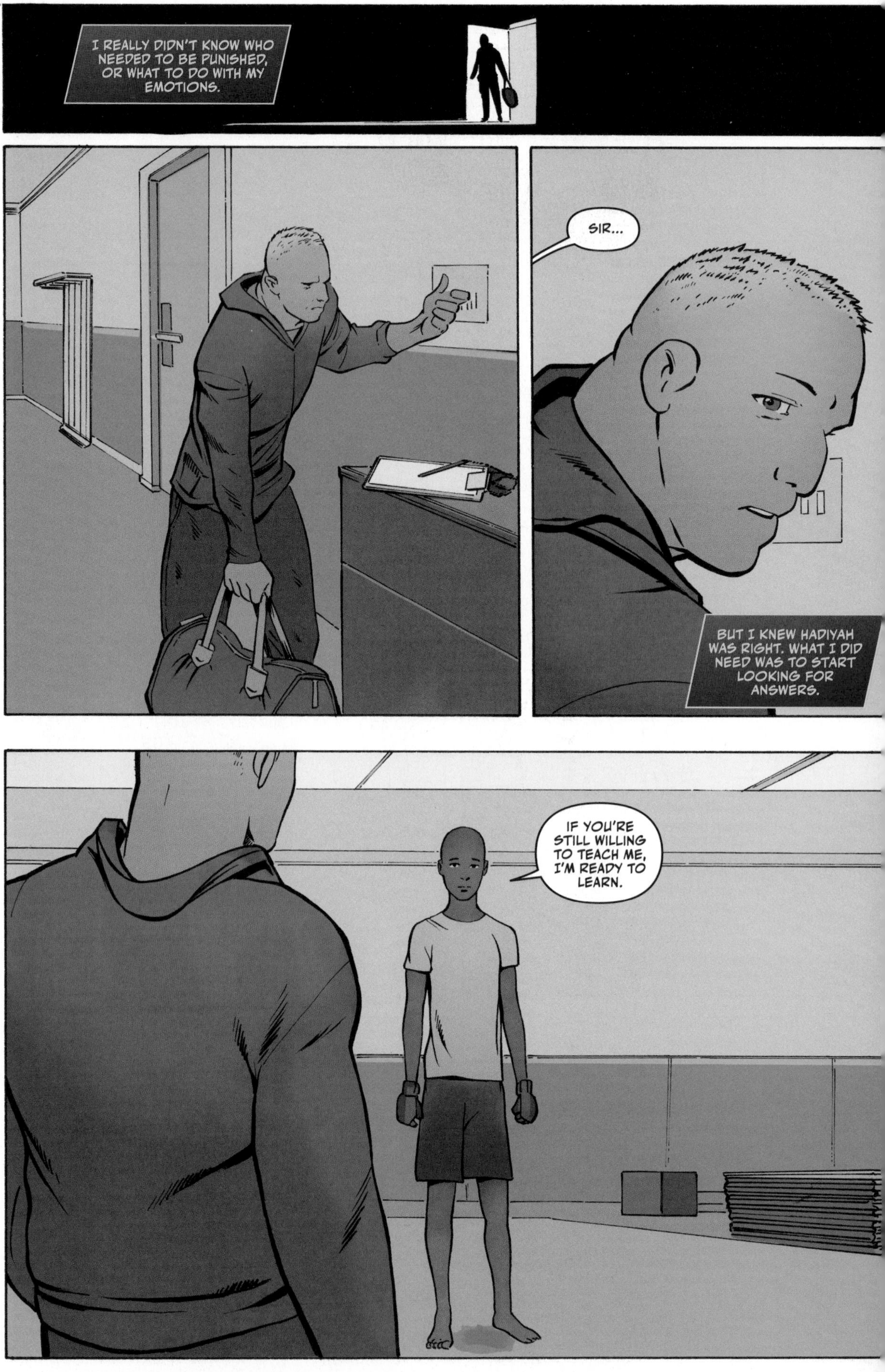
I REALLY DIDN'T KNOW WHO NEEDED TO BE PUNISHED, OR WHAT TO DO WITH MY EMOTIONS.
SIR...
BUT I KNEW HADIYAH WAS RIGHT. WHAT I DID NEED WAS TO START LOOKING FOR ANSWERS.
IF YOU'RE STILL WILLING TO TEACH ME, I'M READY TO LEARN.

The Next Batman: Second Son #4
Cover Art by **JORGE MOLINA**

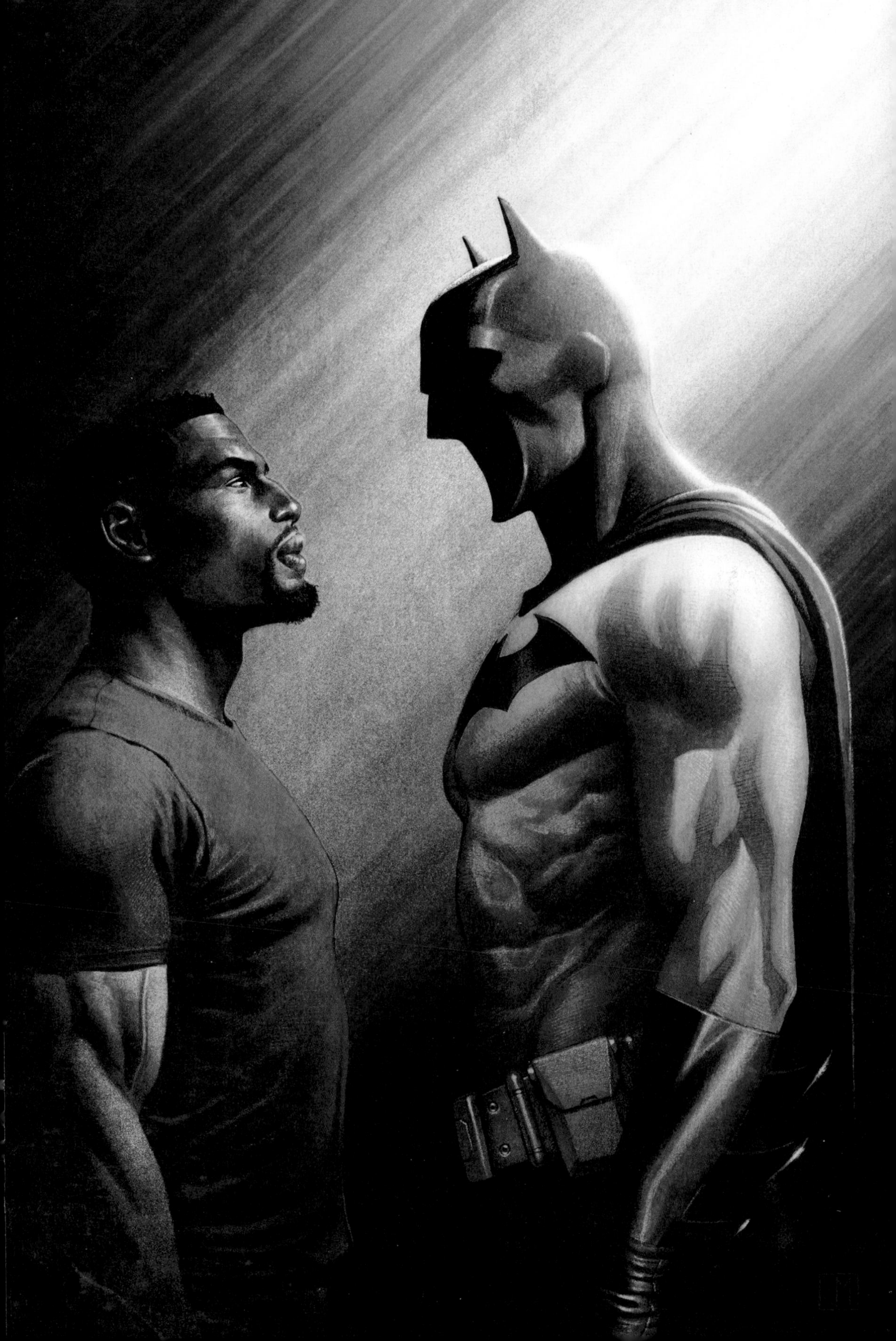

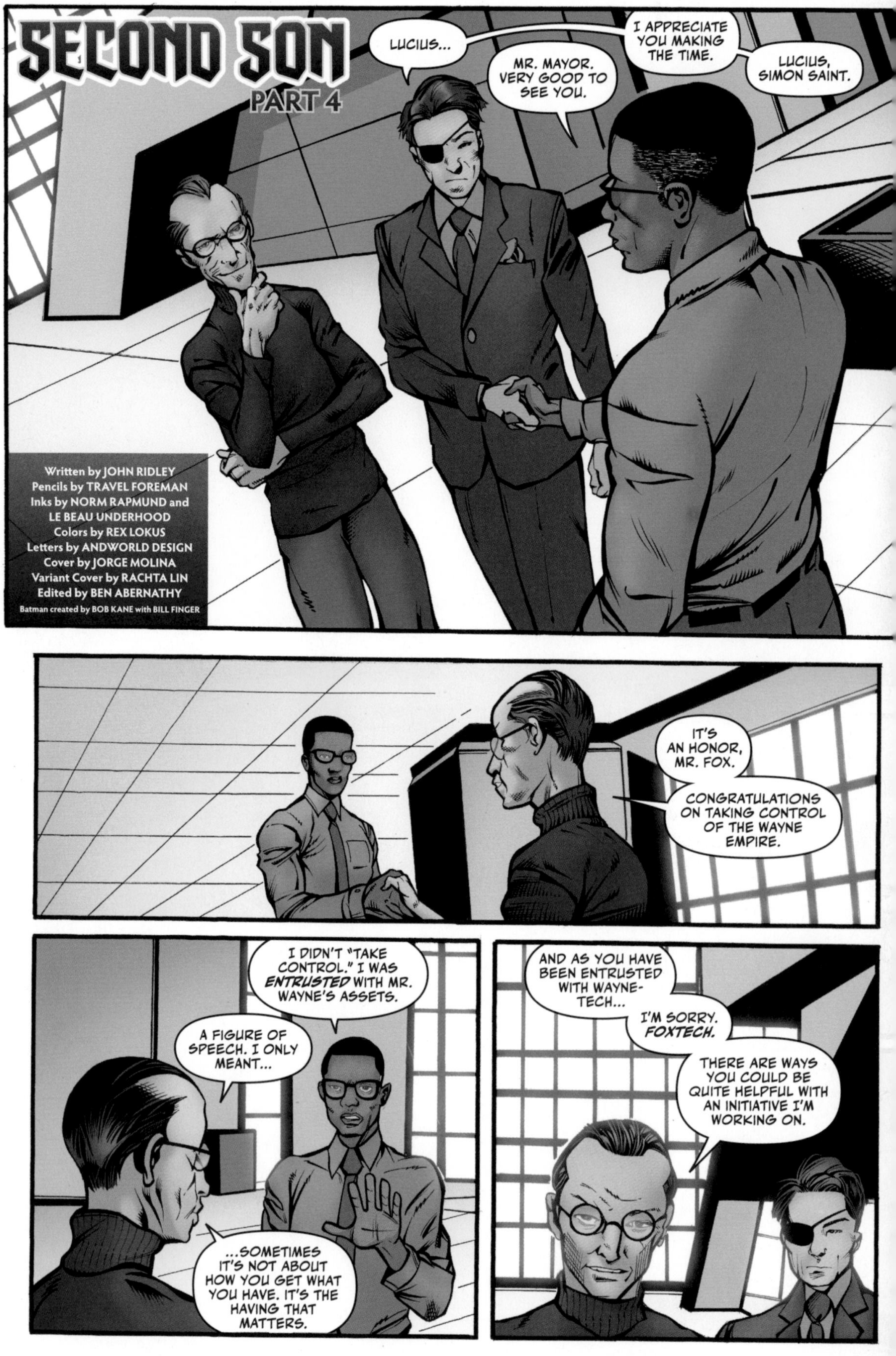
SECOND SON
PART 4
LUCIUS...
MR. MAYOR. VERY GOOD TO SEE YOU.
I APPRECIATE YOU MAKING THE TIME.
LUCIUS, SIMON SAINT.
Written by JOHN RIDLEY
Pencils by TRAVEL FOREMAN
Inks by NORM RAPMUND and LE BEAU UNDERHOOD
Colors by REX LOKUS
Letters by ANDWORLD DESIGN
Cover by JORGE MOLINA
Variant Cover by RACHTA LIN
Edited by BEN ABERNATHY
Batman created by BOB KANE with BILL FINGER
IT'S AN HONOR, MR. FOX.
CONGRATULATIONS ON TAKING CONTROL OF THE WAYNE EMPIRE.
I DIDN'T "TAKE CONTROL." I WAS *ENTRUSTED* WITH MR. WAYNE'S ASSETS.
A FIGURE OF SPEECH. I ONLY MEANT...
...SOMETIMES IT'S NOT ABOUT HOW YOU GET WHAT YOU HAVE. IT'S THE HAVING THAT MATTERS.
AND AS YOU HAVE BEEN ENTRUSTED WITH WAYNE-TECH...
I'M SORRY. *FOXTECH.*
THERE ARE WAYS YOU COULD BE QUITE HELPFUL WITH AN INITIATIVE I'M WORKING ON.

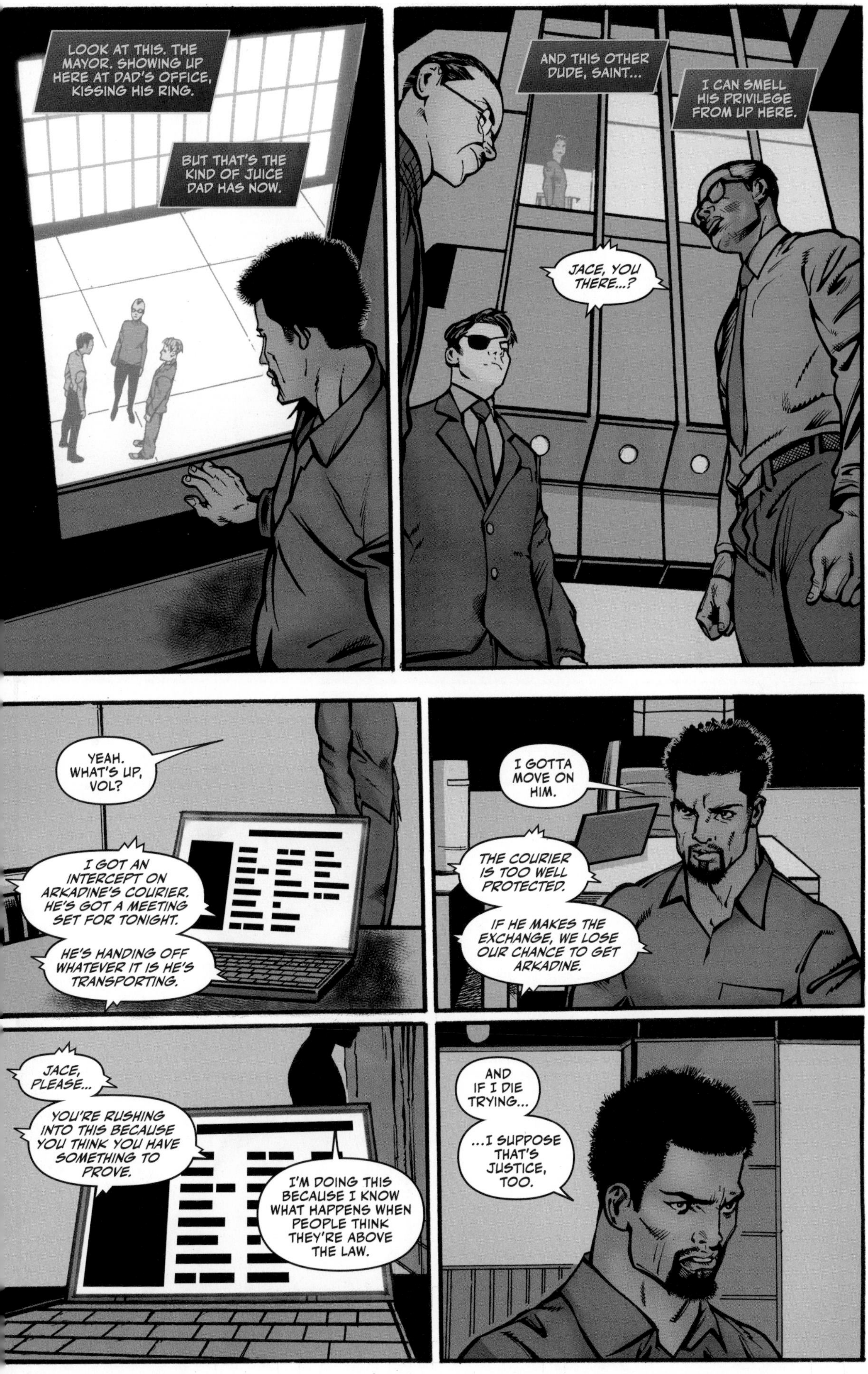
LOOK AT THIS. THE MAYOR. SHOWING UP HERE AT DAD'S OFFICE, KISSING HIS RING.
BUT THAT'S THE KIND OF JUICE DAD HAS NOW.
AND THIS OTHER DUDE, SAINT...
I CAN SMELL HIS PRIVILEGE FROM UP HERE.
JACE, YOU THERE...?
YEAH. WHAT'S UP, VOL?
I GOT AN INTERCEPT ON ARKADINE'S COURIER. HE'S GOT A MEETING SET FOR TONIGHT.
HE'S HANDING OFF WHATEVER IT IS HE'S TRANSPORTING.
I GOTTA MOVE ON HIM.
THE COURIER IS TOO WELL PROTECTED.
IF HE MAKES THE EXCHANGE, WE LOSE OUR CHANCE TO GET ARKADINE.
JACE, PLEASE...
YOU'RE RUSHING INTO THIS BECAUSE YOU THINK YOU HAVE SOMETHING TO PROVE.
I'M DOING THIS BECAUSE I KNOW WHAT HAPPENS WHEN PEOPLE THINK THEY'RE ABOVE THE LAW.
AND IF I DIE TRYING...
...I SUPPOSE THAT'S JUSTICE, TOO.

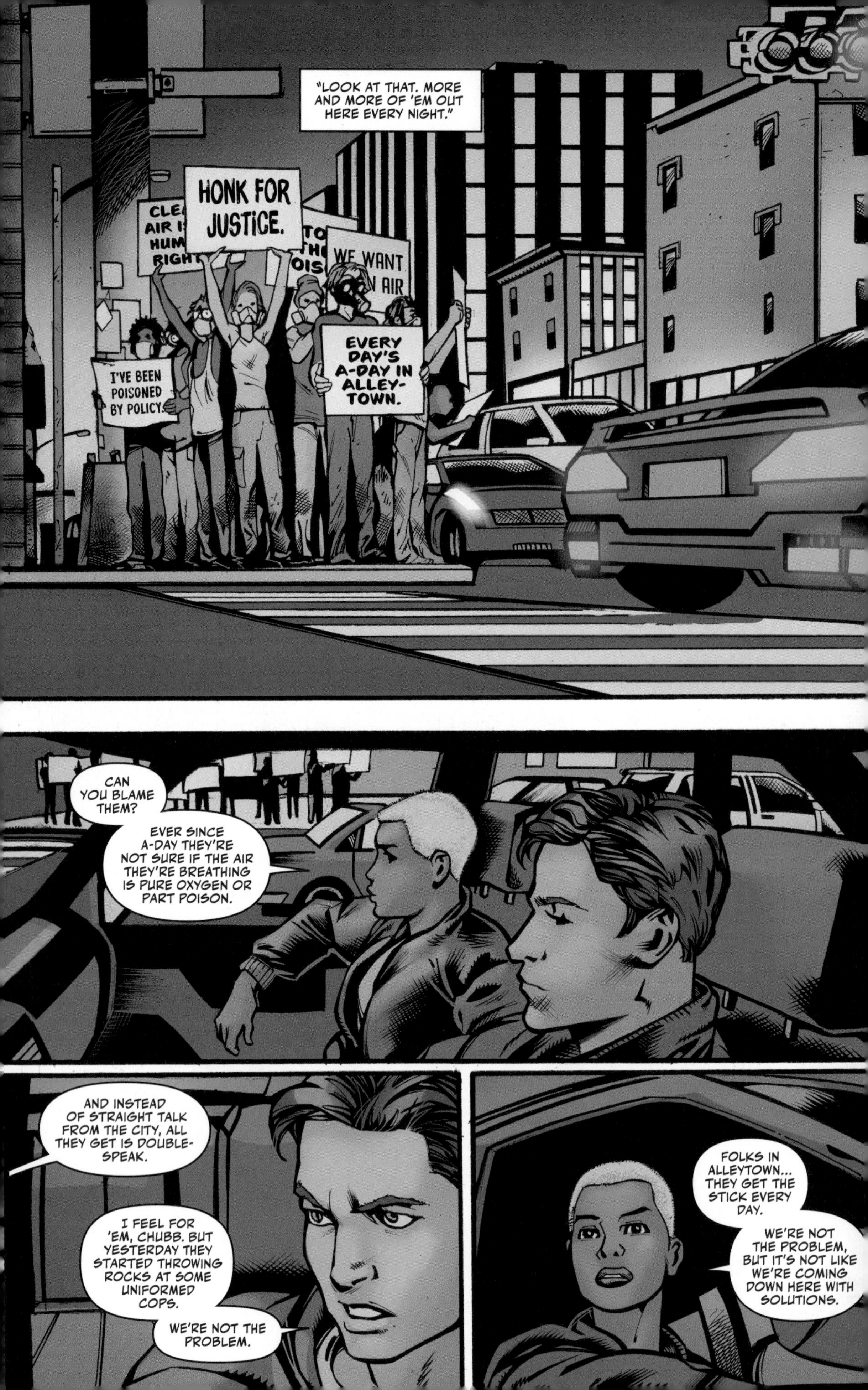
"LOOK AT THAT. MORE AND MORE OF 'EM OUT HERE EVERY NIGHT."
HONK FOR JUSTICE.
I'VE BEEN POISONED BY POLICY.
EVERY DAY'S A-DAY IN ALLEY-TOWN.
WE WANT
CAN YOU BLAME THEM?
EVER SINCE A-DAY THEY'RE NOT SURE IF THE AIR THEY'RE BREATHING IS PURE OXYGEN OR PART POISON.
AND INSTEAD OF STRAIGHT TALK FROM THE CITY, ALL THEY GET IS DOUBLE-SPEAK.
I FEEL FOR 'EM, CHUBB. BUT YESTERDAY THEY STARTED THROWING ROCKS AT SOME UNIFORMED COPS.
WE'RE NOT THE PROBLEM.
FOLKS IN ALLEYTOWN... THEY GET THE STICK EVERY DAY.
WE'RE NOT THE PROBLEM, BUT IT'S NOT LIKE WE'RE COMING DOWN HERE WITH SOLUTIONS.

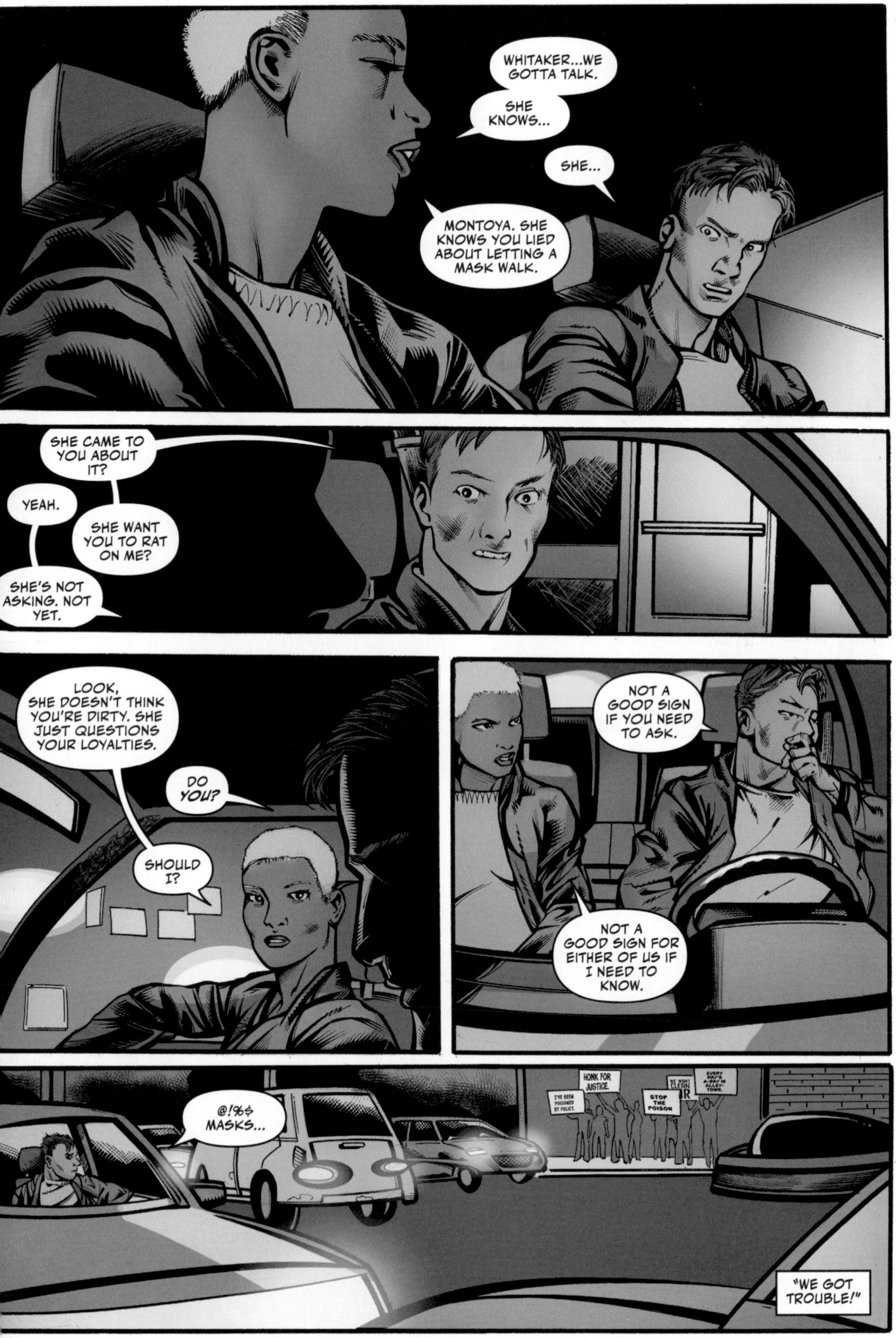
WHITAKER...WE GOTTA TALK.
SHE KNOWS...
SHE...
MONTOYA. SHE KNOWS YOU LIED ABOUT LETTING A MASK WALK.
SHE CAME TO YOU ABOUT IT?
YEAH.
SHE WANT YOU TO RAT ON ME?
SHE'S NOT ASKING. NOT YET.
LOOK, SHE DOESN'T THINK YOU'RE DIRTY. SHE JUST QUESTIONS YOUR LOYALTIES.
DO *YOU?*
SHOULD I?
NOT A GOOD SIGN IF YOU NEED TO ASK.
NOT A GOOD SIGN FOR EITHER OF US IF I NEED TO KNOW.
@!%$ MASKS...
I'VE BEEN POISONED BY POLICY.
HONK FOR JUSTICE.
STOP THE POISON
WE WANT CLEAN
EVERY DAY'S A-DAY IN ALLEY-TOWN.
"WE GOT TROUBLE!"

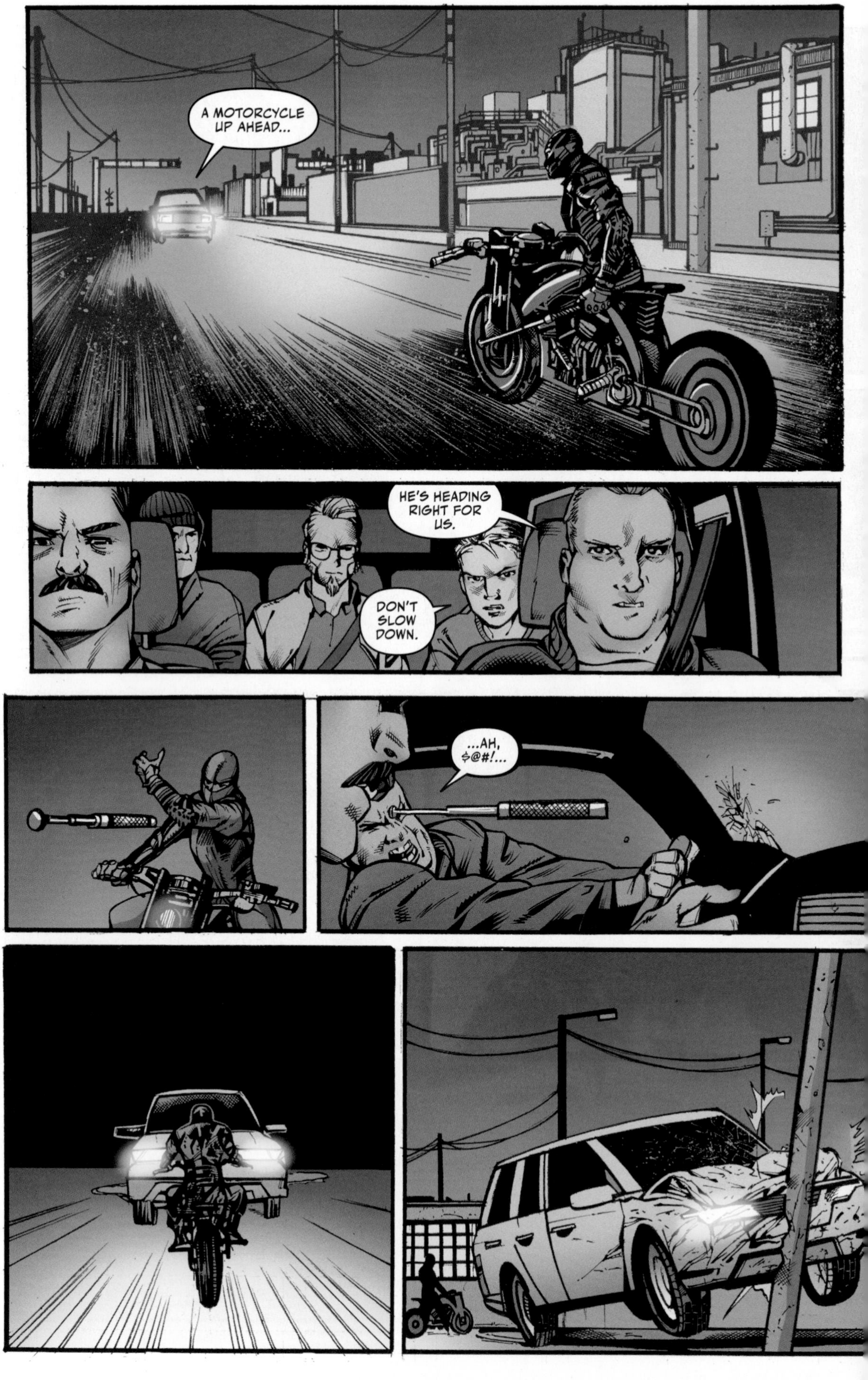
A MOTORCYCLE UP AHEAD...
HE'S HEADING RIGHT FOR US.
DON'T SLOW DOWN.
...AH, $@#!...

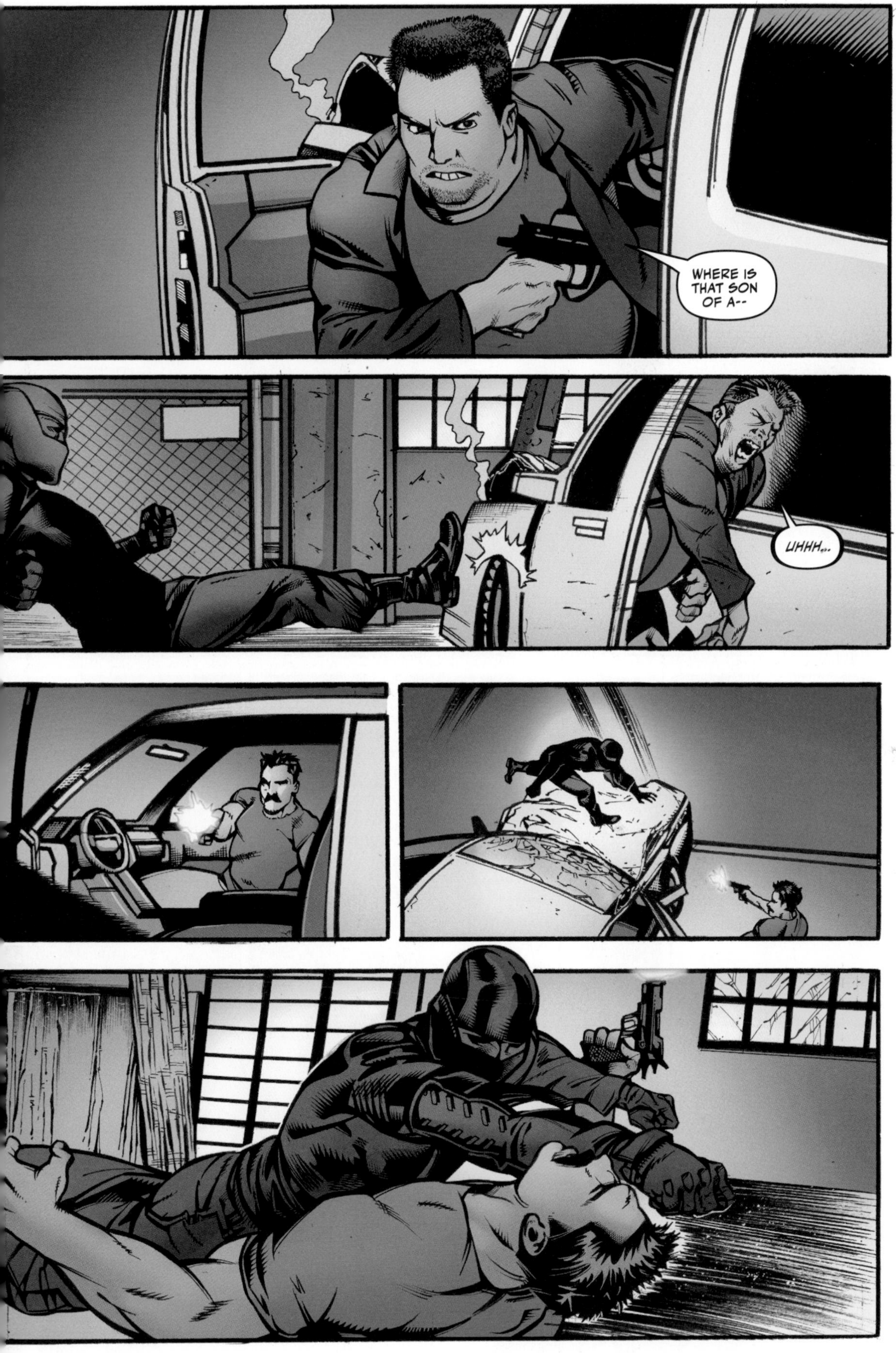
WHERE IS THAT SON OF A--
UHHH...

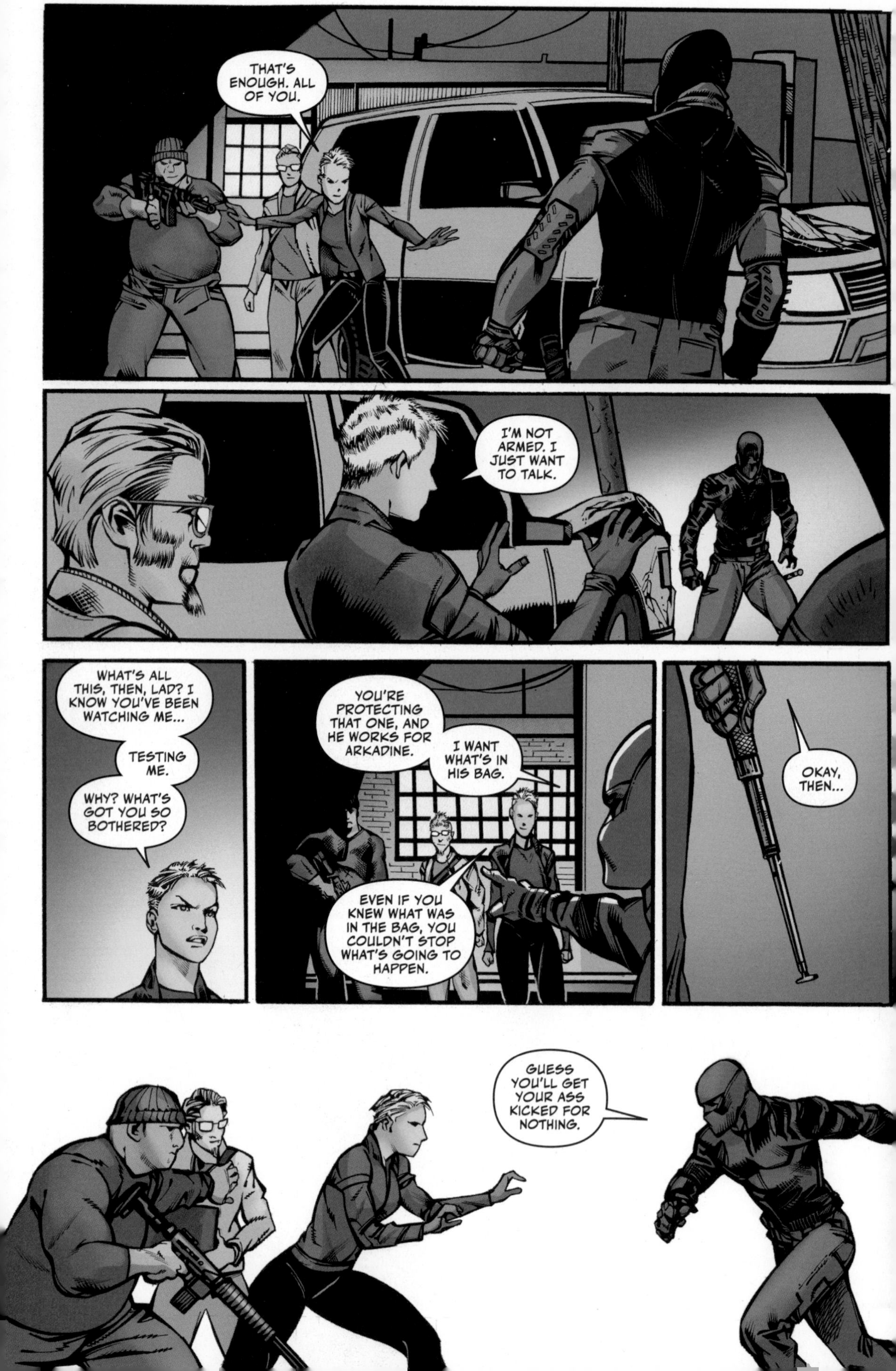
THAT'S ENOUGH. ALL OF YOU.
I'M NOT ARMED. I JUST WANT TO TALK.
WHAT'S ALL THIS, THEN, LAD? I KNOW YOU'VE BEEN WATCHING ME...
TESTING ME.
WHY? WHAT'S GOT YOU SO BOTHERED?
YOU'RE PROTECTING THAT ONE, AND HE WORKS FOR ARKADINE.
I WANT WHAT'S IN HIS BAG.
EVEN IF YOU KNEW WHAT WAS IN THE BAG, YOU COULDN'T STOP WHAT'S GOING TO HAPPEN.
OKAY, THEN...
GUESS YOU'LL GET YOUR ASS KICKED FOR NOTHING.

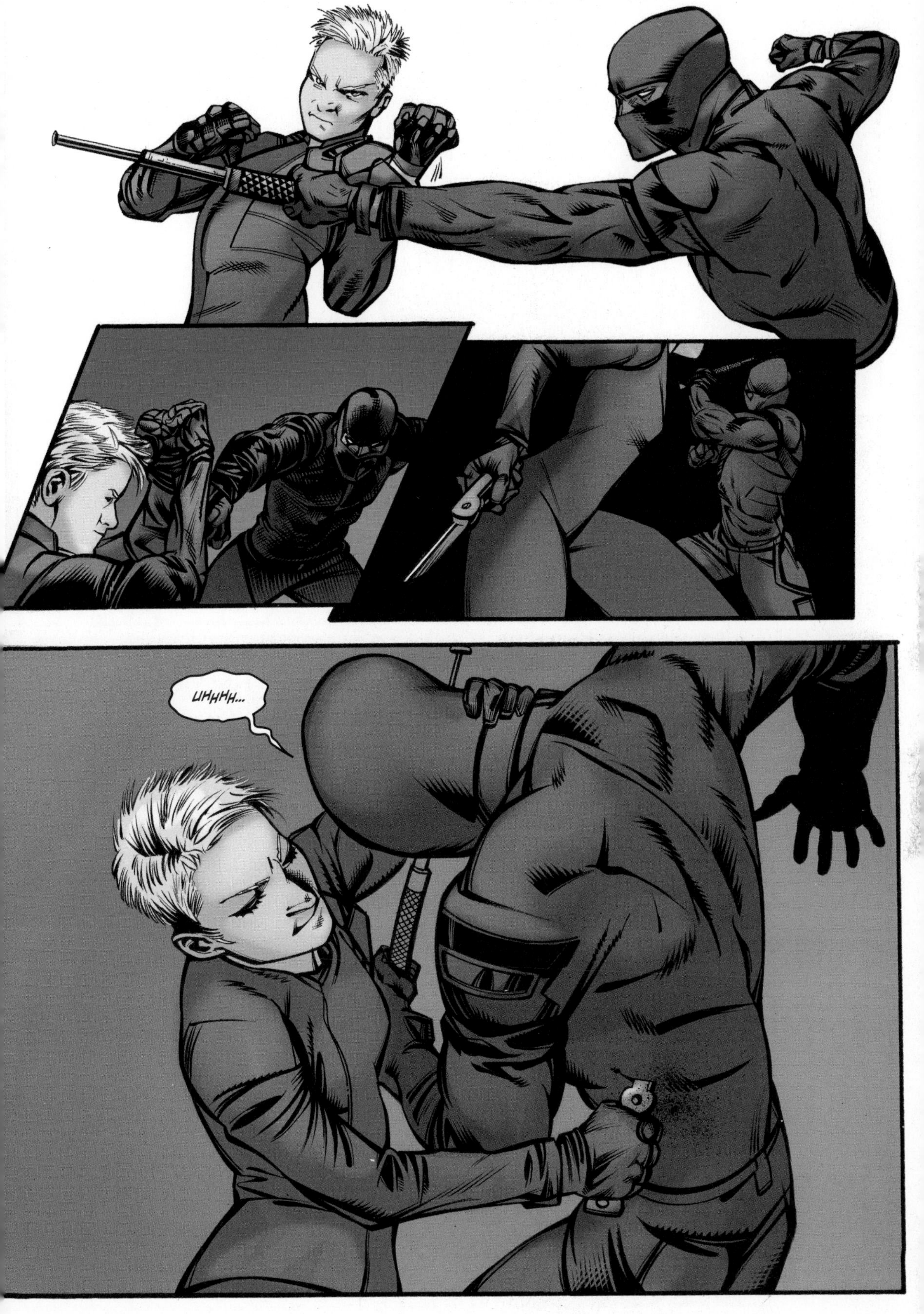
UHHHH...

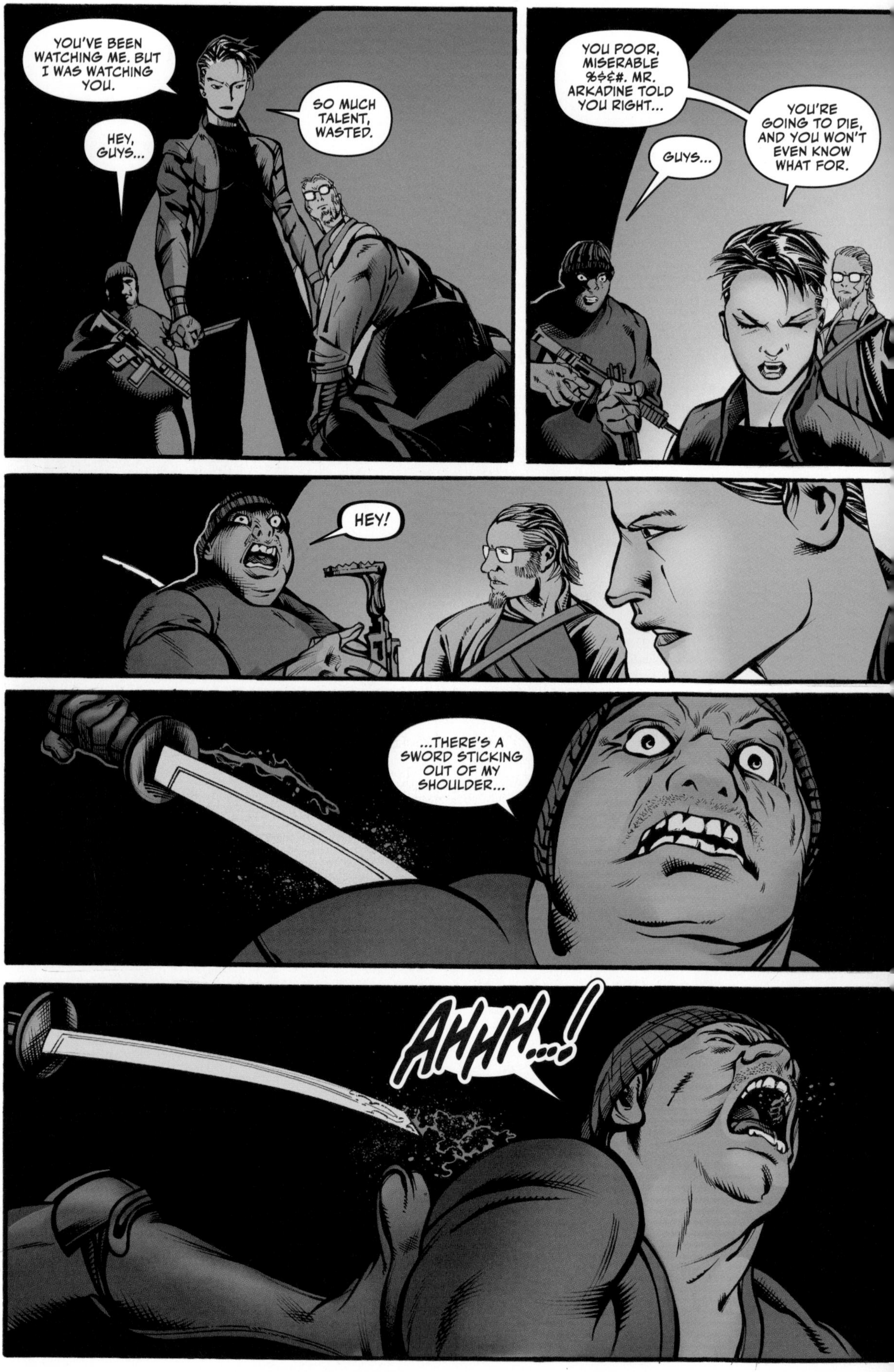
YOU'VE BEEN WATCHING ME. BUT I WAS WATCHING YOU.
HEY, GUYS...
SO MUCH TALENT, WASTED.
YOU POOR, MISERABLE %$&#. MR. ARKADINE TOLD YOU RIGHT...
GUYS...
YOU'RE GOING TO DIE, AND YOU WON'T EVEN KNOW WHAT FOR.
HEY!
...THERE'S A SWORD STICKING OUT OF MY SHOULDER...
AHHH...!

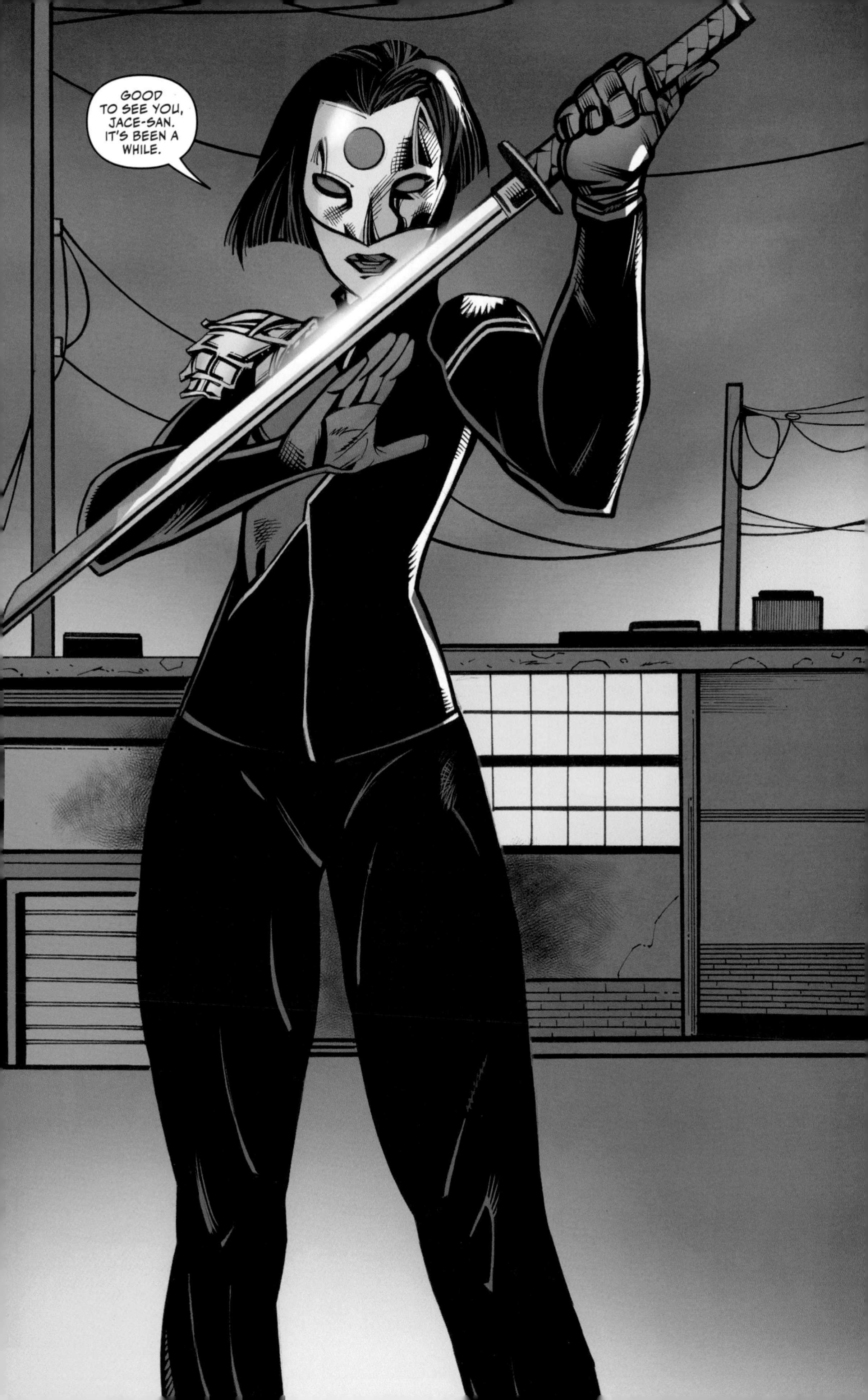
GOOD TO SEE YOU, JACE-SAN. IT'S BEEN A WHILE.

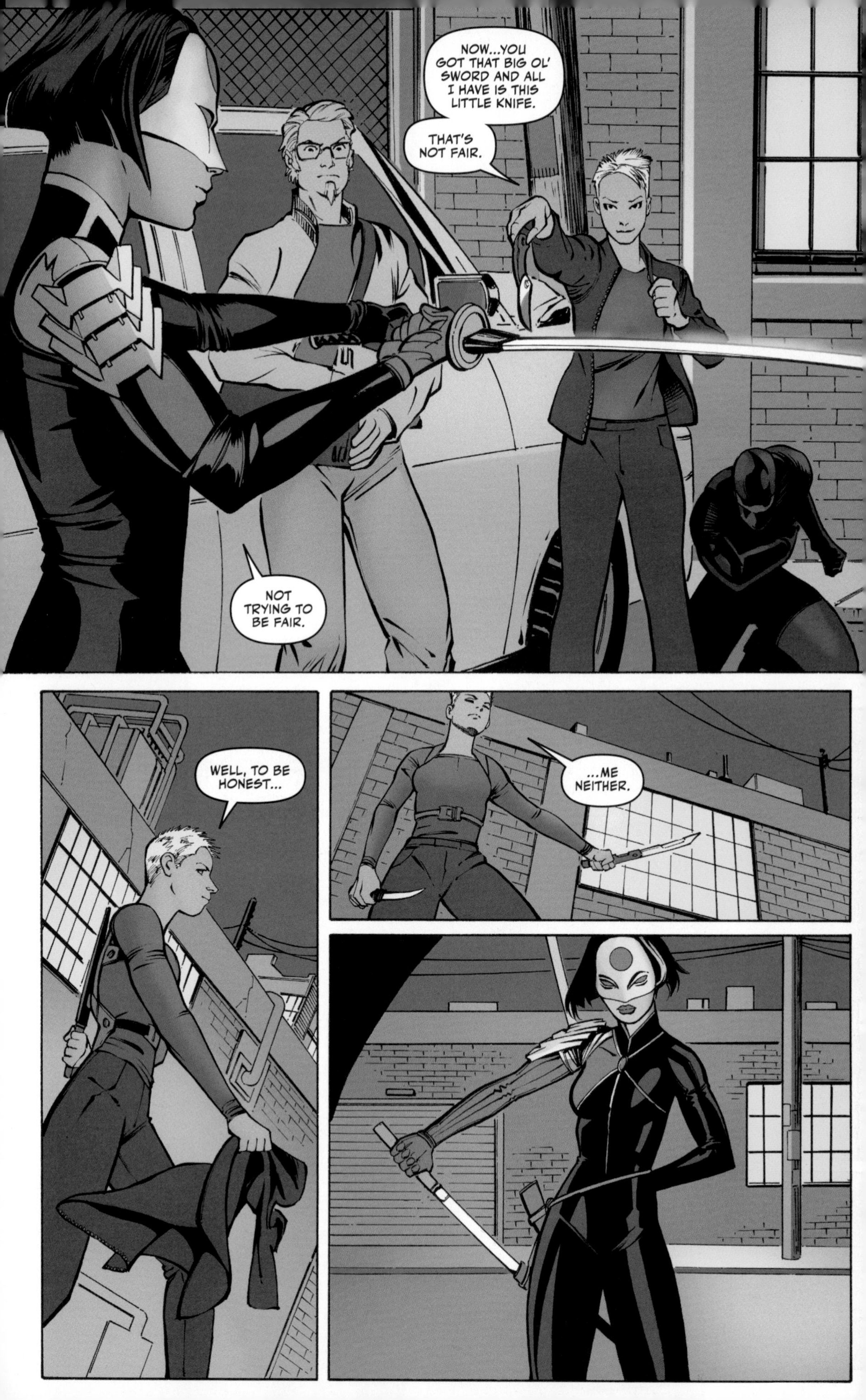
NOW...YOU GOT THAT BIG OL' SWORD AND ALL I HAVE IS THIS LITTLE KNIFE.
THAT'S NOT FAIR.
NOT TRYING TO BE FAIR.
WELL, TO BE HONEST...
...ME NEITHER.

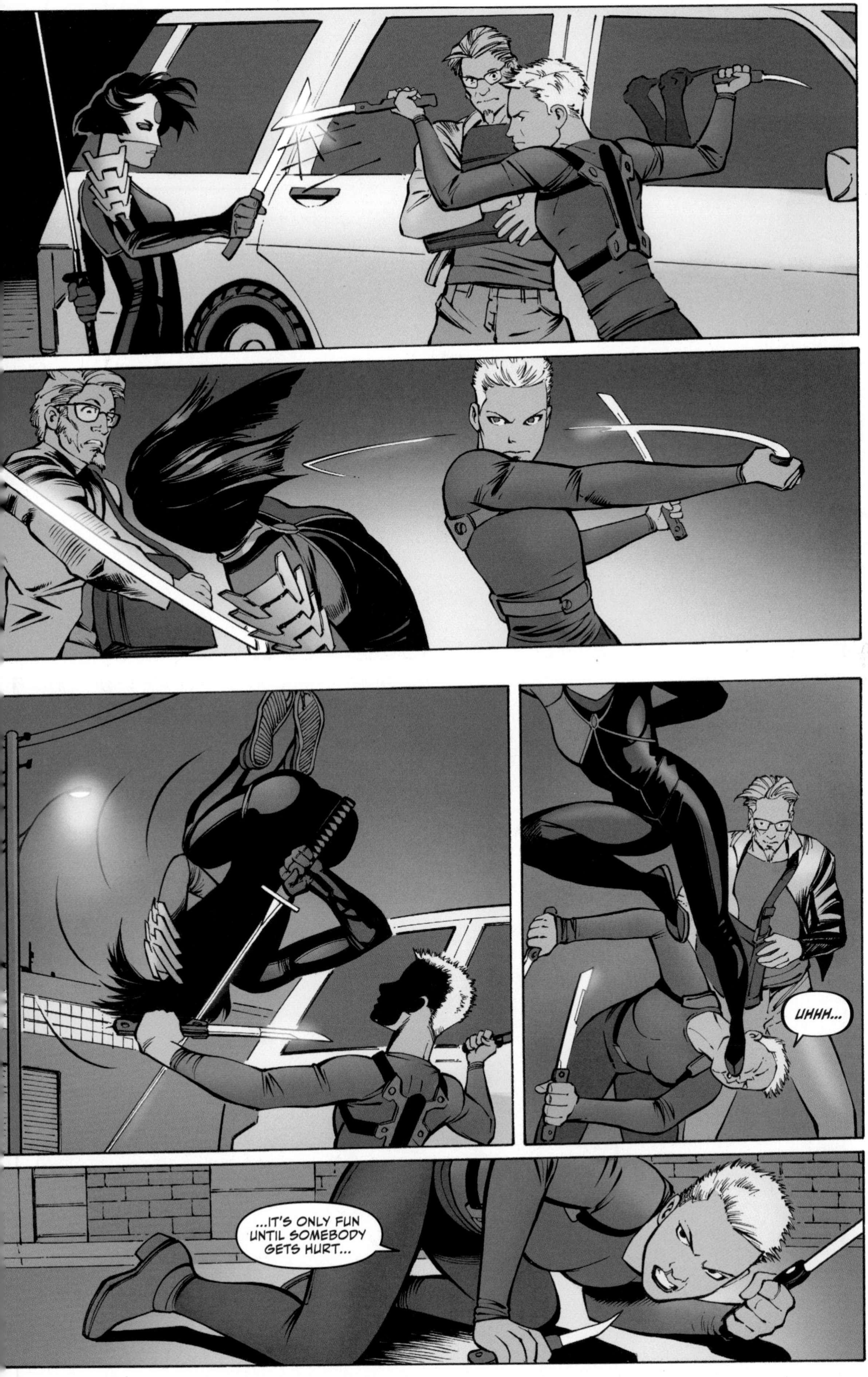
UHHH...
...IT'S ONLY FUN UNTIL SOMEBODY GETS HURT...

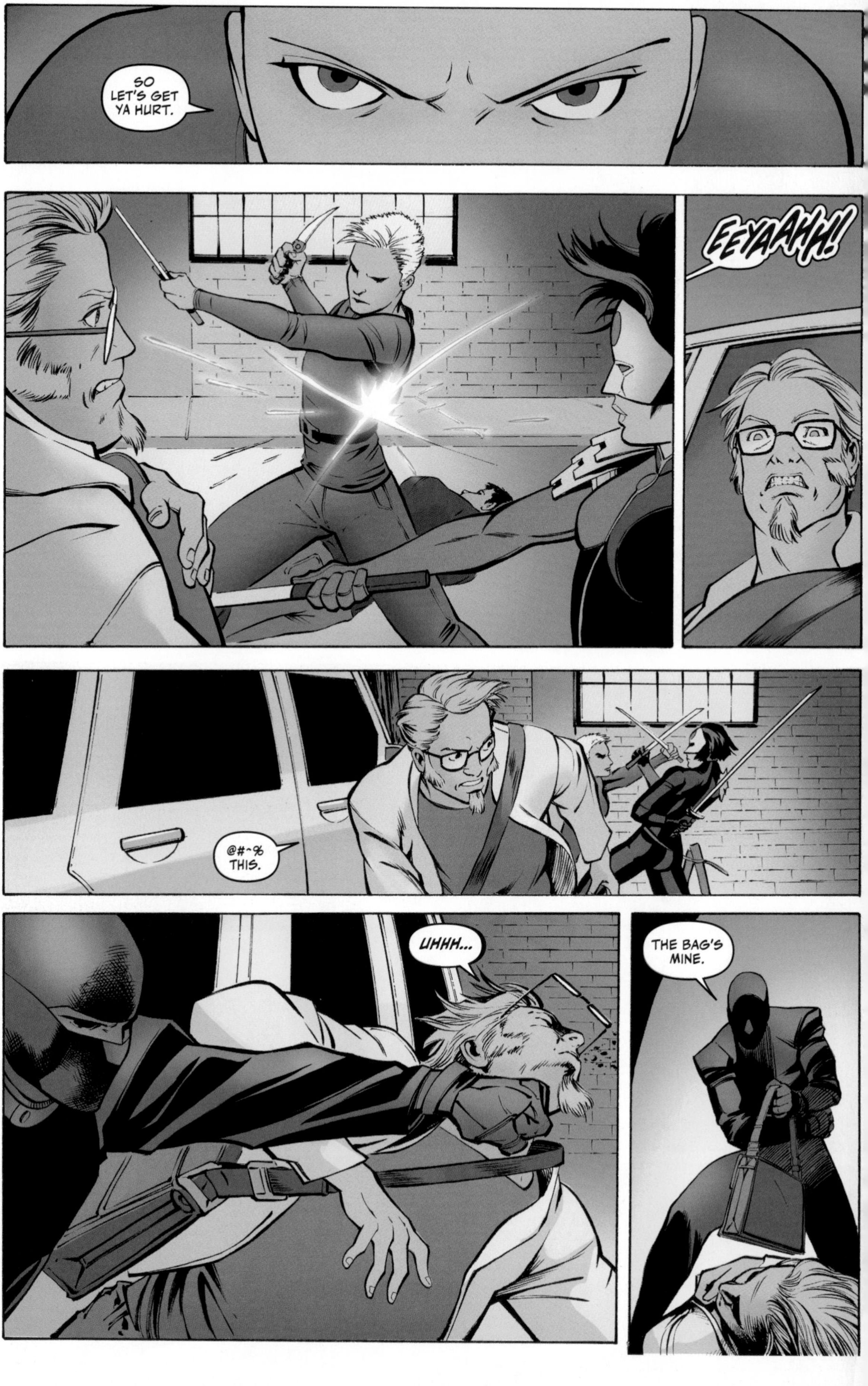
SO LET'S GET YA HURT.
EEYAAHH!
@#~% THIS.
UHHH...
THE BAG'S MINE.

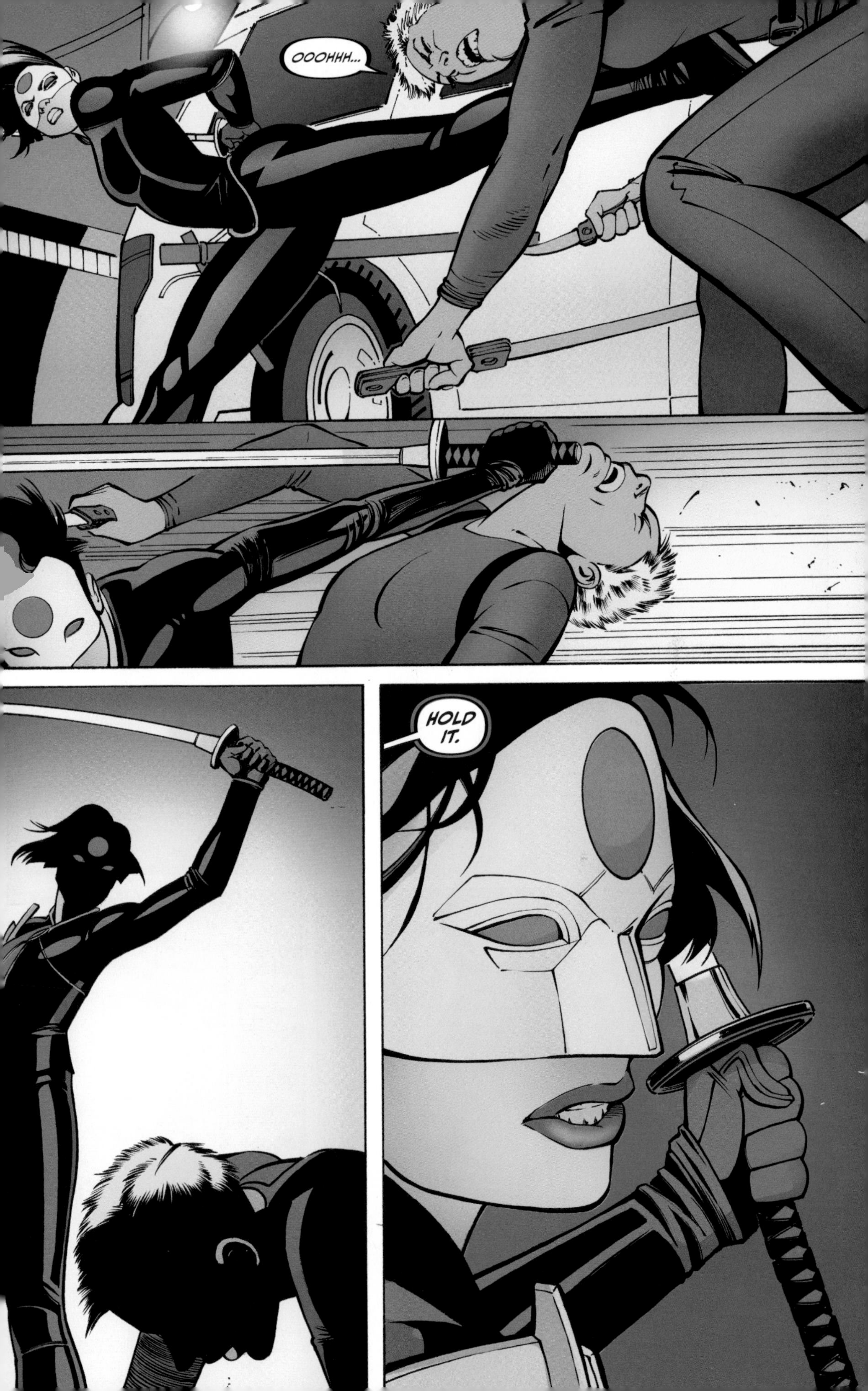
OOOHHH...
HOLD IT.

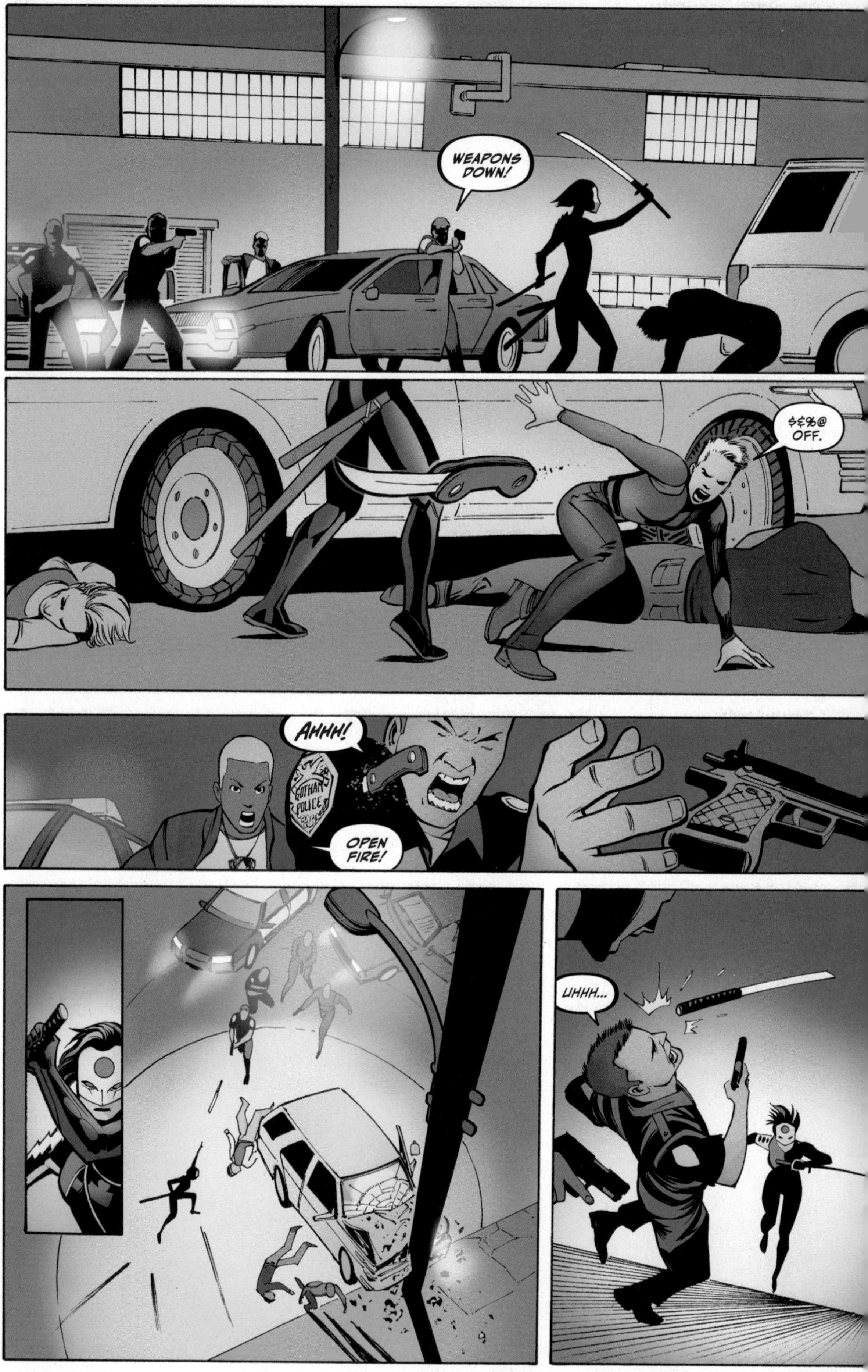
WEAPONS DOWN!
$&%@ OFF.
AHHH!
OPEN FIRE!
UHHH...

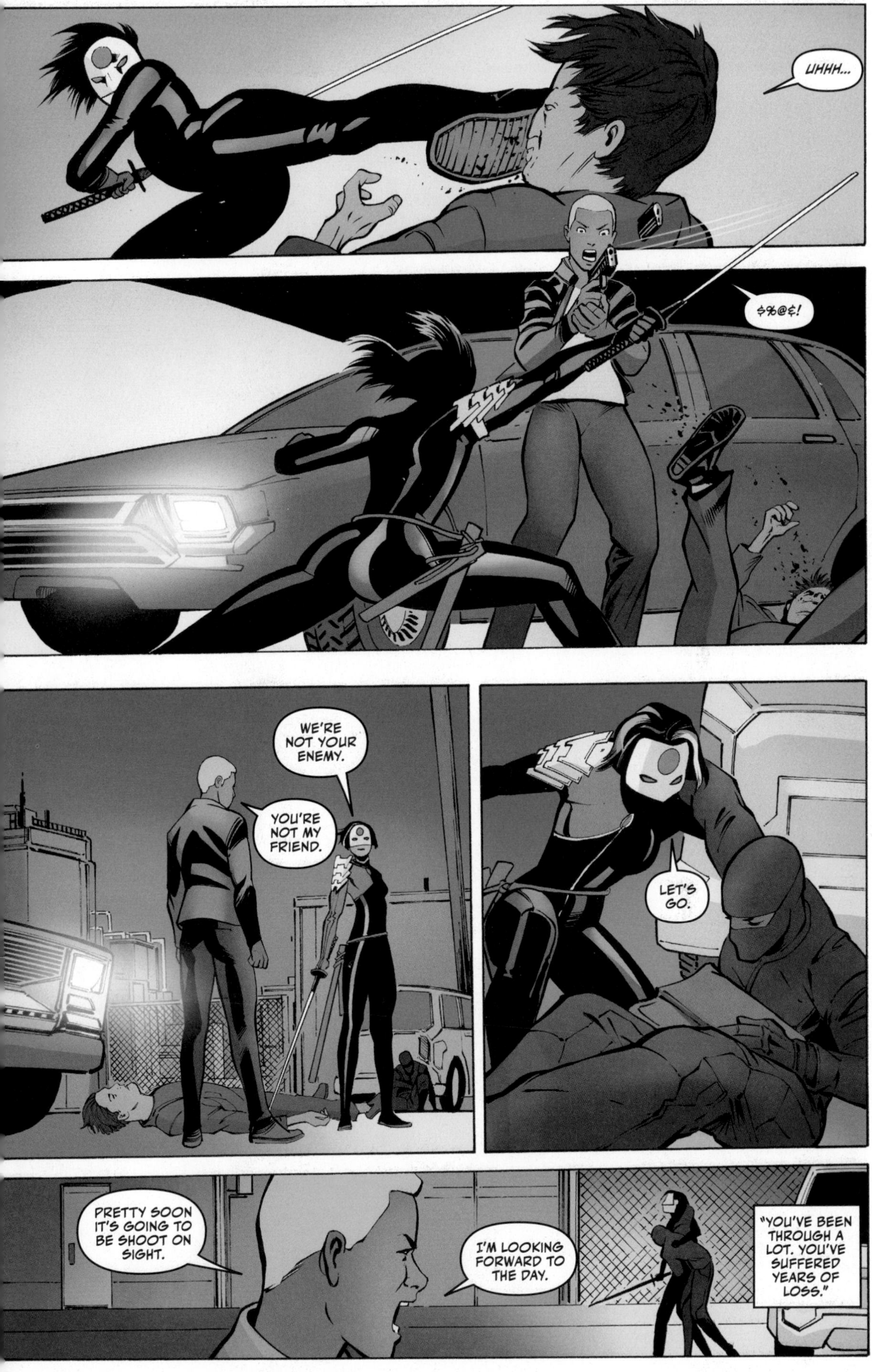
UHHH...
$%@¢!
WE'RE NOT YOUR ENEMY.
YOU'RE NOT MY FRIEND.
LET'S GO.
PRETTY SOON IT'S GOING TO BE SHOOT ON SIGHT.
I'M LOOKING FORWARD TO THE DAY.
"YOU'VE BEEN THROUGH A LOT. YOU'VE SUFFERED YEARS OF LOSS."

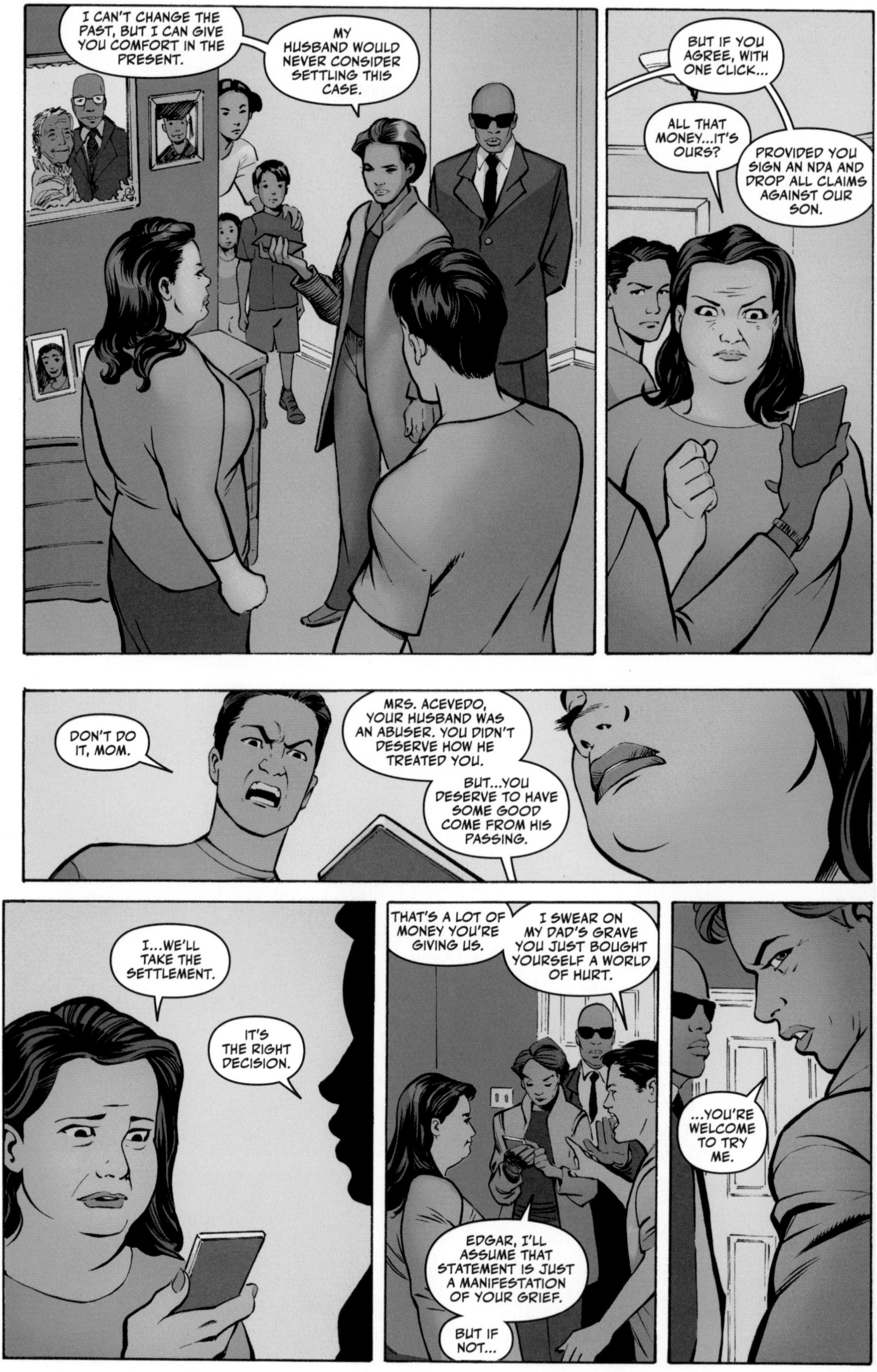
I CAN'T CHANGE THE PAST, BUT I CAN GIVE YOU COMFORT IN THE PRESENT.
MY HUSBAND WOULD NEVER CONSIDER SETTLING THIS CASE.
BUT IF YOU AGREE, WITH ONE CLICK...
ALL THAT MONEY...IT'S OURS?
PROVIDED YOU SIGN AN NDA AND DROP ALL CLAIMS AGAINST OUR SON.
DON'T DO IT, MOM.
MRS. ACEVEDO, YOUR HUSBAND WAS AN ABUSER. YOU DIDN'T DESERVE HOW HE TREATED YOU.
BUT...YOU DESERVE TO HAVE SOME GOOD COME FROM HIS PASSING.
I...WE'LL TAKE THE SETTLEMENT.
IT'S THE RIGHT DECISION.
THAT'S A LOT OF MONEY YOU'RE GIVING US.
I SWEAR ON MY DAD'S GRAVE YOU JUST BOUGHT YOURSELF A WORLD OF HURT.
EDGAR, I'LL ASSUME THAT STATEMENT IS JUST A MANIFESTATION OF YOUR GRIEF.
BUT IF NOT...
...YOU'RE WELCOME TO TRY ME.

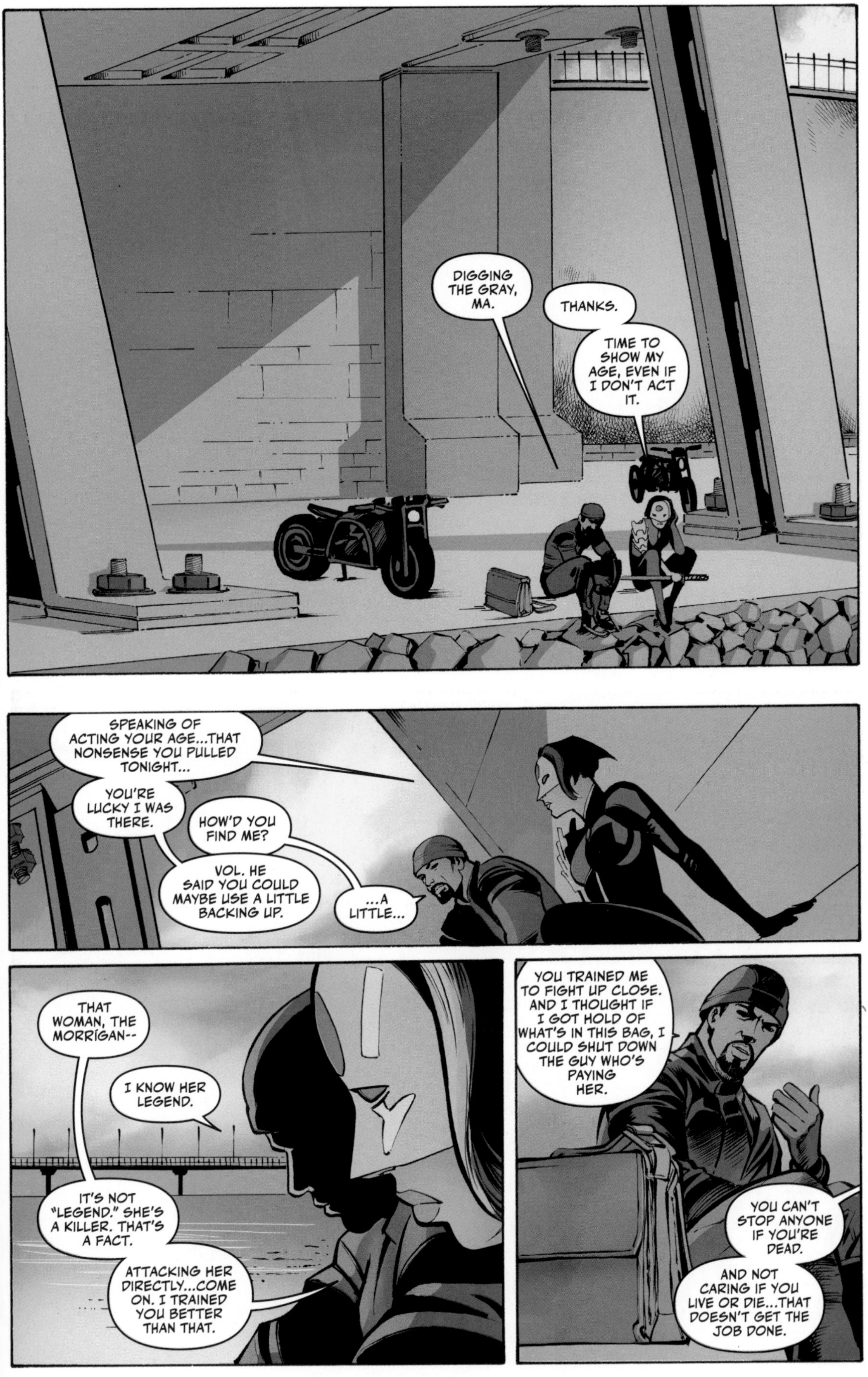
DIGGING THE GRAY, MA.
THANKS.
TIME TO SHOW MY AGE, EVEN IF I DON'T ACT IT.
SPEAKING OF ACTING YOUR AGE...THAT NONSENSE YOU PULLED TONIGHT...
YOU'RE LUCKY I WAS THERE.
HOW'D YOU FIND ME?
VOL. HE SAID YOU COULD MAYBE USE A LITTLE BACKING UP.
...A LITTLE...
THAT WOMAN, THE MORRIGAN--
I KNOW HER LEGEND.
IT'S NOT "LEGEND." SHE'S A KILLER. THAT'S A FACT.
ATTACKING HER DIRECTLY...COME ON. I TRAINED YOU BETTER THAN THAT.
YOU TRAINED ME TO FIGHT UP CLOSE. AND I THOUGHT IF I GOT HOLD OF WHAT'S IN THIS BAG, I COULD SHUT DOWN THE GUY WHO'S PAYING HER.
YOU CAN'T STOP ANYONE IF YOU'RE DEAD.
AND NOT CARING IF YOU LIVE OR DIE...THAT DOESN'T GET THE JOB DONE.

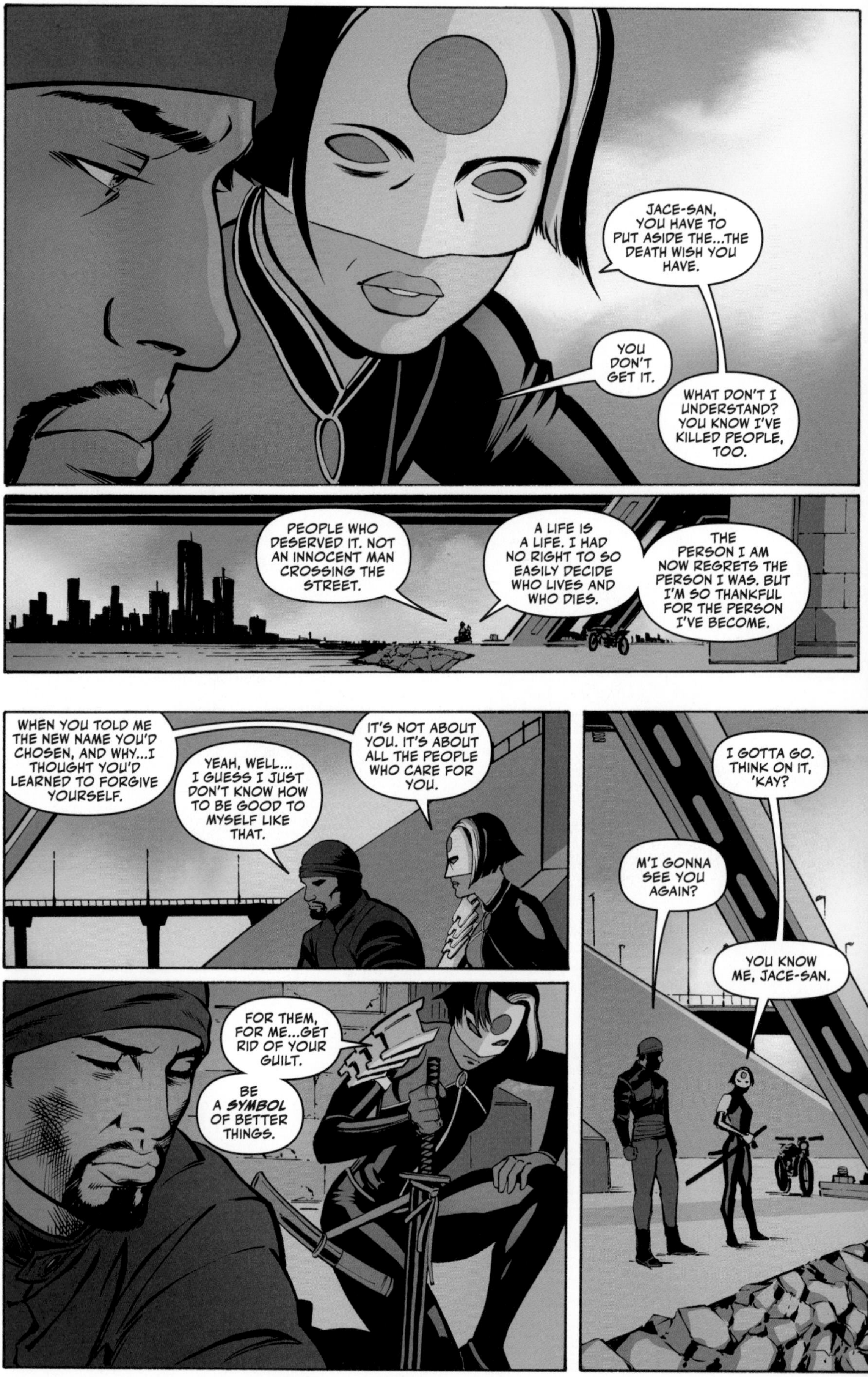
JACE-SAN, YOU HAVE TO PUT ASIDE THE...THE DEATH WISH YOU HAVE.
YOU DON'T GET IT.
WHAT DON'T I UNDERSTAND? YOU KNOW I'VE KILLED PEOPLE, TOO.
PEOPLE WHO DESERVED IT. NOT AN INNOCENT MAN CROSSING THE STREET.
A LIFE IS A LIFE. I HAD NO RIGHT TO SO EASILY DECIDE WHO LIVES AND WHO DIES.
THE PERSON I AM NOW REGRETS THE PERSON I WAS. BUT I'M SO THANKFUL FOR THE PERSON I'VE BECOME.
WHEN YOU TOLD ME THE NEW NAME YOU'D CHOSEN, AND WHY...I THOUGHT YOU'D LEARNED TO FORGIVE YOURSELF.
YEAH, WELL... I GUESS I JUST DON'T KNOW HOW TO BE GOOD TO MYSELF LIKE THAT.
IT'S NOT ABOUT YOU. IT'S ABOUT ALL THE PEOPLE WHO CARE FOR YOU.
FOR THEM, FOR ME...GET RID OF YOUR GUILT.
BE A *SYMBOL* OF BETTER THINGS.
I GOTTA GO. THINK ON IT, 'KAY?
M'I GONNA SEE YOU AGAIN?
YOU KNOW ME, JACE-SAN.

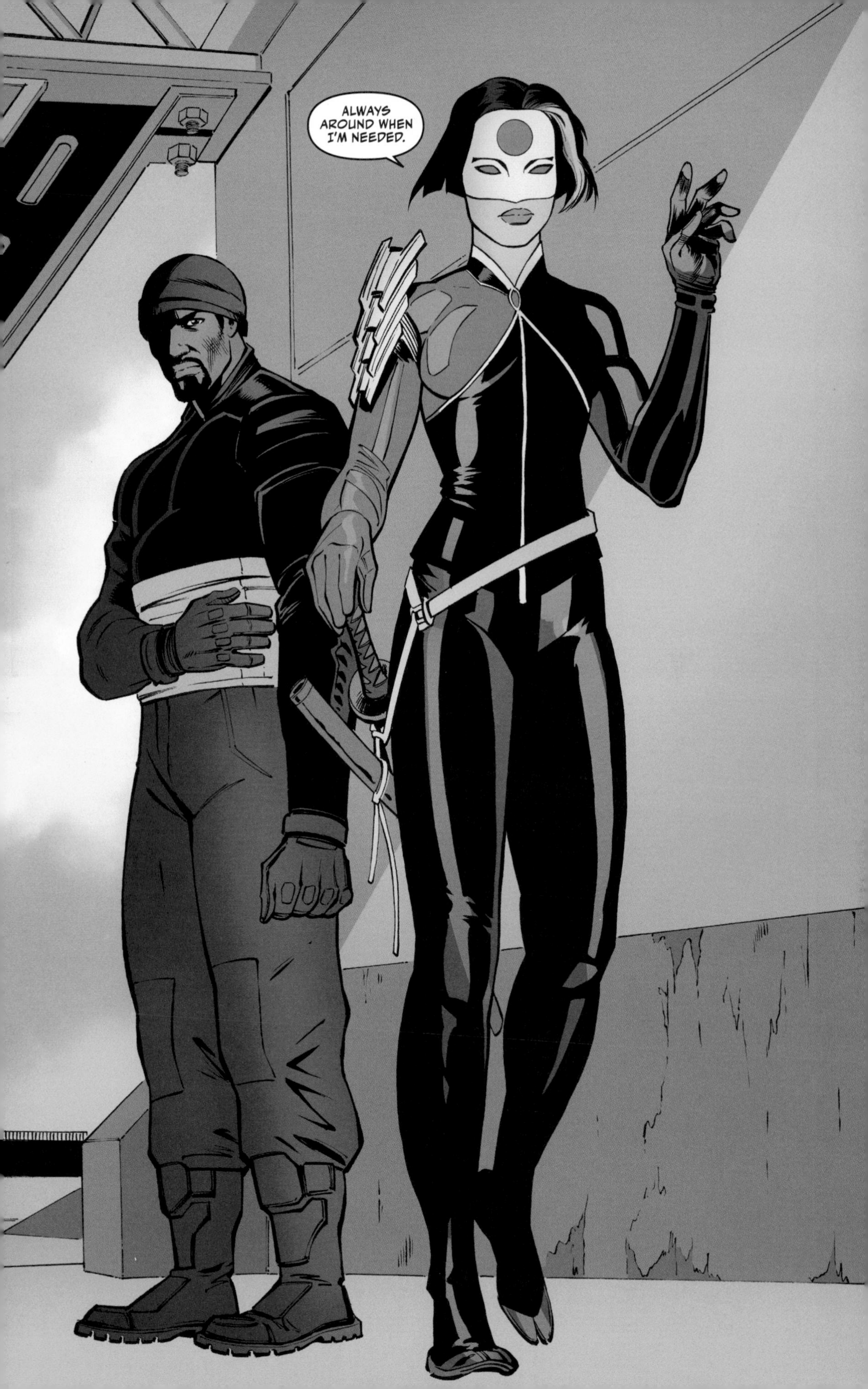
ALWAYS AROUND WHEN I'M NEEDED.

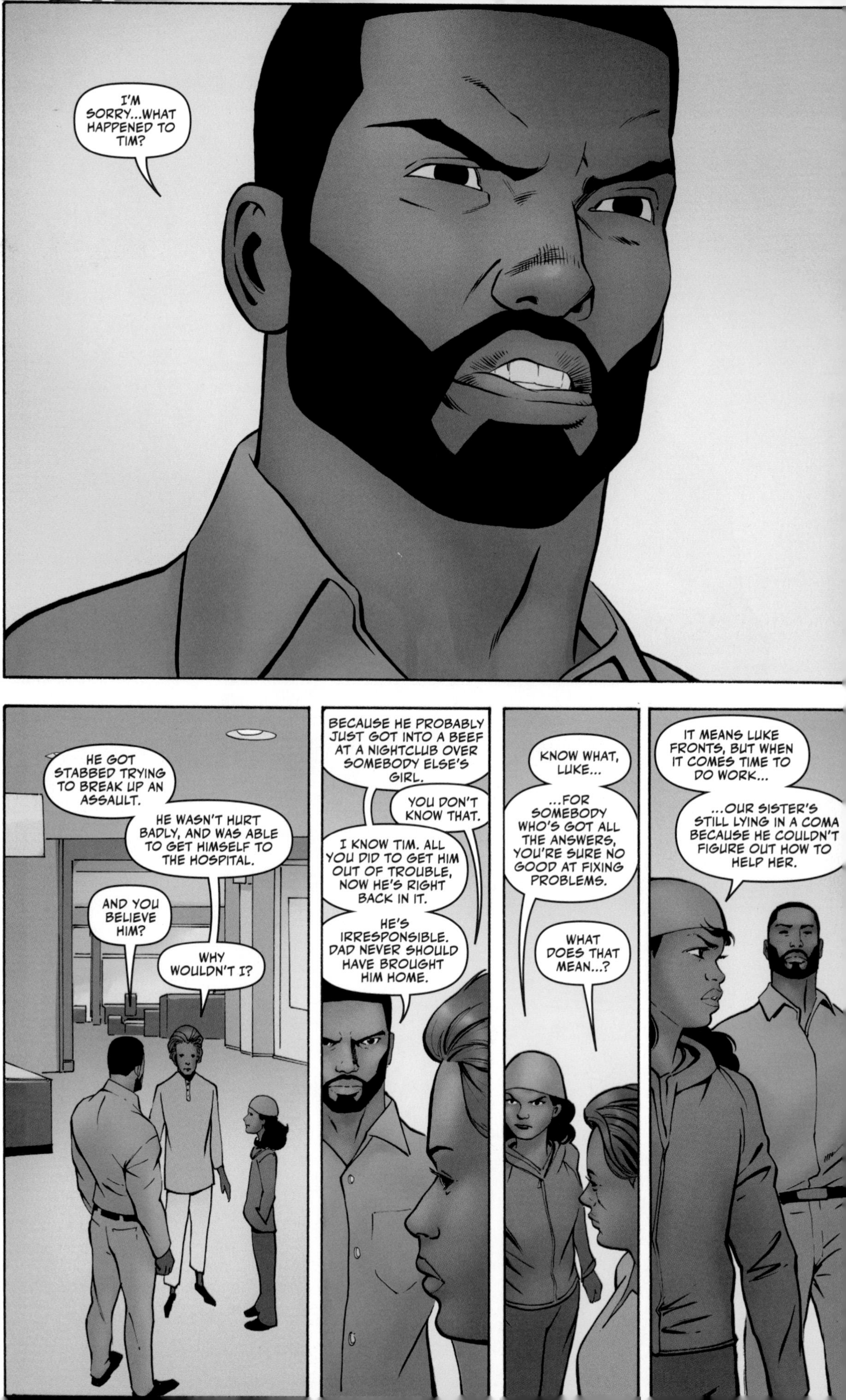

I'M SORRY...WHAT HAPPENED TO TIM?
HE GOT STABBED TRYING TO BREAK UP AN ASSAULT.
HE WASN'T HURT BADLY, AND WAS ABLE TO GET HIMSELF TO THE HOSPITAL.
AND YOU BELIEVE HIM?
WHY WOULDN'T I?
BECAUSE HE PROBABLY JUST GOT INTO A BEEF AT A NIGHTCLUB OVER SOMEBODY ELSE'S GIRL.
YOU DON'T KNOW THAT.
I KNOW TIM. ALL YOU DID TO GET HIM OUT OF TROUBLE, NOW HE'S RIGHT BACK IN IT.
HE'S IRRESPONSIBLE. DAD NEVER SHOULD HAVE BROUGHT HIM HOME.
KNOW WHAT, LUKE...
...FOR SOMEBODY WHO'S GOT ALL THE ANSWERS, YOU'RE SURE NO GOOD AT FIXING PROBLEMS.
WHAT DOES THAT MEAN...?
IT MEANS LUKE FRONTS, BUT WHEN IT COMES TIME TO DO WORK...
...OUR SISTER'S STILL LYING IN A COMA BECAUSE HE COULDN'T FIGURE OUT HOW TO HELP HER.

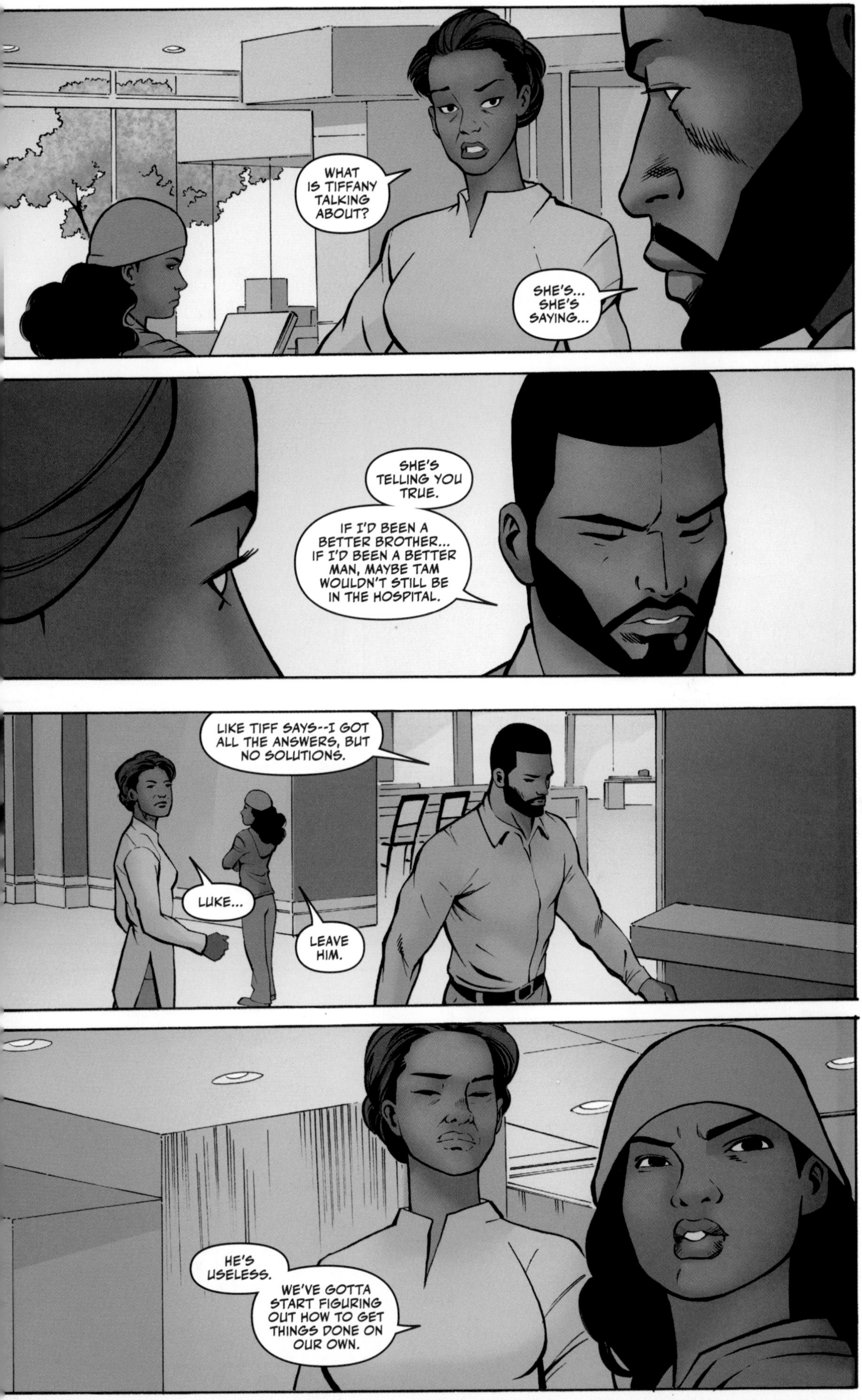
WHAT IS TIFFANY TALKING ABOUT?
SHE'S... SHE'S SAYING...
SHE'S TELLING YOU TRUE.
IF I'D BEEN A BETTER BROTHER... IF I'D BEEN A BETTER MAN, MAYBE TAM WOULDN'T STILL BE IN THE HOSPITAL.
LIKE TIFF SAYS--I GOT ALL THE ANSWERS, BUT NO SOLUTIONS.
LUKE...
LEAVE HIM.
HE'S USELESS.
WE'VE GOTTA START FIGURING OUT HOW TO GET THINGS DONE ON OUR OWN.

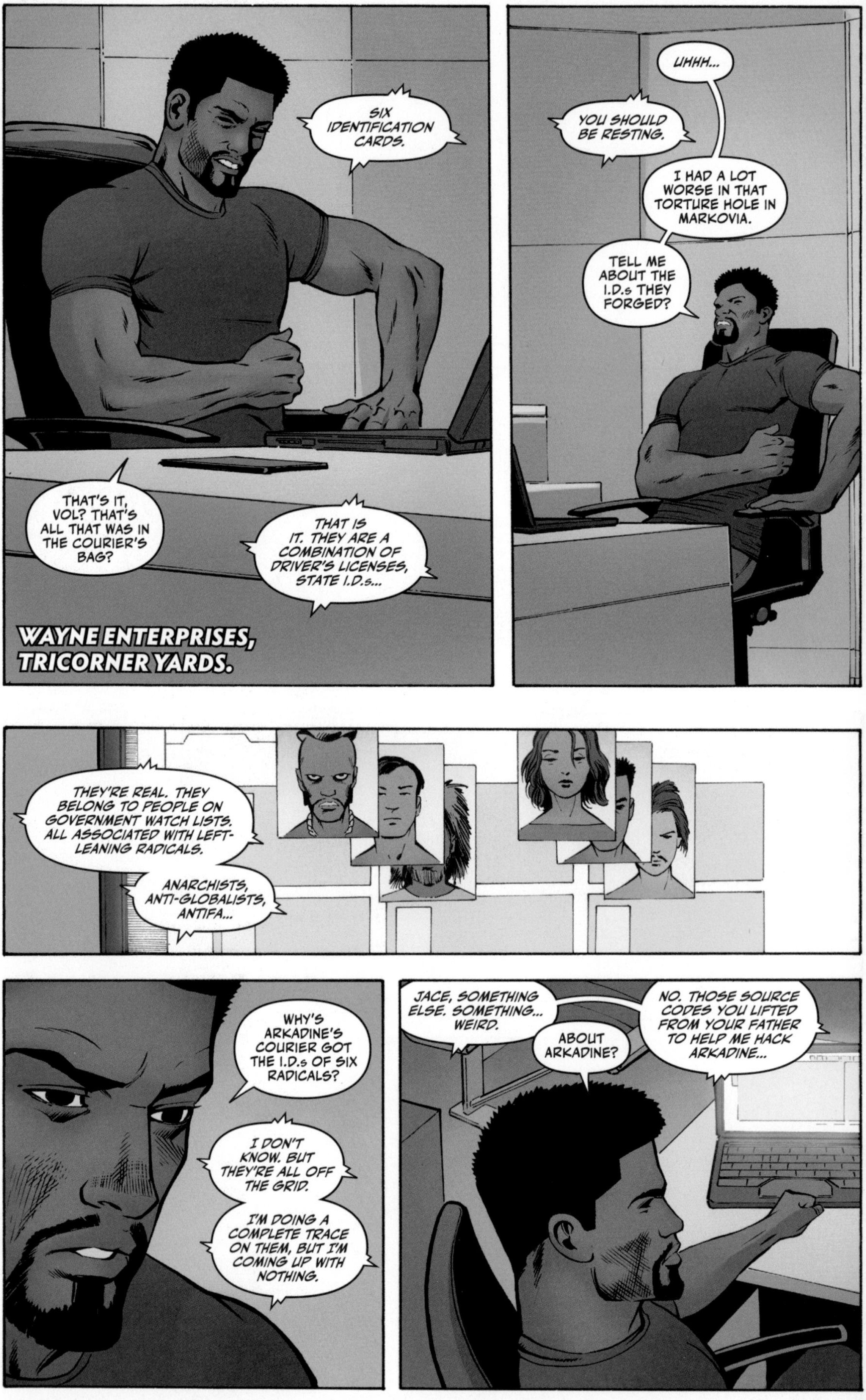
SIX IDENTIFICATION CARDS.
THAT'S IT, VOL? THAT'S ALL THAT WAS IN THE COURIER'S BAG?
THAT IS IT. THEY ARE A COMBINATION OF DRIVER'S LICENSES, STATE I.D.s...
WAYNE ENTERPRISES, TRICORNER YARDS.
UHHH...
YOU SHOULD BE RESTING.
I HAD A LOT WORSE IN THAT TORTURE HOLE IN MARKOVIA.
TELL ME ABOUT THE I.D.s THEY FORGED?
THEY'RE REAL. THEY BELONG TO PEOPLE ON GOVERNMENT WATCH LISTS. ALL ASSOCIATED WITH LEFT-LEANING RADICALS.
ANARCHISTS, ANTI-GLOBALISTS, ANTIFA...
WHY'S ARKADINE'S COURIER GOT THE I.D.s OF SIX RADICALS?
I DON'T KNOW. BUT THEY'RE ALL OFF THE GRID.
I'M DOING A COMPLETE TRACE ON THEM, BUT I'M COMING UP WITH NOTHING.
JACE, SOMETHING ELSE. SOMETHING... WEIRD.
ABOUT ARKADINE?
NO. THOSE SOURCE CODES YOU LIFTED FROM YOUR FATHER TO HELP ME HACK ARKADINE...

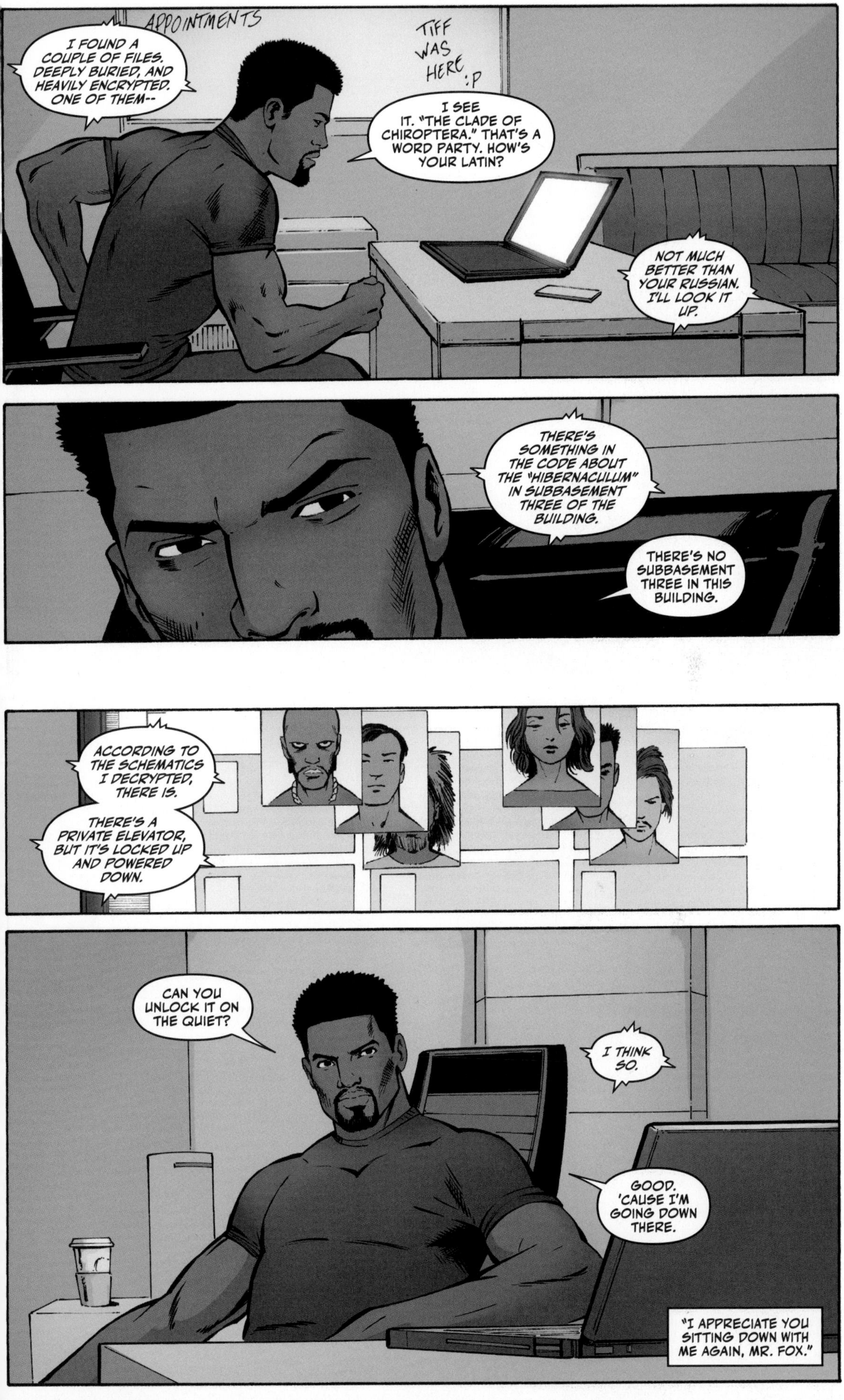
APPOINTMENTS
TIFF WAS HERE :P
I FOUND A COUPLE OF FILES. DEEPLY BURIED, AND HEAVILY ENCRYPTED. ONE OF THEM--
I SEE IT. "THE CLADE OF CHIROPTERA." THAT'S A WORD PARTY. HOW'S YOUR LATIN?
NOT MUCH BETTER THAN YOUR RUSSIAN. I'LL LOOK IT UP.
THERE'S SOMETHING IN THE CODE ABOUT THE "HIBERNACULUM" IN SUBBASEMENT THREE OF THE BUILDING.
THERE'S NO SUBBASEMENT THREE IN THIS BUILDING.
ACCORDING TO THE SCHEMATICS I DECRYPTED, THERE IS.
THERE'S A PRIVATE ELEVATOR, BUT IT'S LOCKED UP AND POWERED DOWN.
CAN YOU UNLOCK IT ON THE QUIET?
I THINK SO.
GOOD. 'CAUSE I'M GOING DOWN THERE.
"I APPRECIATE YOU SITTING DOWN WITH ME AGAIN, MR. FOX."

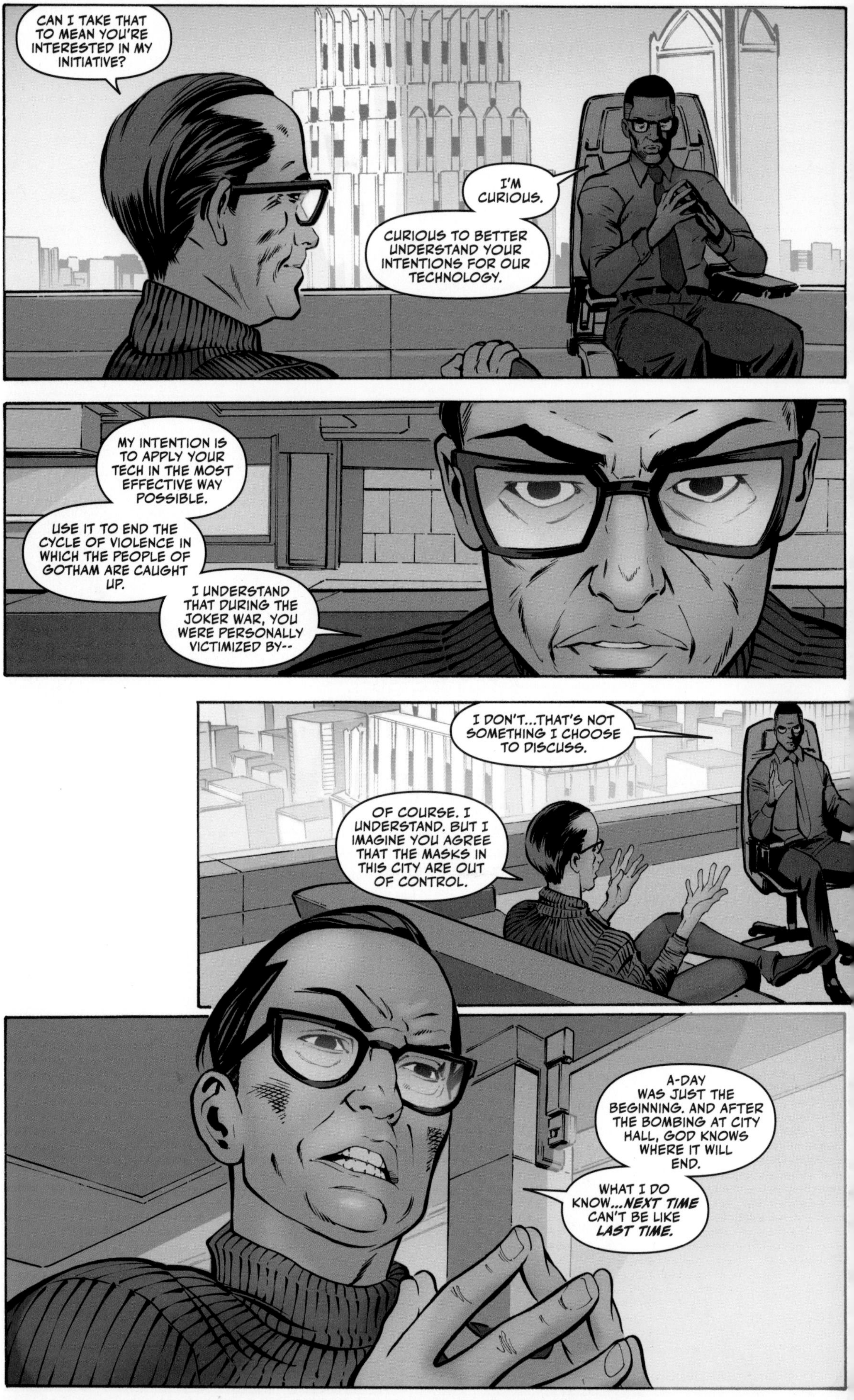
CAN I TAKE THAT TO MEAN YOU'RE INTERESTED IN MY INITIATIVE?
I'M CURIOUS.
CURIOUS TO BETTER UNDERSTAND YOUR INTENTIONS FOR OUR TECHNOLOGY.
MY INTENTION IS TO APPLY YOUR TECH IN THE MOST EFFECTIVE WAY POSSIBLE.
USE IT TO END THE CYCLE OF VIOLENCE IN WHICH THE PEOPLE OF GOTHAM ARE CAUGHT UP.
I UNDERSTAND THAT DURING THE JOKER WAR, YOU WERE PERSONALLY VICTIMIZED BY--
I DON'T...THAT'S NOT SOMETHING I CHOOSE TO DISCUSS.
OF COURSE. I UNDERSTAND. BUT I IMAGINE YOU AGREE THAT THE MASKS IN THIS CITY ARE OUT OF CONTROL.
A-DAY WAS JUST THE BEGINNING. AND AFTER THE BOMBING AT CITY HALL, GOD KNOWS WHERE IT WILL END.
WHAT I DO KNOW...*NEXT TIME* CAN'T BE LIKE *LAST TIME.*

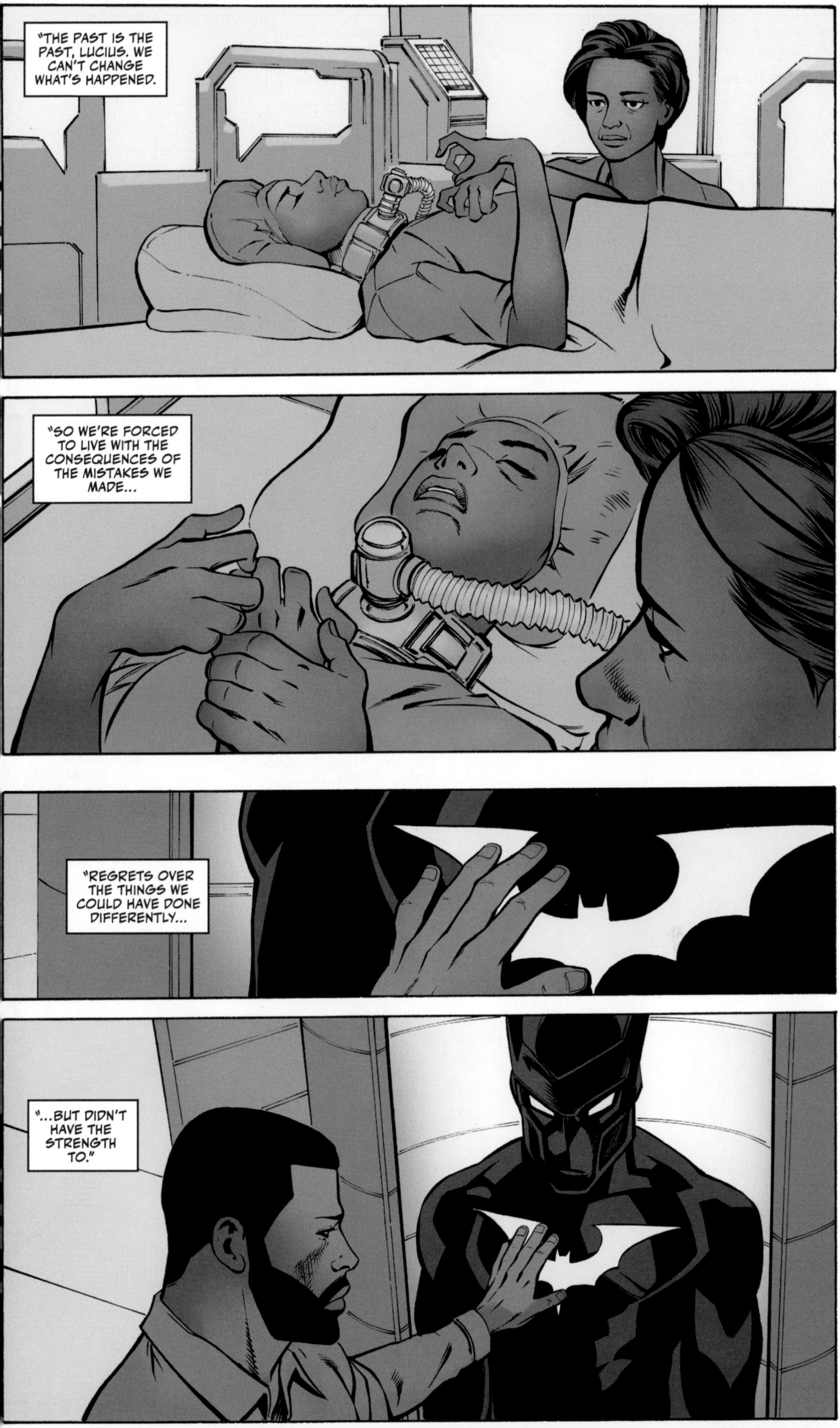
"THE PAST IS THE PAST, LUCIUS. WE CAN'T CHANGE WHAT'S HAPPENED.
"SO WE'RE FORCED TO LIVE WITH THE CONSEQUENCES OF THE MISTAKES WE MADE...
"REGRETS OVER THE THINGS WE COULD HAVE DONE DIFFERENTLY...
"...BUT DIDN'T HAVE THE STRENGTH TO."

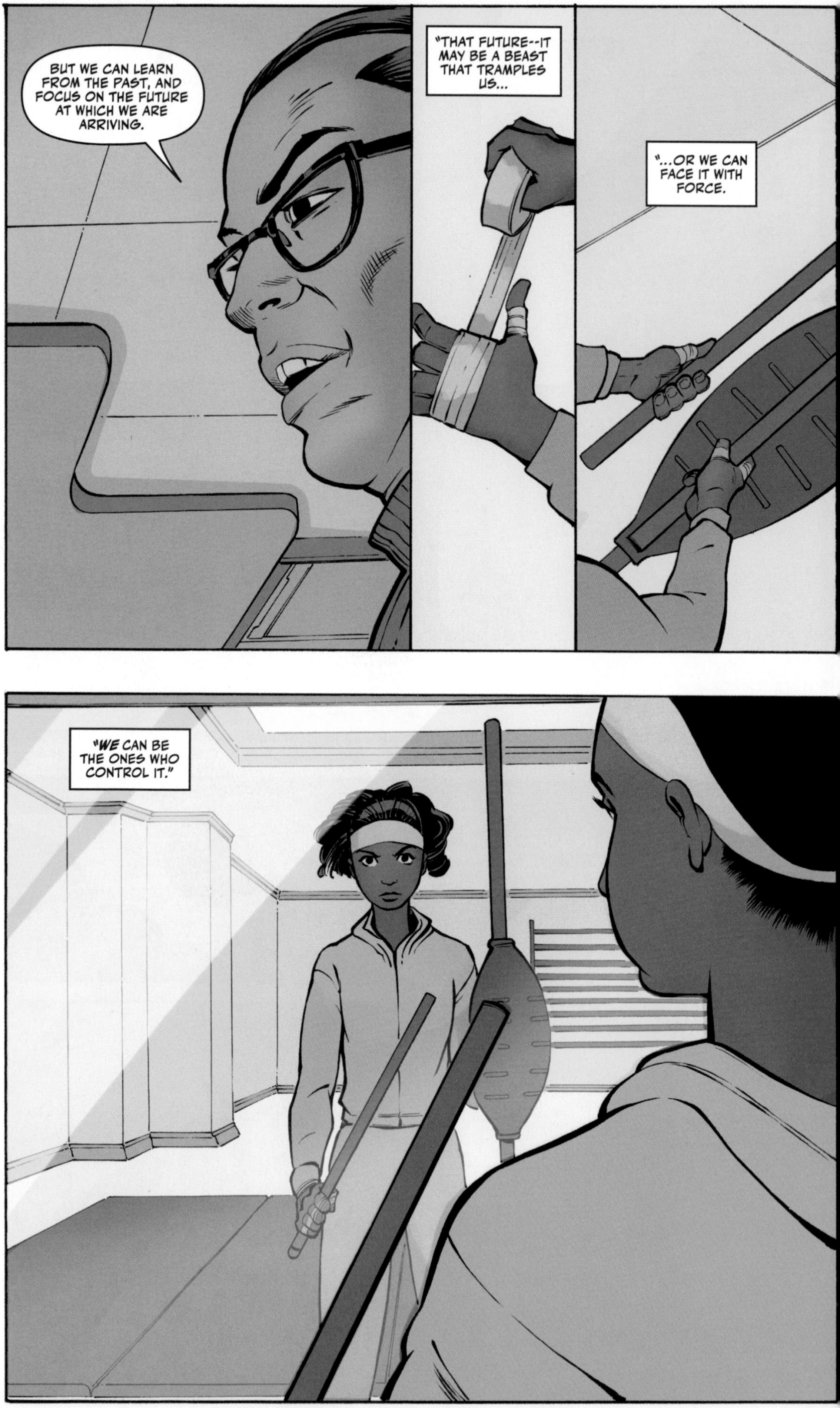
BUT WE CAN LEARN FROM THE PAST, AND FOCUS ON THE FUTURE AT WHICH WE ARE ARRIVING.
"THAT FUTURE--IT MAY BE A BEAST THAT TRAMPLES US...
"...OR WE CAN FACE IT WITH FORCE.
"*WE* CAN BE THE ONES WHO CONTROL IT."

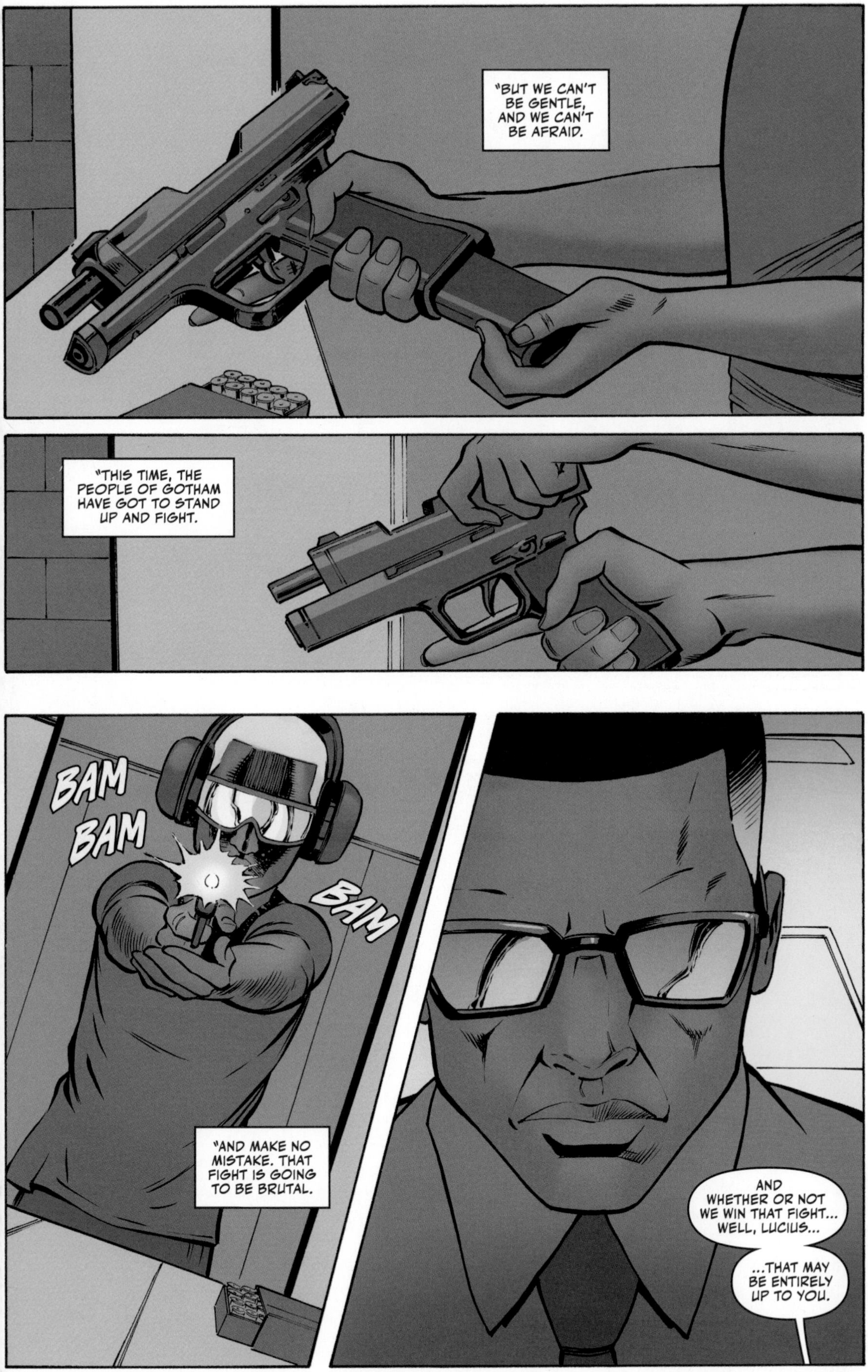
"BUT WE CAN'T BE GENTLE, AND WE CAN'T BE AFRAID.
"THIS TIME, THE PEOPLE OF GOTHAM HAVE GOT TO STAND UP AND FIGHT.
BAM
BAM
BAM
"AND MAKE NO MISTAKE. THAT FIGHT IS GOING TO BE BRUTAL.
AND WHETHER OR NOT WE WIN THAT FIGHT... WELL, LUCIUS...
...THAT MAY BE ENTIRELY UP TO YOU.

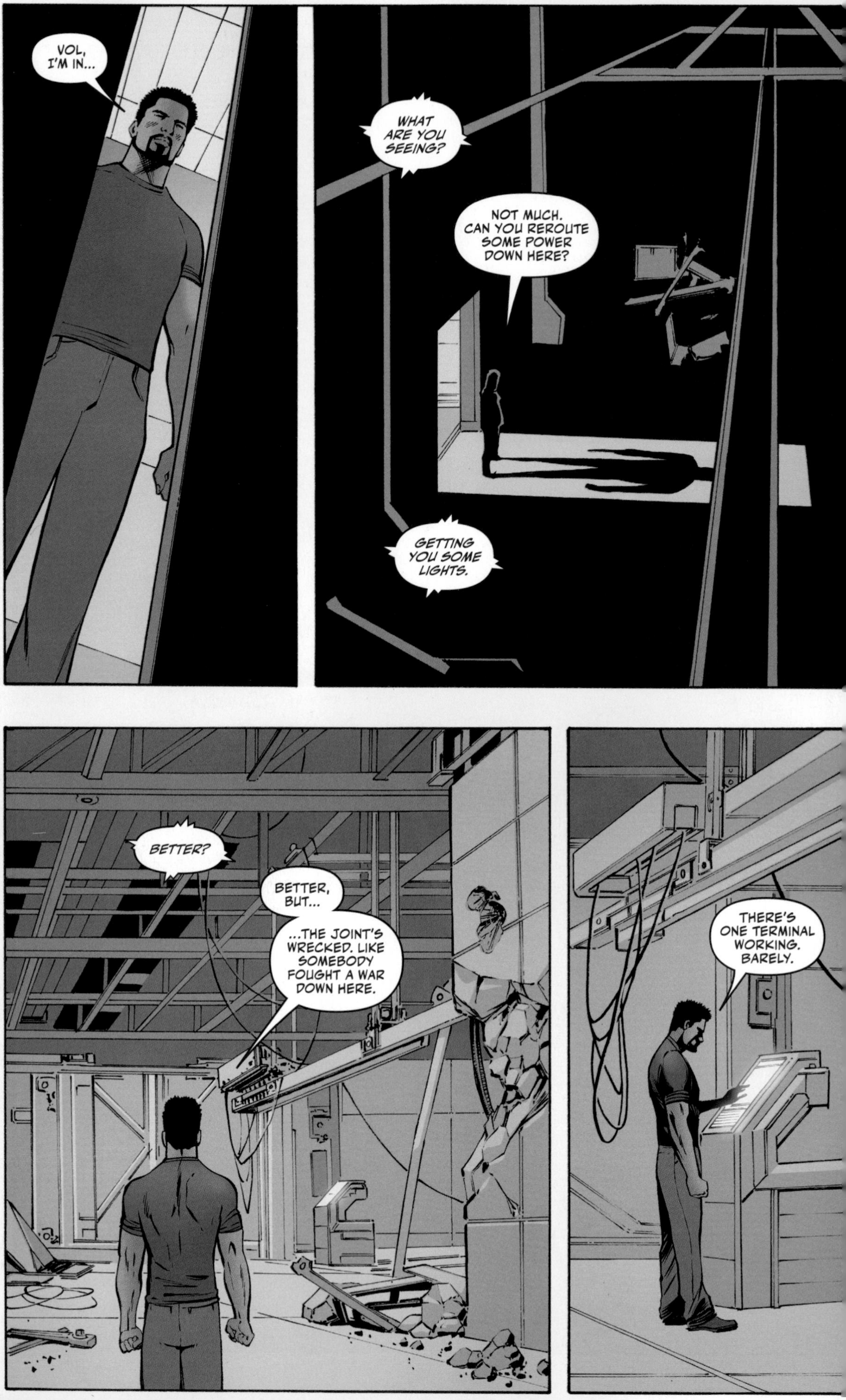
VOL, I'M IN...
WHAT ARE YOU SEEING?
NOT MUCH. CAN YOU REROUTE SOME POWER DOWN HERE?
GETTING YOU SOME LIGHTS.
BETTER?
BETTER, BUT...
...THE JOINT'S WRECKED. LIKE SOMEBODY FOUGHT A WAR DOWN HERE.
THERE'S ONE TERMINAL WORKING. BARELY.

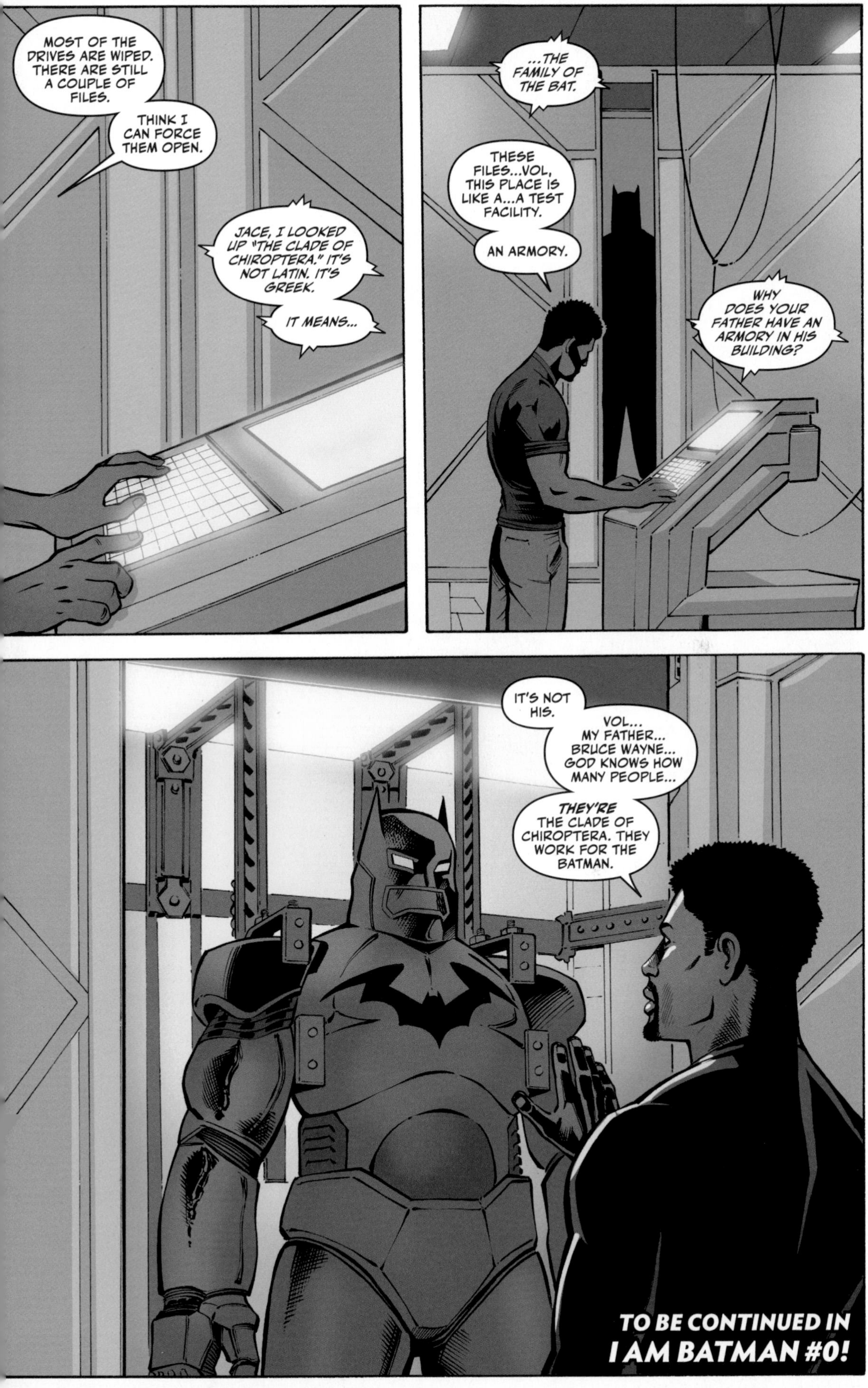
MOST OF THE DRIVES ARE WIPED. THERE ARE STILL A COUPLE OF FILES.
THINK I CAN FORCE THEM OPEN.
JACE, I LOOKED UP "THE CLADE OF CHIROPTERA." IT'S NOT LATIN. IT'S GREEK.
IT MEANS...
...THE FAMILY OF THE BAT.
THESE FILES...VOL, THIS PLACE IS LIKE A...A TEST FACILITY.
AN ARMORY.
WHY DOES YOUR FATHER HAVE AN ARMORY IN HIS BUILDING?
IT'S NOT HIS.
VOL... MY FATHER... BRUCE WAYNE... GOD KNOWS HOW MANY PEOPLE...
THEY'RE THE CLADE OF CHIROPTERA. THEY WORK FOR THE BATMAN.
TO BE CONTINUED IN I AM BATMAN #0!

VARIANT COVER GALLERY

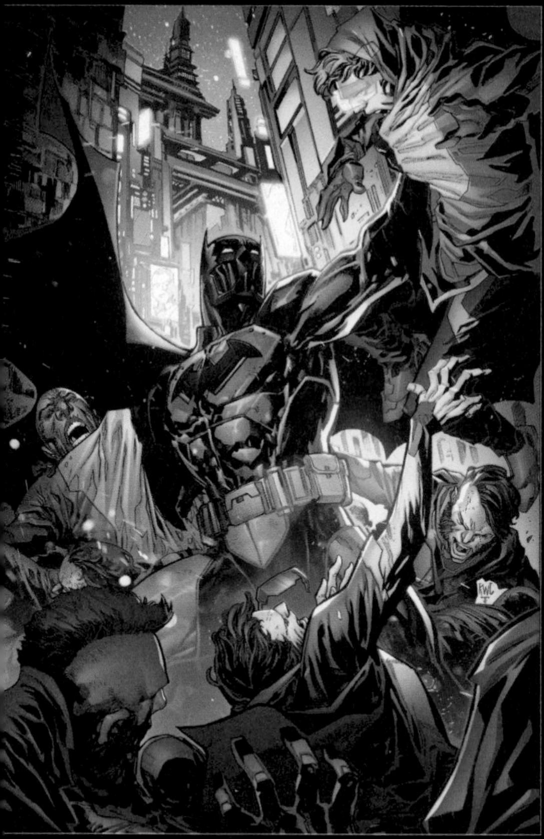

#1 | Variant Cover Art by **KEN LASHLEY** and **DIEGO RODRIGUEZ**

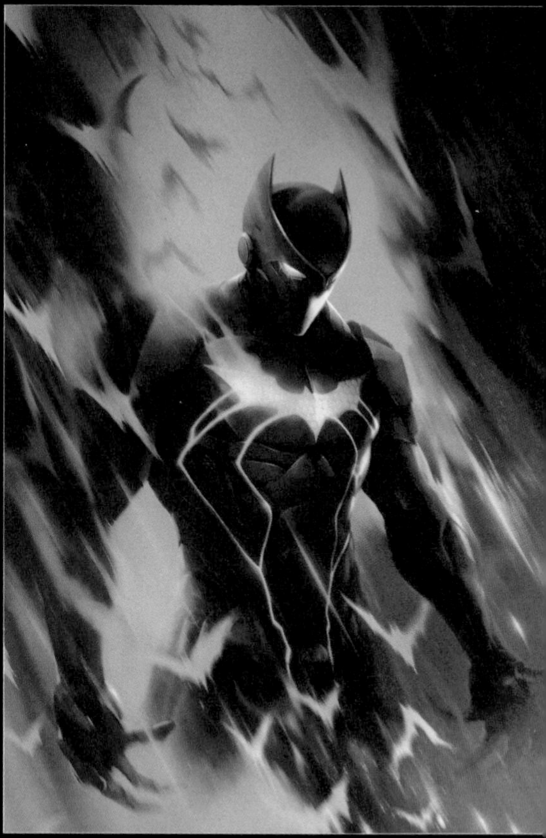

#2 | Variant Cover Art by **FRANCESCO MATTINA**

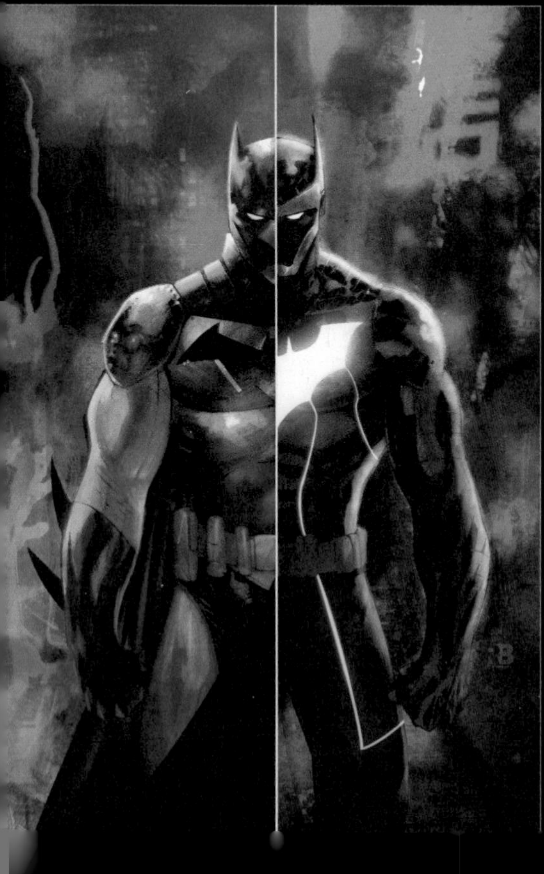

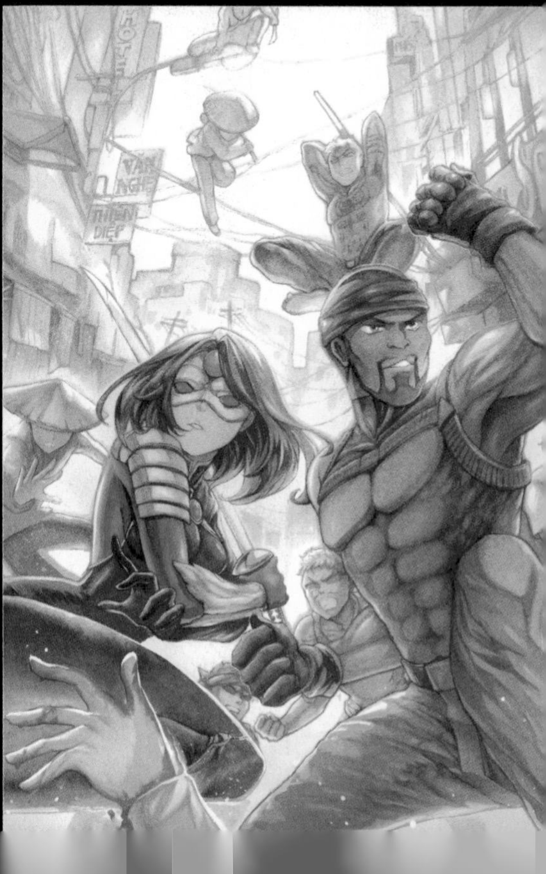